Translating the Crisis

Translating the Crisis discusses the multiple translation practices that shaped the 15M movement, also known as the *indignados* ('outraged'), a series of mass demonstrations and occupations of squares that took place across Spain in 2011 and which played a central role in the recent global wave of popular protest. Through a study of the movement's cultural and intellectual impact, as well as some of its main political evolutions (namely Podemos and Barcelona en Comú), Fernández shows how translation has contributed to the dissemination of ideas and the expansion of political debates, produced new intellectual and political figures, and provided support to political projects.

Drawing on fieldwork, interviews, and a large repertoire of sources in various languages, this monograph provides an in-depth study of the role of translation in the renewal of activist language, the development of political platforms, and the creation of new social references, while also presenting a critical perspective on its limitations and shortcomings. Combining first-hand experience of the Spanish reality with a keen transnational awareness, Fernández offers a nuanced, present-day perspective on the political events taking place in Spain and connects them with wider transformations across the world.

This book is invaluable for scholars and researchers in Translation Studies, Spanish Studies, Social Movement Studies, and Politics.

Fruela Fernández is Assistant Professor in English Studies at Universitat de les Illes Balears (Spain). He is the author of *Espacios de dominación, espacios de resistencia* (2014) and co-editor of *The Routledge Handbook of Translation and Politics* (2018, with Jonathan Evans).

Critical Perspectives on Citizen Media

Series Editors:
Luis Pérez-González, University of Manchester (UK)
Bolette B. Blaagaard, Aalborg University (Denmark)
Mona Baker, University of Manchester (UK)

Critical Perspectives on Citizen Media aims to define and advance understanding of citizen media, an emerging academic field located at the interface between different disciplines, including media studies, sociology, translation studies, performance studies, political science, visual studies and journalism studies. Titles in the series are focused on high-quality and original research, in the form of monographs and edited collections, made accessible for a wide range of readers. The series explores the relationship between citizen media and various cross-disciplinary themes, including but not restricted to, participation, immaterial work, witnessing, resistance and performance. The series editors also welcome proposals for reference works, textbooks and innovative digital outputs produced by citizen engagement groups on the ground.

Translating Dissent
Voices from and with the Egyptian Revolution
Edited by Mona Baker

Citizen Media and Public Spaces
Diverse Expressions of Citizenship and Dissent
Edited by Mona Baker and Bolette B. Blaagaard

Citizen Media and Practice
Currents, Connections, Challenges
Edited by Hilde Stephensen and Emiliano Treré

The Routledge Encyclopedia of Citizen Media
Edited by Mona Baker, Bolette B. Blaagaard, Henry Jones and Luis Pérez-González

Translating the Crisis
Politics and Culture in Spain after the 15M
Fruela Fernández

For more information, visit: https://www.routledge.com/Critical-Perspectives-on-Citizen-Media/book-series/CPCM

Translating the Crisis
Politics and Culture in Spain after the 15M

Fruela Fernández

LONDON AND NEW YORK

First published 2021
by Routledge
2 Park Square, Milton Park, Abingdon, Oxon OX14 4RN

and by Routledge
52 Vanderbilt Avenue, New York, NY 10017

Routledge is an imprint of the Taylor & Francis Group, an informa business

© 2021 Fruela Fernández

The right of Fruela Fernández to be identified as author of this work has been asserted by him in accordance with sections 77 and 78 of the Copyright, Designs and Patents Act 1988.

All rights reserved. No part of this book may be reprinted or reproduced or utilised in any form or by any electronic, mechanical, or other means, now known or hereafter invented, including photocopying and recording, or in any information storage or retrieval system, without permission in writing from the publishers.

Trademark notice: Product or corporate names may be trademarks or registered trademarks, and are used only for identification and explanation without intent to infringe.

British Library Cataloguing-in-Publication Data
A catalogue record for this book is available from the British Library

Library of Congress Cataloging-in-Publication Data
Names: Fernández, Fruela, 1982- author.
Title: Translating the crisis : politics and culture in Spain after the 15M / Fruela Fernández.
Description: London ; New York : Routledge, 2020. | Series: Critical perspectives on citizen media | Includes bibliographical references and index.
Identifiers: LCCN 2020023594 | ISBN 9781138310841 (hardback) | ISBN 9781003105121 (ebook)
Subjects: LCSH: Translating and interpreting–Political aspects–Spain. | Translating and interpreting–Social aspects–Spain. | 15-M (Organization) | Protest movements–Spain–History–21st century. | Social movements–Spain–History–21st century.
Classification: LCC P306.97.P65 .F37 2020 | DDC 322.4/40946–dc2 3
LC record available at https://lccn.loc.gov/2020023594

ISBN: 978-1-138-31084-1 (hbk)
ISBN: 978-1-003-10512-1 (ebk)

Typeset in Bembo
by Taylor & Francis Books

Project supported by a 2018 Leonardo Grant for Researchers and Cultural Creators, BBVA Foundation

The Foundation accepts no responsibility for the opinions, statements, and contents included in the project and/or the results thereof, which are entirely the responsibility of the author

Contents

List of illustrations viii
Acknowledgements ix

    Introduction: Translating the crisis   1
1 The many voices of opposition: Activism and translation in a global context   11
2 Translation-as-tradition: The 15M between past and present   26
3 The 'commons': Rethinking collective agency   49
4 Towards the care strike: Translation and the rise of the feminist movement   69
5 Sea, sun, and dissent: Activist critiques of the 'Spanish model'   90
6 Podemos: Successes and contradictions of a 'translational' party   107
7 Conclusion: The ongoing task of translation   129

Bibliography 137
Index 166

Illustrations

Figures

2.1	Poster for the 2018 edition of the Feria del Libro Político de Madrid, designed by Emma Gascó.	39
2.2	Mural in support of the 2015 Greek referendum (Langreo, Asturias).	41
3.1	The motto 'Omnia Sunt Communia' written on the wall of a university restroom (Universidad Complutense, Madrid).	57
3.2	Detail of the book cover for *La Carta de los Comunes*.	58
3.3	Fragment of a leaflet advertising a course on the commons (La Hidra Cooperativa 2017).	59
4.1	Excerpt of Feminismos Sol's leaflet calling for a 'care strike' in 2012.	83
4.2	Multilingual leaflet produced by the Aragonese 8M committee calling for a 'care strike'.	86
5.1.	Excerpt of a multilingual climate-change leaflet by *Contra el diluvio* (Catalan version).	103

Tables

2.1	Books published by selected series of politically committed publishers: translated books vs. books originally written in Spanish (January 2011 – October 2019)	42
4.1	Number of ISBN licenses for books in Spanish (both originals and translations) under the rubric 'Feminism'	76
4.2	Number of books (translations into Spanish vs. Spanish originals) on feminist topics published by politically committed publishers	77

Acknowledgements

This research was conducted across four institutions, which attests to the precarity of my generation, especially in Southern Europe. It commenced at Hull University, progressed at Newcastle University, evolved at Universidad Complutense, and concluded at Universitat de les Illes Balears. I would like to thank many friends and colleagues who have contributed in different ways to this project over the many years of its development. Javier López Alós, Jonathan Evans, Isabelle Touton, Olga Castro, Vicente Rubio-Pueyo, and Lino González Veiguela read different sections of the text and provided invaluable comments. Nicole Doerr kindly gave me her advice in the final stage of the project. My approach also benefitted from conversations, recommendations, and informal exchanges of ideas with Katryn Evinson, Hibai Arbide, Sophie Noël, Alex Niven, Marianne Maeckelbergh, Pete Baker, David Charlston, Silvia Nanclares, and Luis Moreno Caballud. Special thanks go to César Rendueles, Amador Fernández-Savater, Germán Cano, Isidro López, Ernesto Castro, Nerea Fillat, Juanma Agulles, Salvador Cobo, and Jordi Maíz, who agreed to be interviewed as part of my fieldwork. As on other occasions, Joseph Lambert meticulously proof-read and style-edited the manuscript. At an institutional level, I am grateful to Nigel Harkness for supporting my leave application at Newcastle University and to Carlos Fortea for backing my visiting fellowship at Universidad Complutense.

Whilst every effort has been made to trace copyright holders, this has not been possible in all cases. Any omissions brought to the publisher's attention will be remedied in further editions. In this sense, I am grateful to a number of people and collectives who gave their permission to reproduce copyrighted materials in this book: the designer Emma Gascó for her poster; La Hidra Cooperativa for their leaflet; and Contra el Diluvio for the excerpt from their translated leaflet. Unfortunately, I was unable to receive a response from ADEPAVAN regarding the photograph from their mural in Chapter 2; nevertheless, I am greatly indebted to their political work. The rest of the materials reproduced in this book were issued under Creative Commons licences.

While they have been greatly reworked and expanded, some materials used in different sections of this book have previously appeared in 'Podemos: politics as a "task of translation"', *Translation Studies* 11(1): 1–16 (2018) and 'Toolbox, tradition, and capital: the many roles of translation in contemporary Spanish politics', *Translation Studies* 13(3): 352–368 (2020). Thanks to the editors of the journal for permission to reuse these materials.

I am indebted to Mona Baker, Luis Pérez-González, and Bolette Blaagaard for their interest in my project and for their excellent editorial work. Beyond the limits of the monograph, I would also like to thank Mona for her inspiration and encouragement over the years.

Over a lengthy part of the book, Francina Payeras was my best support and a constant source of laughter. T'estim.

Introduction
Translating the crisis

Over the last decade, the notion of 'crisis' has been a central part of our lives. From the economic crisis that started in 2008 to heated discussions on an impending climate crisis and the multiple political crises that several countries have experienced, our time is characterised by a widespread malaise, a sense of fragility and uncertainty that seems to restrict our ability to predict how events and situations will develop – in fact, the global crisis triggered by the new coronavirus disease (COVID-19) as this book goes into production has only served to enhance this feeling. In the light of these series of recent changes, several theorists have argued that even our perception of time, which was already undergoing major transformations, has changed altogether. While 'Bifo' Berardi (2011) has claimed that we are living 'after the future', as we are no longer psychologically able to conceive it, the late Zygmunt Bauman (2017) suggested that we have moved from a belief in 'utopias' to one based on 'retrotopias': instead of holding the modern view that the future 'will always be better', we are returning to the ancient conception of the past as a lost 'golden age'.

While the frailty and disruption caused by this sense of crisis are hard to deny, a historical detour can often shed new light on contemporary events. As Reinhart Koselleck (2006, 358) reminded us, the word 'crisis' – like many other cognates: *crisi, Krise, crise* – derives from the Ancient Greek κρίσις (krísis), which generally referred to a separation, a decision, or a judgment. The latter meaning was particularly relevant, as it encompassed both the legal context in which a matter had to be judged and the decisive choice that an individual – a doctor, a military leader, or a judge – made in a complex situation. After the 17th and 18th centuries, the term found its way across numerous European languages, undergoing a process of expansion in meaning and becoming incorporated into the lexicon of politics, economy, and history (*ibid.*). Within this diversity of senses, however, a few constants can be traced: a 'crisis' marks a relevant moment for a society, either as an end or as a 'transition', and it is always subject to 'disagreements' between different interpretations, as the assessment of its origins and causes depends 'on the judgmental criteria used to diagnose that condition' (Koselleck 2006, 361).

Although historical awareness is unlikely to dismiss our malaise and uncertainty about the present, it can contribute to providing it with a new *political* component. As Koselleck shows, there is no unique and all-encompassing explanation for any given crisis; neither its origins, nor the answers to it, are indisputable or predetermined. Quite the contrary, in fact, as they depend on those 'judgmental criteria' that are deployed to understand it. In this sense, therefore, interpretations of the 'crisis' are manifold and can be *challenged*. For instance, the psychoanalyst Jorge Alemán has vocally opposed the notion of an 'economic crisis', claiming it is merely a disguise for a new process of economic accumulation (Alemán 2018, 15–17). According to Alemán, this process is based on accusing citizens and societies of overspending and 'living beyond their means', which makes them lose 'the confidence of the markets'. Subsequently, in order to 'restore' this 'confidence', they are forced to make adjustments and sacrifices. However, as we have seen on multiple occasions, this 'confidence' proves to be elusive and citizens never know whether the increasing number of cuts and waves of austerity will ever be enough to 'restore' it.

Between 2011 and 2016, a series of mass protests took to the streets across a wide variety of nations with the very purpose of defending a different understanding of the crises that their countries were experiencing. Often subsumed under the rubric of the 'movement of the squares' (Gerbaudo 2017), the actions, problems, and social composition of these protests were extremely diverse. While some of these movements faced 'ageing dictatorships' (Gerbaudo 2017, 55), as in the case of the Arab uprisings (Egypt, Tunisia, or Libya), others criticised the shortcomings of democratic systems (Flesher Fominaya 2017), as in Greece, Spain, and the United States. However, they all shared an intense repudiation of local and global elites, blaming them for placing their own interests before those of the majority of the people. As unemployment skyrocketed, prices increased, and basic services underwent drastic cuts, these movements aimed to give each 'crisis' a fairer and more collective response from below.

In this context of global unrest and critique, this book focuses upon the Spanish 15M movement and its afterlives to trace and understand the role of translation in the construction and evolution of a whole set of citizen responses to the 'crisis'. As will be discussed over the following pages, translation – understood not only as a linguistic, but also a conceptual and political practice – has played a central, yet frequently unacknowledged role in these popular responses, which range from the development of a new activist lexicon to experiments with forms of protest and collective agency, the development of alternative means of communication, or a conscious way of seeking commonality with other collectives, among many others. In discussion and debate with researchers on other social movements (such as Baker 2016a, 2016b and Doerr 2018), I will argue that, through this variety of translational engagements with social reality, Spanish citizens have contributed to a questioning of official narratives on the 'crisis', while doing their utmost to turn it into an opportunity for change.

Translation within the 15M 'climate'

As Chapter 2 will outline in greater detail, the 15M movement started with a series of occupations of squares and public spaces in May and June 2011 to protest against the consequences and management of the economic crisis. Following the Arab uprisings, the 15M played an important role in the evolution of the movement of the squares, giving rise to its first European and Western 'cluster' (Gerbaudo 2017, 31). Although occupations only lasted a few weeks, the 15M left a profound imprint upon Spanish society. In this sense, it quickly went beyond the strict notion of a movement to become what thinkers have characterised as a 'climate' (Fernández-Savater 2012a) or as a 'political cycle' (Rodríguez 2016, 15–18), in order to emphasise the continuity between the movement and later initiatives. This is the angle that I adopt in this book, understanding the 15M as a contested period of Spanish history with different timings and internal tensions, which will themselves be discussed later in this introduction.

Due to its centrality to Spanish society, there is an abundant and solid bibliography on the 15M and its origins (Sitrin and Azzellini 2014, 121–150; Flesher Fominaya 2015a, 2015b), intellectual debates (Kornetis 2014; Moreno-Caballud 2015; Prádanos 2018), and subsequent evolution (Delclós 2015; Rivero 2015; Antentas 2017), along with collective works covering a wide range of related areas (Cagiao and Touton 2019; Zazo and Torres 2019). However, other than my own work (Fernández 2018, 2020a), little attention has been paid to the important role that translation has played within this new political cycle. As Chapter 1 will show, this is far from surprising considering the general lack of studies on the role of translation in this global wave of protests (Baker 2016b, 10–12).

In the context of this monograph, I understand 'translation' in a broad sense, as required by the variety of materials and the fluid understanding of participants involved. Over recent years, different scholars have argued that translation has become a key signifier across numerous disciplines (Nergaard and Arduini 2011; Blumczynski 2016), in ways that transcend the strictly linguistic practice traditionally associated with it. In previous texts (Fernández 2018; Evans and Fernández 2018, 8–10), I have shown that the concept of translation has a long tradition of usages in the field of politics that frequently exceed standard definitions within Translation Studies. Similarly, Mona Baker (2016b, 3) has noted in the context of the Egyptian revolution that activist notions of translation do not necessarily match with scholarly ones. In this sense, translation will be understood here as the process of replacing a set of source signs with another set of target signs 'on the strength of an interpretation' (Venuti 1995, 18). This process of replacement can be undertaken within the same language or between different languages – what Roman Jakobson (1959, 233) called 'intralingual' and 'interlingual' translation, respectively – but also between theoretical systems and paradigms: for instance, between politics and economics, or between two different philosophical traditions (Boothman 2010, 110–114,

128–130; Lacorte 2010, 214–217), as Marxist thinker Antonio Gramsci had already contended.

Bearing this diversity in mind, this book will trace and analyse the pervasive role of translation, as both a practice and a product, across the political field, following three main lines of study. Firstly, it will show how translation is contributing to the renewal of the activist landscape in Spain through the incorporation of political concepts (such as *comunes* and *cuidados*) in the activist vocabulary and the increasing adoption of intellectual figures (from Silvia Federici to David Harvey, among many others). A second line, strongly connected to the first, will examine the political impact of these practices of translation, as concepts and models inspire new forms of agency (such as the feminist care strike or commons-based collectives) and contribute to the generation of alternative discourses (for instance, against the commodification of housing). Finally, the book will also address the ways in which translation practices aim at finding commonality between different struggles across time and space, highlighting the continuity with historical movements – such as the reappraisal of the early democratic period in Spain and the feminist search for genealogy – or the presence of shared problems in other countries, as is the case with the reception of Latin American populism and the emergence of transnational platforms against 'touristification'. These three lines of enquiry are certainly not exclusive; on the contrary, they tend to overlap and combine, as well as open the way to other important sub-analyses.

A significant element of translation in this context is its diffuse, multi-layered, and multi-channel nature, which I describe through the concept of *expanded translation*. It is clear that our historical time is characterised by an overflow of sources and information, which multiplies and accelerates exchanges, and by a global dominance of English that has blurred 'the boundaries' between 'author and translator' (Bennett and Queiroz de Barros 2017, 365), since authors and readers of texts are increasingly able to generate their own versions and translations without requiring the intervention of a professional translator. In this context, it has become increasingly non-viable to chart the circulation of a concept, an idea, or an author exclusively through a predefined set of translated texts in the traditional sense. As I argue in different sections of this book, a key source for understanding a given process of translation might appear in a derivative text (articles, forewords, summaries, or interviews) or even in other interactions (social media, TV shows, assemblies, activist meetings, and speeches, among others), as a whole mass of instances of linguistic exchange is generated. As such, the construction of meaning and the use of translated concepts, authors, and models implies a collective process, which is non-centralised (multiple agents can join it without previous requirements) yet also unequal (as certain agents enjoy more power and visibility than others). In consequence, the study of expanded translation will tend to focus upon the existence of tensions, oppositions, and imbalances, as they help to outline the main semantic boundaries of each given case.

Translation as an interdisciplinary tool

As is often the case, this project emerged through a combination of inspiring precedents and perceived shortcomings. In particular, the capacity of translation to cut across a variety of disciplines implies an awareness of, and potentially an engagement with, several traditions. For a start, as noted in the previous section, neither the field of Hispanic Studies, nor Translation Studies, had approached the role of translation in this political cycle. However, this does not imply that this research refuses to establish a dialogue with scholarship in these areas. On the one hand, my approach to the Spanish context is strongly embedded in different analyses developed by a set of contemporary scholars, activists, and thinkers across various fields (such as López and Rodríguez 2011; Kornetis 2014; Flesher Fominaya 2015a and 2015b; Moreno-Caballud 2015; Rodríguez 2016, among others), who have espoused a critical perspective of the country's history and politics. On the other, my interest in the evolution of political and activist concepts aligns with an increasing body of literature on the topic, manifested in the emergence of new collective projects that aim to chart the transformation of vocabularies. An invaluable reference would be the *Vocabulaire Européen des Philosophies* (Cassin 2004), adapted into several languages, which posited both the centrality and the limits of translation in the evolution of philosophical concepts. However, my approach is more directly linked to the reassessment of activist vocabulary undertaken by Fritsch, O'Connor, and Thompson (2016), who set out to update Raymond Williams' (1975) *Keywords* project, as well as the study on translated and adapted concepts in the Spanish fields of sexuality and gender proposed by Platero, Rosón, and Ortega (2017). With these two projects, I share the perception that activist language has evolved greatly over recent years, and this necessitates an effort on our part to start a process of mapping and clarification. Finally, although my approach is strictly contemporary, I have also benefitted from reflecting on the collective work developed by the Genealogies of Knowledge project (genealogiesofknowledge.net), based at the University of Manchester, which focuses on the genealogy of social and political concepts across history through processes of translation, retranslation, and mediation. While publications from the project are in progress (Jones 2019 constitutes a perceptive example), the conferences organised in Manchester (2017) and Perugia (2019) were excellent opportunities to engage with other scholars and to refine thoughts on my own work.

Through its focus on the movement of the squares and its afterlives, a third field of engagement for this monograph is political activism and social movements. As will be discussed in Chapter 1, Translation Studies has started to engage with this large area of research over the last decade, addressing the potential of translation and interpreting as an activist tool and contributing to a modest, but very solid body of literature. Surprisingly, however, there have been very few attempts to engage with translation from the field of activism and social movements: Conny Roggeband's 2007 article on transnational exchanges between feminist movements, Olga Malets and Sabina Zajak's

6 Introduction

(2014) framework for the implementation of transnational norms and laws, and Nicole Doerr's (2012, 2018) work, which focuses on the central role of political translation for deliberation within multilingual and multicultural groups. In my view, this absence is partly due to conceptual choices within the discipline of social movements. On the one hand, as Roggeband (2007, 246) has argued, processes of exchange between social movements are frequently conceptualised in terms of 'diffusion', a concept borrowed from communication studies that obscures the complexity of the process, overlooking the role of specific individuals and groups in the adaptation and transformation of ideas and concepts. On the other hand, several scholars have adopted the concept of 'brokerage', defined by Sydney Tarrow (2013, 19) as 'the process through which a third party acts to create a connection between two other actors who would remain unconnected except through the action of the broker'. 'Brokerage' represents a wider-reaching notion than 'diffusion', as it focuses on the active role of agencies, organisations, and individuals in the process of communication. In this vein, for instance, Romanos (2016) has analysed how Spanish migrants in the US served as brokers between the 15M and Occupy Wall Street, contributing to the incorporation and adoption of practices previously explored at the occupations in Spain. Nevertheless, as this monograph will show, 'brokerage' still fails to acknowledge the *transformative* nature of translation, which rests both on subjective (e.g. the ideas and perspectives held by translators) and contextual factors (linguistic, social, and political differences). In the light of this absence, this monograph also aims at advocating the potential benefits of the translational framework for research in movement studies.

The lack of engagement between social movements and translation becomes even more striking if we consider the importance of 'translation' as a concept in political theory. As argued in Chapter 6, there is an important lineage of thinkers who have conceptualised political activity in terms of 'translation', ranging from Antonio Gramsci's reflections on 'translation' and 'translatability' as both opportunities and constraints to political praxis (see Boothman 2010 and Lacorte 2010 for a reconstruction) to contemporary approaches by Judith Butler (2000), Boaventura de Sousa Santos (2006, 131–147) or Michael Hardt and Antonio Negri (Negri and Hardt 2009, 340–351), among others. Beyond multiple differences in objectives and approach, this heritage of debates has popularised the usage of 'translation' as a concept that emphasises the importance of establishing practices of communication and a shared political language that allows understanding between a variety of social agents seeking social transformation. As I argued earlier, these processes of reflection are not only paramount to my own approach, but also play a significant role in discourses mobilised by activists and politicians studied in this book.

Times, levels, and languages of the 15M climate

Earlier in this introduction, I noted that my approach to the 15M is not restricted to the concrete movement that emerged in 2011, but rather addresses the 15M as a 'climate' or historical period where multiple collectives coexist. Adopting this framework of analysis, however, requires a certain mapping to orientate readers. Emmanuel Rodríguez (2016) has proposed to divide the political cycle into a 'movement' phase (2011–2013) – marked by the occupation of the squares, the anti-eviction movement *Plataforma de Afectados por la Hipoteca* (Flesher Fominaya 2015b), and the *Mareas* ('Tides') in defence of public education and healthcare (Iglesias-Onofrio, Rodrigo-Cano and Benítez-Eyzaguirre 2018)— and a 'party' phase (2014–2016), dominated by the creation of Podemos and the development of wide municipalist platforms at a local level (Rubio-Pueyo 2017), such as Barcelona en Comú or Ahora Madrid. The collective Fundación de los Comunes (2018, 10–11) has added a third phase to this periodisation, beginning in 2017–2018 and marked by a revitalisation of non-institutional struggles, such as the feminist movement (see Chapter 4) or the pensioners' movement (Alejos Escarpe 2018).

Although this temporal framework is fundamentally sound, I consider the stance taken by Diego Sztulwark to be more productive. In his analysis of the Argentinean crisis, Sztulwark (2019, 91) claims that an approach based on 'linear sequences' should be replaced by the 'coexistence of temporalities' – instead of seeing politics as a line that progresses across history, we need to focus upon a variety of events that coincide in time, but have their own patterns and dynamics. In this sense, viewing the 15M as a historical period defined by the notion of coexistence allows us to grasp the continuous interaction between citizens, activist collectives, and various forms of political groupings more vividly. Instead of placing these interactions in the strongly delimited phases of the temporal outline, this perspective acknowledges that each group evolves in a given way, which is nevertheless subject to exchanges and tensions with the rest. Besides, as I demonstrate in the following chapters, citizen platforms and collectives have emerged, mutated, and even disappeared across the whole period, further complicating a strictly linear approach.

The question of times and collectives dovetails with the place of citizen media within the materials of this book. In the opening volume of the series in which this monograph appears, Baker and Blaagaard (2016, 16) proposed an ambitious definition of citizen media that encompassed both 'physical artefacts, digital content, practices, performative interventions and discursive formations produced by unaffiliated citizens' and 'the sets of values and agendas that influence and drive the[se] practices and discourses'. Although this monograph is not directly grounded in the field of citizen media, it certainly covers a variety of such media as they interact with other political and cultural formations. Within the context of this book, I would argue that the majority of my case studies could be placed over a continuum of citizen practices, siding with Baker and Blaagaard's (2016, 2) assumption that any conceptualisation of citizen media is 'inevitably porous'. At one end, there would be those interventions that could be understood as proper citizen media, such as the 15M occupations, urban commons (like *La Ingobernable*, studied in Chapter 3), or the numerous examples of citizens spontaneously interacting around meanings, translations, and concepts within different networks (discussed, for instance, in Chapter 6). At the other end, I would place the evolutions of citizen media that have solidified to the point of becoming institutionalised, as would be the case of Barcelona en Comú (discussed in Chapter 3 and Chapter 5) and certainly Podemos (Chapter 6). While sharing some of the concerns and practices that characterised them in their emergence as citizen-led platforms, these formations are now subject to a whole set of inner tensions, power imbalances, and institutional responsibilities that frequently place them in contradiction with the causes and values they originally supported. In between those poles, it would be possible to place a whole set of citizen groupings that have generated a certain degree of affiliation through their persistence over time, while managing to retain their independence from institutions and corporations, such as cooperatives (addressed in Chapter 3) and the various activist groups and platforms analysed in Chapters 4 and 5.

A final caveat is required in terms of the languages and cultures used in this text. As the reader might know, Spain is a multilingual state. While Spanish (also known as Castilian) is the only official language across the country, four other languages are co-official in different communities: Galician (in Galicia), Basque (in the Basque Country and neighbouring areas of Navarra), Catalan (in Catalonia, Valencia, and the Balearic Islands), and Aranese, a variety of Occitan spoken in north-western Catalonia. Another two languages – Asturian and Aragonese – are protected in different regions, although they lack any special status. Therefore, addressing translation practices within this diversity requires a certain degree of choice. In this sense, I have aimed to strike a balance between the opposing necessities of precision and representativeness. In the analysis of politically committed publishers, which is developed in Chapter 2 and re-emerges in Chapter 4, I have focused exclusively on translations into Spanish, which constitute the largest part of the publishing field. Due to the particularities of the cultural and political contexts, flows of translation into other languages would have required separate analyses. However, in the reconstruction of political concepts, discourses, and activist groups conducted in different chapters, I have incorporated an important number of Catalan-speaking examples, as well as cases from Galician, Basque, and Asturian. Unless otherwise noted in the bibliography, all translations from these quoted examples are my own.

The role of critique in politicised research

As readers might have already guessed, this research draws upon an essential part of my life over recent years: innumerable hours of reading and writing, but also of attending meetings, conferences, and assemblies, joining rallies and sit-ins, contributing to debates, giving talks and seminars. It was not primarily a scholarly interest that drew me towards this topic; writing this book was rather a consequence of my involvement in political and activist life. Therefore, I prefer to dismiss from the start the false pretence that this book might have been written from a detached, supposedly objective position. However, unlike what certain dogmatics tend to believe, dismissing objectivity does not imply falling into the trap of a partial and self-celebratory work. On the contrary, my goal has been precisely to develop a critical and consistent analysis of my own generation's political achievements and failures. The difference between the militant author, the activist, and the professional political agent lies precisely in the possibility of distance and retreat. When the struggle is over, when the assembly leaves in disarray or an election is lost, the author can go back to their writing space – no matter how precarious this might be – and re-examine facts with different eyes, without aiming to justify or condone them. The agenda, the agreements or dissents, the strategy or the party line are no longer valid as measures of rightness or wrongness. And it is there and then, in the confrontation between the lived experience and the tools of reflective thought, where a contingent and temporary lesson might emerge and be useful for ourselves and for others.

Structure of the book

As discussed in this introduction, the present monograph establishes a dialogue with the fields of Translation Studies, Hispanic Studies, and Social Movements, which implies that I have aimed at addressing potential readers across all three domains. With this purpose in mind, I have not assumed any background knowledge and have provided a clear context for the main debates in the book. Inevitably, this implies that each reader will face the book from a different disciplinary angle, finding greater relevance in some sections than in others. Nevertheless, I hope that my take on these issues will also be of interest in those cases that are more familiar to the reader.

The first chapters of the book establish the foundations for later analyses. Chapter 1 presents the particularities of activism under globalisation before providing an in-depth overview of the relationships between translation and activism in this historical period, highlighting both the existing bibliography and potential gaps in research. In Chapter 2, I reconstruct the social and cultural characteristics of the 15M movement, uncovering a number of strands for the study of the larger 'climate' that has followed. Relying on approaches from different disciplines, I understand the 15M as a period characterised by renewed political engagement and disaffection with the immediate past, which creates an acute need for new concepts, references, and models in which translation plays a key role. In the final section of Chapter 2, I apply this lens to the renewed momentum of politically committed publishers and highlight their importance in the 15M climate.

The following three chapters focus on the centrality of translation practices for political activity within this period. Despite their differences, all three share a focus on the process of expanded translation of key concepts for activism and politics, as well as a concern for the ways in which political action incorporates translational components. Chapter 3 presents a detailed study of the 'commons' – a paradigm for horizontal and collaborative action – and its complex translation between languages, but also between theory and practice, without neglecting its conflicts and tensions. Importantly, the concept of the 'commons' will interact with other notions in Chapters 4 and 5, showing the interdependence of activist vocabulary. Chapter 4 addresses the importance of translation in the evolution of the feminist movement through the study of its genealogical practices and the centrality of the concept of 'care' in the development of the 2018 feminist strike. Chapter 5, meanwhile, covers a variety of activist collectives that share an opposition to the Spanish economic model, based upon the commodification of housing and mass tourism.

Finally, Chapter 6 provides a case study of the political party Podemos, created in 2014 as a response to the new political cycle that opened in 2011. As will be argued, Podemos represents a unique example of a 'translational' party, as an important part of its foundations, early discourse, and communicative practices are indebted to translation. At the same time, Podemos offers an opportunity to address the limits that certain understandings of translation can pose to political activity. In this sense, the party offers a cluster of some of the most relevant examples of translation practice in this period, yet also some of its clearest failures and distortions, thus providing an appropriate counterpoint to previous chapters.

Across Chapters 2 to 6, I have interspersed the main sections with independent textboxes, a common practice in the social sciences. Textboxes provide an opportunity for the discussion of lengthier examples that would perhaps break up the reading experience if analysed within the main text, but deserve more attention than a footnote, which all too frequently escape the attention of readers. In some cases, the textbox functions as an expansion on an issue that has been mentioned, while in others it serves as a counter-example, an opposition, or even a criticism to the main line of thought. Since they create intervals between larger sections of discourse, readers are welcome to integrate them into their reading or to address them after they have finished reading a chapter.

1 The many voices of opposition
Activism and translation in a global context

For readers who are not acquainted with the field, the study of translation and interpreting could seem to be mainly concerned with linguistic and textual issues. Although this has been occasionally the case, there is an important strand within Translation Studies that has engaged with the promotion of dissent and the impact of power inequalities upon linguistic practices for many decades. In a previous publication (Evans and Fernández 2018, 4–8), my co-author and I called it 'a secret history of translation studies' in order to emphasise the relatively marginal role of this heritage of thought while simultaneously aiming to emphasise its continuity over time. As we pointed out there, this line of reflection addresses issues as diverse as the role of translation in colonialism, the relationship between translation and resistance to power, or the role of translators within these structures.

Approaches to translation and interpreting as forms of activism provide a contemporary extension to this 'secret history', even if the branch itself is relatively recent and the available bibliography is modest in comparison with other strands of research. In this chapter, I will outline how activism has evolved in our current historical period, characterised by the combined impact of globalisation and neoliberalism. As I will argue, this impact itself represents an object of confrontation for activist endeavours. Secondly, I will present different approaches to activist translation and interpreting, before moving into a survey of existing research that connects translation and interpreting with activism against the negative effects of globalisation, which is precisely where I place the 15M movement and its later evolutions within this monograph.

Understanding activism in a globalised context

'Activism' is a concept that has been used extensively in social debates over recent decades. Its meaning, however, is frequently 'emotional and ill-defined' (Baker 2018, 453), the term being characterised by 'its inherent slipperiness'. In the context of this book, it will be understood as a broad set of activities undertaken by individuals – generally, although not exclusively organised as a group or community – who aim to change the current state of affairs in the name of a given cause. A key characteristic of activism is the fact that it 'goes beyond conventional politics' (Martin 2007, 20), that is, it does not follow the standard channels for political action, which in the case of democratic systems are generally assumed to be parties, elections, unions, and similar platforms. However, as will be seen, boundaries between activism and standard politics have become blurred over recent years, with the emergence of citizens' platforms that run for local and regional elections (in the Spanish case, the whole spectrum of the so-called 'municipalismo') or that even become actual parties, as in the complex case of Podemos, which will be analysed and discussed in Chapter 6.

A key characteristic of activist groups is that they tend to be 'set up outside the mainstream institutions of society', since their agendas 'explicitly challenge the dominant narratives of the time' (Baker 2006a, 462). In other words, activism vigorously opposes the key pillars of a given society (the institutions) as a way of promoting a different social model. Activist goals can range from merely influencing public opinion by raising awareness on a topic to more vocal actions, such as exposing an injustice, denouncing individuals or collectives, and even providing help and support to certain social groups. In this sense, therefore, activism is not a recent development, but it has rather 'been present throughout history, in every sort of political system' (Martin 2007, 19). In fact, as explored later in this chapter, the study of translation has occasionally attempted to read back 'activist' endeavours in past periods on the basis of this commonality.

Bearing in mind the long history of activism, this chapter will focus exclusively on activism under globalisation, which is another 'contested concept' (Steger 2013, 1), and for which multiple definitions and periodisations coexist. In this monograph, I privilege an understanding of globalisation as an advanced stage in the evolution of capitalism that began in the 1970s, enabled by the evolution of technology, a transformation of regulatory practices, and the increasing development of transnational frameworks. From this angle, therefore, globalisation will be here understood as an economic and political project that has enabled the implementation of neoliberalism on a global scale (Harvey 2005).

A decisive step for the advent of globalised neoliberalism has been the development of a completely new infrastructure for finance, capital, communication, migration, and travel (Pieterse 2009, 9). This was enabled by a 'boom in information and communications technologies' (*ibid.*) and the facilitation of commercial exchanges that has accompanied the implementation of several common regulatory frameworks, such as the establishment of the European Common Market (1993), the North American Free Trade Agreement or NAFTA (1994), and the World Trade Organization (1995). In this way, globalisation is characterised by discourses of 'exchange' and 'movement', as increasing flows of capital, goods, people, and information have become the cornerstone of the social and economic system.

As a consequence of these processes, the globalised world is characterised by a blurring of economic and political boundaries, as the market is no longer 'enclosed within' or 'embedded' in each administrative unit. On the contrary, nation-states have become 'jurisdictional claims *in a unitary world market*' (Arrighi, Hopkins and Wallerstein 1989, 6; my italics), since neoliberalism has unified the world into a single political and economic system within which nation-states have lost important degrees of sovereignty and become secondary actors, mostly in charge of law-enforcement and security. As Joseph Stiglitz (2002, 21; my italics) put it in an oft-cited phrase, under neoliberal globalisation we have 'global governance *without* global government'. This is thanks to a 'growth in the density of the interstate system' – with the approval and enforcement of the frameworks mentioned earlier, among others – and has in turn led to 'an enmeshing' of the internal and the external processes (Arrighi, Hopkins and Wallerstein 1989, 43–44). In other words, political and economic processes under globalisation tend to acquire an international and global dimension that reduces the potential for local and regional opposition, a characteristic that will have important consequences for activism. At the same time, this process leads to greater tension between citizens and governments, as the latter are elected by the former yet are frequently allied with a variety of elites (creditors, investors, and banks, among others). Colin Crouch (2004) conceptualised this process of disaffection through the notion of 'post-democracy', which emphasises the increasingly restricted and technical role of democratic processes within nation-states. Meanwhile, Wolfgang Streeck (2015, 11–13) has provocatively claimed that contemporary governments need to address the demands from two constituencies or 'peoples': the *Staatsvolk* ('the people of the state') and the *Marktvolk* ('the people of the market'). As will be seen, the 'post-democratic' disaffection and the split within this 'double' constituency will be major themes for activism too.

With its emphasis on exchanges, globalisation is also characterised by the advent of what has been called 'network society' (Castells 2000) or, with more negative overtones, 'communicative capitalism' (Dean 2017, 6). Through global networks and information technology, contemporary capitalism is altering most aspects of human life, from the dissemination of knowledge to the organisation of society. Daily life is structured through an unending and constantly expanding list of technologies across multiple fields, such as communication, language learning, friendship and romance, transportation, budget and tax payment, or workplace management, to name a few. This transformation is obviously not neutral, as it implies that capital has a 'new capacity', one that is certainly unprecedented, to 'capture the activities through which we reproduce our social lives' (Dean 2017, 7), monetarising and extracting benefit from every human action. In fact, it has been strongly argued that data and information generated by users of technology in their daily routines have become the most important commodity of our time (Wark 2019, 1–6) as they enable processes such as social control, prediction of habits, automation of jobs, and product placement.

Finally, a major criticism of globalisation revolves around the way in which it has resulted in greater inequality (Harvey 2005, 16–18), fostering the enrichment of the upper echelons of society and a more unfair distribution of wealth. As the authors of the World Inequality Report 2018 have emphasised, 'income inequality has increased rapidly in North America, China, India, and Russia' since 1980, while growing 'moderately in Europe' (Alvaredo, Chancel, Piketty, Saez and Zucman 2018, 5). In their view, 'this increase in inequality marks the end of a post-war egalitarian regime which took different forms in these regions'. Along with the rebuttal of this post-Second World War system, based upon extensive welfare and social distribution, the globalised expansion of neoliberalism goes hand in hand with the increasing 'economisation' of reality, that is, a conception of every human and social element in economic and market terms. The idea that neoliberalism does not simply constitute an 'ideology' or an 'economic model', but rather a 'political' and 'governing rationality' was first addressed by Michel Foucault in his 1978–1979 lectures at the Collège de France (Foucault 2004) and has been further explored by authors like Dardot and Laval (2009) and Wendy Brown (2015). From this angle, neoliberalism is understood as a mode of governance that goes far beyond the economy, as it transforms values, behaviours, subjects, and social relationships within a framework of constant competition. This restructuring of 'reality' leads in turn to the imposition of what has been called 'capitalist realism' (Fisher 2009, 1–2): an ideological framework under which capitalism is presented as 'the only viable political and economic system', thus legitimising its inherent inequalities and discrediting any attempt 'even to *imagine* a coherent alternative to it' (*ibid.*).

On the basis of this brief outline, it is possible to highlight certain specificities of activism under globalisation that will form the backbone of my approach in this chapter and, more widely, throughout this monograph. In my understanding, 'globalised' activism is characterised by three factors: an awareness of the need for global solidarity and cooperation in order to oppose the consequences of globalisation, an evolution beyond the traditional definition of the working classes, and an ambiguous relationship with the technological evolution of globalisation.

The first element is the most obvious, since one of the defining activist movements under globalisation has been the so-called 'alter-globalisation', 'global justice', or 'anti-globalisation' movement (Hands 2010, 142). This developed at the end of the 1990s and early 2000s (Della Porta 2007; Reitan 2007) through massive demonstrations against transnational institutions such as the World Trade Organization, the World Bank, or the G8. The activist platforms grouped under this rubric found their origins in the denunciation of various aspects of globalisation – such as the signature of NAFTA, the activities of the International Monetary Fund, the piling up of poor countries' foreign debt, or rising inequality – and emphasised 'a critique of the democratic deficit of the supranational bodies and global institutions' that have fostered globalisation, as well as a rejection 'of the market-oriented policies of these institutions' (Wennerhag 2010, 28). Alter-globalisation also espoused the first critique of the above-mentioned 'capitalist realism' through its emphasis on the existence of alternatives: one of its most quoted slogans was 'Another World is Possible', which synthesised both the global character of the struggle and the strong correlation between globalisation and the opposition to its negative effects.

The so-called 'movement of the squares' (Gerbaudo 2017) or 'anti-austerity and pro-democracy protests' (Flesher Fominaya 2017, 2–4) that took to the streets of many global cities in the years following the 2008 economic crisis can be understood as being closely related to the global justice movement. This 'array of popular and anti-establishment protest movements' between 2011 and 2016 (Gerbaudo 2017, 32) involved the occupation of public spaces across a great variety of countries (Egypt, Tunisia, Libya, Greece, Spain, the United States, Turkey, and France, to name just a few) to protest against the social consequences of the crisis, such as major cuts to public services and investments. As was the case with the alter-globalisation movement, these actions espoused a strong international perspective – as I will discuss in Chapter 2, there were frequent references to and borrowings from other movements taking place at the time – and a rejection of the centrality of neoliberal economy. Furthermore, they criticised their governments for betraying democracy and placing the interests of the elites (either national or international) before those of the people, which highlighted the tension evoked earlier between *Staatsvolk* and *Marktvolk*. Although there are certain differences between both movements (Gerbaudo 2017, 19–25), we may view the global justice movement and the movement of the squares as two 'waves' of the same 'epoch of contention' (Wolfson and Funke 2016, 62) against the consequences of globalisation.

A second salient aspect of activism under globalisation is the defence of diversity (cultural, sexual, racial, environmental, and linguistic), which ties in with both the birth of alter-globalisation and the ascent of identity politics. Although the claims of oppressed and minority groups played an important role in traditional protests, they have acquired a central role under globalisation. On the one hand, this is connected to the ongoing decline of traditional progressive movements, mostly centred upon the working class and the conditions of labour. This transition has been at the core of many discussions regarding political action (such as Laclau and Mouffe 1985 or Butler 2000) and will resonate in different sections of this book. On the other hand, the increasing expansion of capitalism across the globe, with its associated threats to traditional environments and ways of life, has also firmly placed the protection of diversity in the spotlight.

A well-known concept, 'identity politics' refers to 'a wide range of political activity and theorizing founded upon the shared experiences of injustice of members of certain social groups' (Heyes 2018). It came to the fore in the 1960s and 1970s with 'the emergence of large-scale political movements' such as 'second wave feminism, Black Civil Rights in the U.S., gay and lesbian liberation, and the American Indian movements' (*ibid.*). The appearance of these groups demanding recognition of their difference would later feed into anti-globalisation concerns for the fate of indigenous and traditional peoples across the world, who see their ways of life threatened in the name of capitalist expansion. In fact, indigenous peoples have always been strongly represented in the World Social Forum, an annual meeting of activists and civic organisations that started in 2001, which is strongly linked to the global justice movement (Santos 2006). Based upon this double strand of dissent, many of the most significant activist movements that have taken shape in recent decades have espoused the claims of collectives that are oppressed, threatened, or discriminated against. Prominent examples would be Black Lives Matter (Lebron 2017), which campaigns against systemic racism and violence towards black people in the US, and the global feminist movement *Ni Una Menos* ('Not even one [woman] less'), which started in Argentina in 2015 (Gago and Cavallero 2017) to protest violence and discrimination against women and has later expanded to many countries across the world (the Spanish case will play an important role in Chapter 4 of this book).

Finally, a third defining characteristic of activism under globalisation is its relationship with technology, a factor that cuts across a variety of campaigns and causes. Like any other human endeavour, activism is conditioned to a great extent by technology (Hands 2010, 23), and technological change is a key determining factor for globalisation. While previous generations of activists relied on means of communication that were strongly time and location dependent (e.g. letters, pamphlets, books, or newspapers), the advent of new media, such as the internet, mobile phones, and social networking, has made communication quicker and easier, enabling activists to coordinate their activities in unprecedented ways. Although this was already a characteristic of the alter-globalisation movement (Tarrow 2006, 116–117, 136–138, 210–212 *passim*), the role of social media such as Facebook, Twitter, and YouTube became paramount for the organisation and coordination of protests during the movement of the squares (Gerbaudo 2012), as well as for the international dissemination of these events (Romanos 2016). However, the centrality of technological means for new protests has also been criticised for its 'cyberfetishism', which equates media and network presence with tangible results in everyday life (Rendueles 2013; Morozov 2013). In this sense, the proven ability of governments to ban access to certain sites (Xiao 2011) and even to shut down the internet (Ritzen 2018) as a means of stifling dissent should serve as a cautionary tale against an excessive faith in technology. In fact, growing awareness of its potential abuses and misuses has generated an important strand of activism that focuses specifically on technology, such as data activism (Gutiérrez 2018), which utilises data infrastructure as a way of denouncing an injustice or raising awareness of a risk, and hacktivism (Karagiannopoulos 2018), a rather loose set of practices that put traditional hacking (i.e. illicitly taking control of a computer, website, or computing system) at the service of a given cause. The group Anonymous, which has launched cyberattacks against a variety of corporations and governments, and the Wikileaks project, which has leaked secret information on sensitive matters (such as the US-led wars in Afghanistan and Iraq), can be seen as notable examples of this type of activism.

Translation, interpreting, and activism: approaches and main areas of research

The conceptualisation of translation and interpreting as forms of activism is relatively recent, going back to the beginning of the 21st century. Despite the relative paucity of research on the topic, interest is clearly growing, as shown by an increasing number of publications (Brownlie 2010; Baker 2018; Carcelén-Estrada 2018) aimed at charting the field, and even the proposal of an 'activist turn' (Wolf 2012), in line with previous 'turns' in the history of the discipline. In this section, I will sketch two main approaches to activism within the field, according to their focus on the individual or the collective, before reviewing the existing bibliography on the contribution that translation and interpreting have made to activist movements that oppose the consequences of globalisation, focusing upon the 'two waves' of anti-globalisation: the 1990s global justice movements and the 2010s movement of the squares.

Approaches to 'activism' in Translation Studies

As Brownlie (2010, 46) has argued, research on activism in Translation Studies can be divided into two main groups: on the one hand, the study and reappraisal of 'activist' translators and interpreters; on the other, the role of translation and interpreting in the advocacy of certain political causes. This division involves, in turn, two further oppositions: the past versus the contemporary and the individual versus the collective.

A notable example of the first trend of study is a much-cited piece by Maria Tymoczko (2000), which offers the first explicit attempt — though one that is at times rather unclear and self-centred — to discuss translation as a form of activism. By looking at how numerous Irish translators reworked the myth of the hero Cú Chulainn across several decades and put it at the service of various ideological projects, Tymoczko argues that activist and engaged translation should be understood 'as a sort of speech act' (2000, 26), that is, a textual construction that has effects upon external reality through its 'involvement in conflict or battle' (31). Other scholars (Milton 2006; Guo 2008; Cheung 2010) have shared her textual approach, studying the ways in which past translators can be understood as activists through the production of translations that are aimed at eliciting social change.

The second strand of research on the topic has focused strictly on contemporary activism, placing greater significance on communities. A major reference in this area is Mona Baker's work and her 'narrative' approach. In her seminal book *Translation and Conflict*, Baker (2006b) argues that narratives — 'everyday stories we live by' (Baker 2006b, 3) — are paramount to the functioning of societies, as they form the basis of exchange, mediation, and transmission of knowledge, ideologies, and attitudes. At the same time, narratives are also 'dynamic', which implies that at any given time it is possible to find 'a variety of divergent, criss-crossing, often vacillating narratives' (*ibid.*) that coexist. Since narratives are fundamental to the legitimacy of the status quo, a central method in undermining a regime is to challenge 'the stories that sustain [it]' through the articulation of 'alternative stories' (*ibid*.) – a point at which, as Baker shows, translation and interpreting can play a central role. In an article published in the same year, Baker (2006a) linked the notion of narrative with activism by looking at 'narrative communities': communities of translators and interpreters who have been brought together by a shared narrative that aims to transform social reality (2006a, 471–472). In Baker's view, this 'emerging pattern of communities' is characterised by both a political commitment and an awareness of the transnationality of struggles – a defining characteristic of globalised activism, as I have argued –, since they understand that contemporary conflicts 'reverberate across the planet and, almost without exception, are played out in the international arena' (472).

The existing bibliography on activist communities constitutes a major point of reference in the field. Given its clear link to the problematic of globalisation, it is addressed at various points in the following sections and chapters. For the time being, it is important to highlight a main divide. While on the one hand, we can find communities whose members identify themselves *professionally* as translators and interpreters, and who put their skills at the service of a given cause (De Manuel Jerez, López Cortes and Brander de la Iglesia 2004; Baker 2006a, 2013; Boéri 2008, 2012), on the other we have communities formed by *non-professional* translators and interpreters, who nevertheless use their linguistic abilities and their shared knowledge for political purposes (Pérez-González 2010, 2016; Baker 2016b). In this sense, with the evolution of technology over recent decades, the potential for activist networks to become fluid and no longer bound to a shared place has increased exponentially, even redefining the very notion of 'community'. For instance, Neilson (2009) has reflected on the potential of 'open translation' with the emergence of platforms such as Tlaxcala and Global Voices, which are based on 'free and open source software tools' and are loosely defined, since anyone sharing their values is welcome to join the collective practice. Pérez-González (2010) has gone even further, highlighting the emergence of what he calls 'ad-hocracies of activist translators', that is, groups of individual users who start cooperating online on translational tasks without any previous knowledge of each other. Nevertheless, as will be discussed in the following sections, this trend has not meant the end of activist communities in a more traditional sense, including those that are location-based.

Translation and interpreting within the alter-globalisation movement

As discussed, the alter-globalisation or global justice movement was born in the 1990s in opposition to the consequences of neoliberal globalisation. Its truly transnational constitution and the variety of movements that came together implied, in turn, a great diversity of languages and a need for mediation services. In fact, it could be argued that translation and interpreting were the truly enabling means for these movements. As a British activist attending a transnational meeting in Spain in 1997 remarked:

> With me were delegates from the Karnataka State Farmers Association, Indonesia's land reform struggle, the landless peasant movement Sem Terra from Brazil, Bolivian mine-workers, Ogoni people from Nigeria, Gorlbeen anti-nuclear activists – to name but a few. [...] *As teams of translators gave meaning to the voices of the voiceless I began to realise that our struggles which at first appeared so different were intricately linked.* In spite of the cultural and language differences between us I made friends. A week later [,] representatives of hundreds of groups had committed themselves to taking action together.
>
> (quoted in Reitan 2007, 43; my italics)

This reflection brings to the fore a key element of activism in a globalised world: under the unitary market created by neoliberalism, citizens across multiple locations face similar economic and political pressures that might seem completely different on the surface, but are inextricably linked to the overarching capitalist system. In this sense, translation and interpreting are tools that *reveal the commonality* between different struggles.

A major strand of research on this phase of the alter-globalisation movement has focused on the work of an organisation of voluntary interpreters, Babels, which was 'set up in September 2002 by a group of activists linked to the French branch of the alternative globalization network, ATTAC' (Baker 2006a, 474). Babels labelled itself as 'an international network of volunteer interpreters and translators' who had the goal of using 'their skills and expertise for the benefit of those social and citizens' movements that adhere to the charter of principles of the Social Forums' (Babels n.d.). As such, Babels coordinated interpreting services at various Social Forums – the main meeting of the global justice movement – between 2002 and 2014. However, this cooperation ended in 2014. In 2015, Babels refused to offer their volunteer services at the World Social Forum (WSF) due to the lack of consultation and dialogue on behalf of the organisation (Babels 2015). Furthermore, in 2016 they again declined to participate due to a controversial decision by the WSF organising committee to offer interpretation only into French, English, and Spanish – described by Babels as 'three colonial languages' – and a lack of both sufficient equipment and funding (Babels 2016).

As these examples show, Babels has been characterised by frequent conflict throughout their existence. In 2005, Peter Naumann, a German professional interpreter who had worked at a number of WSFs before the arrival of Babels, heavily criticised the collective for their interpretation services in 2005, which he characterised as lacking professionalism and showing poor quality. From a narrative perspective, Boéri (2008) analysed this controversy and argued that each position was shaped by different understandings of commitment, which in turn led to different conceptions of conference interpreting. While Babels showed strong '[c]ommitment to participation and horizontality', Naumann manifested 'commitment to expertise and rationality' (Boéri 2008, 43). The former leads to a vision of 'a horizontal world' where interpreting is 'the product of the collective participation of individuals from a wide range of backgrounds', while the latter espouses 'an expertise-based hierarchical world' in which 'conference interpreters are portrayed as an elite of gifted individuals' (44). These tensions between 'horizontality' and 'verticality' – understood in this context as non-hierarchical versus hierarchical social structures – have plagued Babels on more than one occasion. At the London Social Forum in 2004, Babels released a statement criticising the organisation of the Forum; yet this communiqué had only been written and approved by certain members, which led to 'dissatisfaction among volunteers', as some of them 'felt they had not been informed of the organizational process nor consulted with respect to Babels' statement' (Boéri 2012, 276), effectively contradicting the network's commitment to horizontality and member participation.

From a different perspective, Babels and, by extension, translation and interpreting have been studied as a central factor for enhancing inclusion and fostering more democratic practices in political deliberation. Through the comparison of monolingual national activist meetings and multilingual meetings at the European Social Forum (ESF), Doerr (2012) has argued that the presence of interpreters at the ESF created a more welcoming space for newcomers and minorities. In this case, the need for a slower pace of deliberation in order to accommodate interpreting services between different languages fostered a more attentive and inclusive attitude among participants (Doerr 2012, 13–16). By contrast, monolingual deliberations were more strongly characterised by 'hierarchical settings that reproduced inequalities of class, gender, and ethnicity' (18).

Moving beyond Babels and the alter-globalisation movement, Doerr would later develop and expand this argument in her book *Political Translation* (2018), in which she analyses the work of a variety of grassroots 'political translators' who diverge from the supposed 'neutrality' that some users expect from them and 'openly intervene to challenge cultural and linguistic power asymmetries' (Doerr 2018, 4). In this way, Doerr posits an understanding of 'political translation' as 'a broad set of practices designed to address marginalization based on gender, class, race, and other differences' (6). Importantly, she also focuses on the tension experienced by 'institutional political translators' (79–93), that is, members of given communities who lose their credit among the people that they were supposed to help as they progressively become embedded in the trappings of institutional politics. In my view, the notion of 'institutional political translators' offers a useful tool to explore the conflicts between contemporary activism and standard politics. In different sections of this monograph and particularly in Chapter 6, I will analyse similar cases of translational tensions.

Finally, the World Social Forum itself has been studied as a translational space. Understanding the concept in a wider sense that goes beyond interlingual translation, Portuguese sociologist Boaventura de Sousa Santos has argued that translation can be 'the procedure that allows for mutual intelligibility' among multiple experiences of the world, such as the ones that came together at the WSF, 'without jeopardizing their identity and autonomy' or 'reducing them to homogeneous entities' (Santos 2006, 131–132). In this sense, Santos sees translation as the element that can bring together a diverse range of movements that would otherwise run the risk of falling into atomisation (132), by 'reinforcing what is common in the diversity of counter-hegemonic drive' (133).

Along with the WSF, another collective that is central to understanding the alter-globalisation movement was undoubtedly the Mexican Ejército Zapatista de Liberación Nacional ('Zapatista Army of National Liberation'), commonly known as the Zapatistas or EZLN. The EZLN came to the fore on 1 January 1994, the day the North American Free Trade Agreement came into effect, when they issued a declaration against NAFTA and the Mexican government. The EZLN opposed NAFTA on the basis of the threat it presented to the survival of traditional indigenous agriculture, as the agreement would ease 'the influx of cheap goods, particularly corn, from US-based agribusiness' (Wolfson and Funke 2016, 68). After a few days of armed skirmishes against the Mexican army, the Zapatistas retreated to the Lacandon Jungle in Chiapas, from where they have continued to develop their struggle.

Born out of decades of collaboration between a Marxist-Leninist guerrilla and various indigenous movements, the EZLN has drawn upon numerous practices of translation. According to its most widely known spokesperson, Subcomandante Marcos, the Zapatista movement was created through 'the process of translation of this Marxist-Leninist university culture into indigenous culture' (Subcomandante Marcos and Le Bot 1997, 292). Marcos, who also sees himself as a 'translator' (137, 165), claims that 'the true creators of Zapatismo were the translators' (292), as they reformulated and transformed their ideological framework into the many indigenous dialects. At the same time, translation and interpreting were a central element for the armed struggle of the guerrillas, as indigenous groups and Spanish-speaking troops communicated through members of the collective who can translate between languages (173–174).

Along with its emphasis on direct democracy (Wolfson and Funke 2016, 69), the EZLN has played a central role in the alter-globalisation movement through their involvement in media and cyberspace activism. From an early stage, various networks of activists across the world helped to disseminate the EZLN's message by uploading and translating their *comunicados* (communiqués) and related news. An electronic book on the Zapatistas (Autonomedia 1994) had already been put together in 1994 by 'an e-mail coordinated team translating material largely gathered from The Net' (Cleaver 1998), in what was perhaps one of the very first examples of translation cyberactivism. In its introduction, the book was described as follows:

22 *The many voices of opposition*

> [It has been] produced by an all[-]volunteer Editorial Collective, and many of the translations were 'farmed out' to volunteers all over the internet. This book (and much of the publicity about the EZLN[)] would not have been possible without the growing community of politically-minded people on the internet.
>
> (Autonomedia 1994, 1)

Unfortunately, to the best of my knowledge, there is very little research available on the different networks that developed this collective work of translation. Moreover, the evolution of the internet over the last twenty years – with the arrival of new communication systems and the deletion of numerous mailing lists and websites that are no longer in use – suggests that much of this information is probably irretrievable. In an early piece, Shirley (2001, 8, 22) briefly touches upon the role of The Groundwork Collective, a student organisation at the University of California at San Diego, and the National Commission for Democracy in Mexico–USA in the maintenance and translation of the first Zapatista website; neither of these groups appears to be active at the moment. However, translation activism in support of the EZLN is still a dynamic area: the website Enlace Zapatista (Zapatist Link) regularly uploads Zapatista communiqués and related documents, which are translated into a variety of languages (English, Italian, German, French, and, to a lesser extent, Greek and Arabic).

The movement of the squares and the second wave of activist translation

The global economic and social crisis of 2008 led to a period of turmoil that, rather than being over, seems to have since evolved into two distinct phases. As already mentioned, the first of these was the so-called movement of the squares, which comprised a series of 'anti-establishment protest movements' (Gerbaudo 2017, 32) across multiple countries. The Spanish 'indignados' or 15M movement, which is the main subject of this book, was placed within this first phase, and I will discuss its characteristics in greater detail in the following chapter. The second phase involves a series of reactions, which partially overlap with the former in a chronological sense and share some of its anti-establishment concerns – criticisms of corruption and the economic inequalities of globalisation, loss of sovereignty, political disaffection, and uncertainty over the future – while reformulating them in a nationalist and conservative framework, such as the xenophobic strand within the Brexit campaign in the UK (2016), the election of Donald Trump as President of the USA (2017), and the increasing presence of the far-right in European parliaments. To date, very little work has been done on the role of translation within this nationalist strand of anti-globalisation, a notable exception being the ongoing work by Joseph Keady (2018). Therefore, in this section I will focus exclusively on the role of translation and interpreting within the first of these phases.

From the very beginning, translation and interpreting were decisive for the emergence of the 'movement of the squares'. This is particularly true of their need to disseminate information on their own existence and, without them, further processes of imitation and solidarity would have been impossible. Both voluntary and professional translators and interpreters contributed to this dissemination, either by providing linguistic and logistical support to foreign journalists covering the events (as in the case of the so-called 'fixers': Gunter 2011), or by raising international awareness of these causes and developments through the means of translation (Baker 2016a, 2016b; Emmerich 2015; Selim 2016). A variety of international journals and collaborative sites – such as *Open Democracy, Rebelión, Sin Permiso, Révolution Permanente*, or *Paris-Luttes*, to name a few – consistently used translation to provide context and coverage of the various struggles taking place, enhancing the potential commonality between the protests.

This translational density, however, has not been matched by studies in the field. The Egyptian uprisings of 2011 and their aftermath, which played a key role in the birth and evolution of the movement of the squares, are the only event that has generated a noteworthy body of research on translation activism. In 2012, an edited collection (Mehrez 2012) was published following a collective project at the American University of Cairo, compiling university students' translations of chants, slogans, poems, interviews, and communiqués, as well as reflections on the difficulties and nuances of the translational process. In 2016, another edited collection (Baker 2016a) took a more complex angle, bringing together a series of reflections on the translation of the Egyptian revolution across multiple media, including poetry, documentary film, street art, and comics. Within this strand, the activist video collective Mosireen, which incorporated the work of activist subtitlers, has attracted significant attention. One of those volunteer subtitlers (Selim 2016) reflected on the influence of political commitment upon the task of the translator, emphasising how activists at Mosireen worked 'with the intention of building international solidarity networks', 'always with one eye to other uprisings' (84–85).

Meanwhile, Baker (2016c) has studied the work of Mosireen and Words of Women from the Egyptian Revolution to analyse whether subtitling enhances or, on the contrary, undermines these projects' political commitment. Through sustained fieldwork and textual analysis, Baker investigates the lack of awareness towards subtitling on behalf of many activists, the secondary and passive role played by volunteer translators, and how their translations frequently fail to adhere to the principles of solidarity and diversity that underpin the movements. For instance, Baker (2016c, 9–10) shows how the choice of languages for the subtitles, with a strong prevalence of English, has limited the expressions of solidarity that the collectives received, as it precluded the possibility of establishing a fruitful dialogue with other movements taking place across the African continent. Furthermore, collectives are not systematic in their use of translation practices in a way that can reflect the diversity of the speakers interviewed, and subtitlers show a tendency to erase linguistic diversity in favour of coherence and semantic meaning.

For the time being, protest movements in this wave remain largely unacknowledged from this perspective, either from the field of Social Movement Studies or from Translation Studies. In an early piece, Mowbray (2010) analysed the importance of blogs in the international dissemination of information on the Greek riots of 2008, and briefly noted the presence of translation as part of their activity, although there is no reflection on their production and reception. Similarly, Heloïse Nez (2016) noted in her study of the 15M that different documents released by the assemblies were translated into several languages, yet she does not list the language choices or address their production. From a different angle, activist Mark Bray (2013) has proposed an understanding of Occupy Wall Street in terms of intralingual translation, arguing that the movement aimed at translating anarchist ideas into a language that could overcome the ideological prejudices that American audiences might have towards anarchism. Finally, my previous work on the Spanish 15M movement and its evolution (Fernández 2018, 2020a), which feeds into this monograph, constitutes the only available material on the translational aspects of this event.

Conclusions and points of departure

This review of the field of translation as a form of activism under globalisation has highlighted a number of issues and lacunae, many of which this monograph aims to address, while also providing a number of relevant points that will be useful for my analyses. Firstly, it has emphasised how translation is paramount for contemporary activism due to the *global* condition of both the economic and political system (neoliberalism) and of the resistance to it (alterglobalisation, movement of the squares). The increasing unification of governance under neoliberalism means that political action needs to move beyond the traditional notion of the nation-state, which in turn requires significant effort in communication, dissemination, and translation on behalf of activist groups. Indeed, it could be argued that global activism would be impossible without the existence of translation, regardless of the degree of awareness that political agents might have of it. As I argue in various chapters of this book, translation – as a specific form of communication – can be the decisive tool in helping activist groups find *commonality* among their struggles, either at the transnational and interlinguistic level – revealing the unitary nature of the system they are facing under the apparent diversity of their problems – or at the national and intralinguistic level – brokering a common platform of action beyond the multiple demands that they are defending.

A second important element for the contemporary study of activist translation is the multiplication of materials, formats, and means enabled by the increasing use of technology and the communicative nature of capitalism. Along with traditional written means, from books to journals or pamphlets, understanding activist translation now implies moving through social media, blogs, websites, mailing lists, chats, podcasts, and online videos, among other platforms. From the perspective of the researcher, this proliferation has two obvious, and somewhat conflicting, consequences as we must navigate both a seemingly endless list of sources that can be taken into account while recognising the volatility of those same sources due to ongoing editing, potential deletions, or site closures (be they politically motivated or not). At a deeper level, it presents an interesting conundrum: while this multiplication of voices allows for a more nuanced approach to the materials, one must not lose sight of the different degrees of relevance and social reach that each source has. Throughout this book, I have aimed to find a balance between core texts and the variety of fleeting comments and reactions that coexist with them, as I am convinced that this swarm of engagements can shed light on the main argument.

A final element, which is firmly connected with the previous one, is the diversity of translators. Unlike other forms of translation within the field of politics, activist translation is not clearly defined along professional versus non-professional lines, since both forms of translation coexist. As I will show in the following chapters, relevant and valuable examples of activist discourse can appear in the form of a book translated by a professional with a name and a career, but also in a blogpost or social media publication written by an anonymous activist who has linguistic skills but no familiarity with the task. Combining the proliferation of media and the proliferation of producers, the process of translation leads to the space of expanded translation that I evoked in the introduction: an expanding field of exchanges, tensions, and imbalances that defies a linear analysis based on a restricted set of materials.

2 Translation-as-tradition

The 15M between past and present

On Sunday 15 May 2011, a series of large demonstrations took place across Spain. In principle, there was nothing unusual about this: popular protests had become part and parcel of Spanish daily life since the beginning of the economic crisis. The unexpected global recession had revealed the weaknesses of Spain's remarkable economic performance at the turn of the twenty-first century, exposing its heavy dependence on property development and aggressive banking practices (López and Rodríguez 2011, 5–6; see also Chapter 5 in this book). Soaring unemployment, widespread corruption of the political elite, and the implementation of austerity policies had firstly led to an economic crisis and then to a crisis of legitimacy, as citizens began to mistrust and challenge Spanish institutions (Simón 2012). If anything, those May demonstrations offered a vivid confirmation of the crisis, since they had been organised by a network of citizens' platforms, outside of the standard channels of political parties, under a slogan that questioned one of the basic tenets of the system: ¡Democracia Real YA! ('Real Democracy NOW!'). The magnitude of the social rift was clear to see, with a country that was formally considered a democracy no longer deemed a democracy by its own citizens.

Following the demonstration in Madrid, however, something unexpected happened. A small group of protesters – later to be known as 'los 40 de Sol', 'the forty [people] at Sol' – decided to spend the night in the central square of Sol, a highly iconic space for Spanish citizens having been shown on innumerable TV shows and with its tower clock playing a central role during New Year celebrations. In the early hours of Monday 16, a few police agents approached protesters and had a tense exchange with them, before eventually allowing the small group to sleep rough in the square (Sánchez n.d.). As information on the gathering started circulating on social networks, more and more people decided to camp, not only in Madrid but also in other cities across the country (Razquin 2017, 71–72). The following morning, journalists started covering the occupations, giving them yet another boost (Sánchez n.d.). In less than a week, makeshift camps had been formed by protesters in at least sixty Spanish cities, including major capitals like Barcelona and Seville (El País 2011b). Sol Square, the symbolic centre of the movement, brought together up to 28,000 citizens at peak times. The 15M movement was born.

Over the following weeks, occupations galvanised the country, puzzling politicians and observers alike. Camps attracted citizens from various social strata who engaged in open discussions at popular assemblies and committees (Della Porta 2015, 1–2). In this way, they became places for a political practice, common within social movements, that is known as 'prefiguration' (Maeckelbergh 2011). Instead of deferring the construction of their envisaged society to the future, protesters aimed to construct it there and then, in the temporary setting of the squares. If the movement had started by criticising the lack of 'real' democracy in Spain, assemblies became an experiment in 'direct democracy' (Sitrin and Azzellini 2014, 121–150; Della Porta 2015, 157–210), where every person was encouraged to speak and to contribute to the discussion, regardless of their specific background or familiarity with public speaking.[1] Debates led to agreement on a set of concrete demands for democratic regeneration and to reduce politicians' privileges, fight unemployment, or ensure citizens' rights to housing and healthcare, among others (Democracia Real Ya 2011), which were soon supported by a majority of Spanish citizens (Urquizu 2016, 22–25). As noted in the introduction, the 15M quickly mutated from a movement into a 'climate' (Fernández-Savater 2012a) or a 'political cycle' (Rodríguez 2016, 15–18), where multiple initiatives and collectives coexist.

In this chapter, I begin by placing the 15M in a historical perspective in order to contextualise its continuity with other movements and periods. In this way, I aim to debunk (to borrow the term used by Flesher Fominaya 2015a) the widely shared impression that the 15M was simply born out of thin air. This debunking is also relevant in order to fully understand some of the intellectual and cultural characteristics of the 15M 'climate' and its evolutions, in particular its pressing need for new models and references. In the second part of the chapter, I link these processes to the centrality of translation within this new period, paying special attention to the key role played by politically committed book publishers and the way in which translation interacts with local activism.

Placing the 15M within contemporary Spanish history

As mentioned, the emergence of the 15M and its decisive impact came as a surprise for a large part of Spanish society. This unexpected arrival, its 'heterogeneous' nature (Errejón and Mouffe 2015, 63), and the lack of links with traditional political organs such as parties and trade unions sparked multiple debates regarding its social meaning, relevance, and position in the political spectrum. While notable Conservative politicians claimed that the movement was hiding a new 'antisystemic left-wing' (Europa Press 2011a) and suggested it was 'marginal' (El País 2011c) in Spanish politics, the main parties on the traditional left argued for 'the need to listen' to the protesters (Cué and Díez 2011), while encouraging them to stop their non-parliamentary actions and to engage again with traditional institutions (Europa Press 2011b). At the same time, the movement was derided by a Communist party as 'petty-bourgeois' and an 'attack on the main lines of class struggle' (Partido Comunista de los Pueblos de España 2011), while an anarchist collective described it as 'the defence by other means of the status quo' (Cul de Sac 2016, 30; see Chapter 5 in this book).

Beyond the actual relevance of these debates, it was evident that the 15M had to be placed within the global wave of 'anti-austerity and pro-democracy protests' (Flesher Fominaya 2017, 2–4) that followed the eruption of the 2008 economic crisis. In symbolic terms, the strongest encouragement had been the various Arab uprisings and the occupation of Tahrir Square in Egypt (Romanos 2016, 107–109), a source of inspiration that was mentioned by several among the first campers (Sánchez n.d.) and reappeared in numerous signs made by protesters.[2] 'The 15M cannot be understood', claimed three activists at the time (Fernández, Sevilla and Urbán 2012, 17), 'without the experience and the lesson given to the world' by the Arab uprisings. In this sense, the 15M movement would represent a key moment for the movement of the squares, as it translated the occupation model of the Arab uprisings to the global North, opening its first 'cluster' among Western countries (Gerbaudo 2017, 31). In this way, the 15M became a catalyst for other events, inspiring actions in Portugal (Baumgarten 2013, 466), Greece (Douzinas 2013, 12), and the USA (Romanos 2016 and 2018).

However, considering the sociographic data gathered by Della Porta (2015, 49–60), it seems clear that the 15M was much closer to its Western counterparts than to its Middle-Eastern predecessors: while in countries like Egypt protests had a strong working class presence, the 15M and other European actions were mainly composed of young, middle-class, educated workers in precarious professional conditions. In the Spanish case, most protesters belonged to this social stratum (Rodríguez 2016, 32–45; Razquin 2017, 143–144) and were 'alarmed by the ongoing decomposition of the middle class in the face of a process of re-proletarianization' (Fernández, Sevilla and Urbán 2012, 18–19). Meanwhile, other sectors that were equally affected by austerity, such as manual workers, were largely absent from the squares: according to polls, only 9% of Spanish non-specialised workers attended the gatherings (Razquin 2017, 144). Veteran journalist Enric Juliana, who claimed that the 'university component was notable at the 15M', captured this disparity with an interesting comparison: at the squares, 'for every image of Che Guevara there were three of Nietzsche' (Juliana and Palà 2017, 44), that is, the traditional icons of the proletarian left-wing had been replaced by intellectual and cultural references in accordance with the social shift at demonstrations. Although it might not have seemed particularly relevant at the time, this shift in class composition has resonated in later analyses (Rodríguez 2016) and will be important for my study of the cultural limits of the 15M.

While its international links were evident, the national heritage of the protests was not as clear to observers, even if activists themselves could easily retrace it. Although the 15M certainly had a surprising and innovative component, the media's insistence on the novelty and unexpectedness of the movement fit well with the 'spasmodic view of popular history', a recurrent trope criticised by historian E.P. Thompson (1971, 76). According to this way of narrating history, popular movements lack agency and continuity: instead of being 'self-conscious or self-activating', they are 'simple responses to economic stimuli' (*ibid.*). In this sense, placing the 15M exclusively within the wide arch of popular responses that took place across the world in the aftermath of the global crisis would be a way of deactivating part of its potential, reducing it to a single event caused by the uncertainty of the economic situation instead of understanding it as part of a wider heritage of actions against Spanish political and economic elites.

Since the beginning of the 21st century, Spain witnessed the emergence of a considerable number of popular movements that eschewed the rigidity of traditional political structures (Fernández-Savater 2013a, 13), and several of these are considered by analysts to be part of the 15M's genealogy (Amparo Lasén in Fernández-Savater 2013a, 257–261; Rivero 2015, 54–72). They include the 2002 *Nunca Máis* ('Never again') demonstrations that followed a badly managed oil spill off the Galician coast; the controversial 13M (13 March 2004) protests that took place after the Atocha terror bombings in Madrid;[3] students' opposition to the neoliberal policies and the marketisation of education involved in the implementation of the European Higher Education Area in 2008 (Fernández, Sevilla and Urbán 2013); and the protests in 2011 against the passing of the law popularly known as *Ley Sinde*, which imposed heavy fines for peer-to-peer sharing of copyrighted materials. The latter in particular would play an important role in the concrete preparations of the 15M, through the involvement of many hacktivists and supporters of copyleft and free culture (Grueso 2012). Out of the protests against the Sinde law, two platforms were created that greatly influenced political debates before the 15M: #nolesvotes ('#donotvotethem'), which encouraged citizens not to vote for parties that supported the Sinde law (Razquin 2017, 23–33), and Juventud sin Futuro ('Youth without Future'), which had strong links with left-wing activism at universities (Razquin 2017, 46–57). Finally, many activists who had been engaged in collective projects within the Madrid area – such as the cultural lab *Universidad Nómada*, the journal *Ladinamo*, or the self-managed social centres *Patio Maravillas* and *Tabacalera* – would also be highly visible during the 15M and its subsequent political developments (Flesher Fominaya 2015a, 150–156).

A central characteristic of this pre-15M cultural ferment, which went on to produce the movement and the subsequent political climate, has been its prolonged and profound reassessment of Spain's recent history. In particular, activists, artists, writers, and citizens have questioned what could be called the official narrative of a key period for the country: the Transition to Democracy that followed Francoism. The *Transición*, as it is popularly known in Spain, is a contested period in Spanish history, even in terms of its chronology. While most experts agree that it began with the death of the dictator Francisco Franco (November 1975), scholars dispute the exact dates of its conclusion (Vilarós 1998, 1–3). Contenders include the first democratic elections (1977), which were won by the Unión de Centro Democrático, a coalition of several conservative parties with varying degrees of affinity with the dictatorship; the passing of the Spanish Constitution (1978); the landslide victory for the Partido

Socialista Obrero Español in 1982, the first party in government that had direct ties with the Second Spanish Republic (1931–1939), the democratic regime that Franco had unlawfully replaced by force; and the country's entrance to the European Economic Community (EEC, 1986).

Along with its obvious importance as a turning point in Spanish history, the relevance of the *Transición* lies in its force as collective narrative. Although the *Transición* was a major disappointment in terms of the political expectations of many citizens – who would have preferred a republic instead of a monarchy or supported different views on the configuration of the regional system (Garcés 2008, 427–548) – at an institutional level it became what André-Bazzana (2006, 277–280) has called the 'founding myth' of contemporary Spanish society. Over the following decades, this 'myth' has been repeatedly used to garner the ideological support of Spanish citizens, as well as to justify a number of political choices (Fontana 2012, 7), which were presented as necessary for the country at the expense of the population's best interests. As noted in Chapter 1, 'narratives' are fundamental to the legitimacy and persistence of the status quo, which implies that a central method in opposing a political system is to challenge 'the stories that sustain [it]' through the articulation of 'alternative stories' (Baker 2006b, 3), a task that perfectly characterises contemporary approaches to this past.

From the very beginning, the 15M climate has developed a sustained critique of the 'myth' of the *Transición*, both through aesthetic expressions – slogans, graffiti, or posters (see Kornetis 2014, 87–92; Labrador 2014) – and reflective texts, either from a journalistic or a historical perspective (such as Monedero 2011, Martínez 2012, and Rodríguez 2015, among others). Due to their differences regarding format, style, and approach, these critiques do not focus upon the same aspects of the process, yet all of them agree on the incomplete nature of the *Transición*: instead of becoming a full process of democratic regeneration, it was controlled by a 'pact between elites' (Rodríguez 2015, 347–348) – those stemming from the Francoist dictatorship and those supported by the anti-Francoist camp (mainly Socialists and Communists) – that ditched the most controversial and problematic claims, such as the referendum on the political system.[4]

Relying on an economic structure that benefitted from neoliberal measures implemented during the final phase of Francoism (López and Rodríguez 2011, 6–8) and imposing a social discourse that emphasised ideas of 'stability' and 'modernity' (Moreno-Caballud 2015, 53–57), the new state emerging after Francoism became fully integrated within the economic and social framework of the EEC. In so doing, it earned both internal and external legitimacy that obscured the shortcomings of the process and the lack of a clean break with the unequal system created during the dictatorship. In order to emphasise the perceived continuity between Francoist and democratic structures, a concept that has become popular within the 15M climate has been that of 'regime' or 'regime of 78' (Errejón 2013, 180–181), in reference to the year in which the Spanish Constitution was passed. The conceptual choice is certainly provocative, as the word *régimen* immediately evokes the well-known expression *régimen franquista* (Francoist regime) to Spanish listeners. Beyond this polemical aim, there is the argument that a regime needs to be understood as a whole set of apparatuses, power structures, and forms of life (Errejón 2013, 176) that can survive a specific form of government. In this sense, the 15M would be both a cause and a consequence of what political scientists describe as a 'regime crisis' (Simón 2012), in which the foundations 'of the political system' constructed during the *Transición* 'are suffering from serious wear' (Antentas 2017, 107).

Another concept that is important to understanding the 15M from this historical perspective is the notion of the *Cultura de la Transición* ('Culture of the Transition' or CT; Martínez 2012), used to describe the cultural and political framework developed during the Transition to Democracy. Consolidated during the governments of the aforementioned Partido Socialista Obrero Español (PSOE, 1982–1996), critics argue that the CT defined the boundaries of what could and could not be publicly discussed, privileging consensus at the expense of dissent and fomenting institutional and media silence on discourses addressing controversial issues such as the role of the monarchy, the status of other nations within the State (Catalonia, Galicia, and the Basque Country), or the aforementioned continuity between Francoist and democratic structures (Echevarría 2012). Therefore, the CT should be understood as the ideological framework generated by the post-Transition regime in order to legitimise its origins, structure, and imbalances of power. As I have discussed elsewhere (Fernández 2017) and will further elaborate in this chapter, this staunch opposition to the CT should not be equated with a wholesale rejection of the past, but rather of a certain narrative of it.

The intellectual field after the 15M: between dialogue and profit

The 15M's profound social impact, its opposition to the Culture of the Transition, its lack of direct links to traditional political organs, and its commitment to a new, more horizontal culture (Moreno-Caballud 2015, 178–231) resulted in a major transformation of the cultural landscape. This has been strongly expressed through an acute need for new models, references, and tools as the traditional and canonical ones were no longer considered suitable for contemporary realities. As Rodríguez (2016, 60) has cleverly argued, when the movement 'had to invent a new political language', it realised it 'was orphan', which forced it to start searching for political tools through different means. This is not specific to the Spanish case: Donatella Della Porta (2015, 96–102) has noted that this lack of inherited repertoires is a common feature of most anti-austerity movements, which frequently need to develop their own references and elements of identification either by importing them or by resignifying those that are currently available (e.g. banners or songs).

Early on, this openness to new definitions and debates was exemplified through the publication of a significant number of books and pamphlets on the 15M (Juventud sin Futuro 2011; Iglesias 2011; Iglesias and Monedero 2011;

Oliveres 2011; Taibo 2011; Taibo and Domènech 2011; Viejo 2011; Fernández, Sevilla and Urbán 2012; Vivas and Antentas 2011, 2012; Bustinduy and Lago 2013, to mention the most visible) that aimed to discuss the meaning and relevance of the movement. Read retrospectively, a number of characteristics stand out within this set of publications. Firstly, these books prominently featured a number of authors and activists who would later play a leading role in political projects, such as Pablo Iglesias (future secretary general of Podemos), Íñigo Errejón (founder of both Podemos and its later schisms Más Madrid/Más País), Rita Maestre (Madrid city councillor with Podemos and Más Madrid), Jorge Lago (founder of Podemos and owner of the publisher Lengua de Trapo), Isabel Serra (Madrid MP with Podemos), Eduardo Fernández Rubiño (Madrid MP with Podemos and Más Madrid), Raimundo Viejo (former national MP and Barcelona city councillor with the Catalan party En Comú), Gala Pin (former Barcelona city councillor with En Comú), David Fernàndez (former autonomic MP in Catalonia with the left-wing platform CUP), Anna Gabriel (former autonomic MP in Catalonia with CUP), and Miguel Urbán (European MP with Podemos), among others. Although commentators often argue that the 15M should not be equated with any political project, since no organisation would be able to 'represent' the diversity of the movement (Errejón and Mouffe 2015, 63), this continuity points to the way in which the movement contributed decisively to the birth and evolution of future parties and platforms. In this sense, it would not be correct to postulate a clear-cut distinction between movement and later endeavours: as argued in the introduction they need to be seen as part of a series of tensions and engagements.

Secondly, to a certain extent this wealth of publications was designed to privilege certain readings of the 15M at the expense of others. As the editors of one collection put it, protesters needed 'to hold to our own narratives' and 'to tell our own history' (Fernández, Sevilla and Urbán 2012, 7). In this process of framing and explaining the 15M, activists and authors revealed how the temporary alliance between political sensibilities that had been enabled by the movement was due to evolve into different political approaches in the long term, but also how these future platforms and projects were likely to reclaim the spirit of the 15M for their own purposes. In 2011, several activist academics had already argued that the 15M was split into two major 'logics' (Domènech 2011) or 'souls' (Iglesias and Monedero 2011, 102–104; Taibo 2011, 31–37), which sat in opposition primarily due to their understanding of institutional politics: while one aimed at transforming the current system from within, the other advocated a transformation of the system from the outside. This was clearly visible in the divergent interpretations of the 15M motto 'No nos representan' ('They do not represent us'): should it be interpreted in a well-defined, circumscribed sense ('Current politicians do not represent us'), or rather at a deeper level ('No one represents us'), that is, as a rejection of political representation? On the one hand, a number of protesters interviewed claimed that 'people no longer trust representation' (Sitrin and Azzellini 2014, 130–131), suggesting they favoured a strongly horizontal understanding of democracy. On the other hand, members of political parties like Podemos or En Comú would later argue that only a militant minority supported this reading. They claimed that the majority of people who identified with the 15M favoured a less radical interpretation of this critique, which implied that citizens could not be represented by those politicians and under those specific conditions (Errejón interviewed in Mora, Gallego Díaz and Rivero 2015; Expósito 2019, 31–32).

Finally, this flow of books was also promoted by publishers, who saw the 15M as a 'publishing boom' (Díaz de Quijano 2011) and sought texts that could echo the movement's preoccupations as a potential means of increasing sales (Corroto 2014), as the case of the name 'indignados' clearly shows (see below). Along with disputes on the political and social meaning of the movement, this search for economic profit formed the second branch of the logic of appropriation of the 15M that has taken place within the intellectual field and the book industry. As I will show in different cases across this book, this has led to an ambiguous relationship between culture and politics, since dialogues with the movement could also be interpreted to varying degrees as a search for 'militant remunerations' (*rétributions du militantisme*; Gaxie 1977), that is, the symbolic and material benefits that can be extracted from participation in politics. This tension between dialogue and remuneration, between engagement and benefit, which often crystallises in an ambiguous stance that combines aspects of both, will be at the heart of several discussions over the following chapters.

Translational issues within the squares

As I argued earlier, Spanish culture after the 15M is defined by a relative lack of shared models and references, a characteristic trait of many pro-democracy movements of the period. It is therefore not surprising that translation has played a central role within the 15M climate, as has frequently happened in times of 'turning points', 'crises', or 'vacuums' (Even-Zohar 1990b, 47). Translated authors such as Judith Butler (Cabré 2015), Slavoj Žižek (Público 2017), Angela Davis (Gutiérrez and Borraz 2018), and Silvia Federici (Martínez 2018) attracted major attention and spoke to large audiences when they visited Spain, resulting in long queues at the entrance of the venues or forcing organisers to provide additional spaces for listeners. As will be discussed in this section and in later chapters, many translated thinkers (Antonio Negri, Alain Badiou, Jacques Rancière, or Ernesto Laclau, among others) have also been used as points of reference for political debates. In this sense, philosopher and activist Amador Fernández-Savater ties the relevance of these translated authors firmly to the new political climate, claiming that the 'enormous following' generated by their interventions is the expression of 'a social search for questions' (Fernández-Savater 2013a, 203).

During the first weeks of the occupations of the squares (May–June 2011), there were heated debates on how to conceptualise what was happening, and translated texts and concepts functioned as important points of reference in this process (personal interview with philosopher Ernesto Castro, 18 March 2016).

Both onsite and online, protesters and observers mobilised concepts that emphasised the disruptive character of the 15M (see Appleton 2011; Fernández-Savater and García-Ormaechea 2011; CRUCE 2011), such as Alain Badiou's 'événement' ('event') – *evento* or *acontecimiento*, depending on the chosen translation (Badiou 1999) – and Jacques Rancière's (1996) opposition between 'the political' ('le politique') and 'the police' ('la police') (*política/policía*). While Badiou's concept emphasises how something unexpected (the 'event') can reveal a social truth that is hidden behind the structure of reality, Rancière's distinction opposes the emancipating role of politics ('the political') to the controlling role of governance and hierarchies (the 'police').[5] Similarly, another key conceptual discussion – and one that was also present within protest movements in other countries (Prentoulis and Thomassen 2013; Gerbaudo 2017, 89–112) – revolved around Antonio Negri's concept of the 'multitude' (*multitud*) and Ernesto Laclau's reformulation of 'the people' (*pueblo*), which involved differing stances on political strategy, organisation, and participation in party politics (Schavelzon 2015, 7–11).[6] In multiple senses, this showed the continuity between the 15M and the activist landscape that preceded it, as some of these intellectual references – like Rancière or Negri – were already a feature of ongoing discussions before the emergence of the movement (Sánchez Cedillo 2011; Fernández-Savater 2013a, 321–330).

However, another translational process taking place at the time, which concerned the naming of the movement, involved more problematic issues in terms of representation, cultural inequality, and commercial profit. An interesting characteristic of the movement of the squares is the way in which concepts and names associated with specific protests (such as 'Occupy' or 'Tahrir') have been displaced and relocated across linguistic and national borders. This has influenced the way in which new events are perceived while reinforcing the commonality of the various struggles, as in the case of the Turkish hashtag #OccupyGezi or the street sign for 'Tahrir Square' used by protesters at Occupy London (Court 2011). Yet another concept that achieved international success emerged from the Spanish protests: that of *los indignados* ('the indignant', 'the outraged'), a term that was initially used to describe protesters but prompted similar coinages abroad, like the 'Indignados de Lisboa' (Baumgarten 2013, 466) or the Greek translation αγανακτισμένοι ('aganaktismenoi'; Douzinas 2013, 12).

The name 'indignados' was technically a translation, as it was inspired by a pamphlet (*Indignez-vous!*) written by diplomat and concentration camp survivor Stéphane Hessel and translated into Spanish as *¡Indignaos!* in February 2011 (Hessel 2011a). In its criticisms of the consequences of austerity and its direct address to young people, Hessel's book provided a useful shortcut for social commentators to denote a social movement with an unclear shape and boundaries. As such, the concept *indignados* gained major currency in mass media from the early days of the movement and the pamphlet quickly became a bestseller – 350,000 copies of the Spanish translation and 40,000 of the Catalan had been sold by the end of May 2011 (La Vanguardia 2011). Its commercial success prompted the publication of other texts closely mirroring

¡Indignaos! in their format, content, and even naming style, such as Hessel's own ¡Comprometeos! (Get involved!; Hessel 2011b) and the co-authored ¡No os rindáis! (Don't give up!; Hessel and Uría 2013).

Nevertheless, the name *indignados* did not sit well within different sectors of the movement, as many participants had not read the text (Martínez 2016, 144) or did not feel strongly engaged by its content (Mir García 2013). Furthermore, many activists felt that a name focusing exclusively on their 'anger' would be reductive, as it 'overlook[ed] other emotional responses, such as hope and solidarity' (Flesher Fominaya 2015a, 160).[7] In fact, the contrast between the emotional connotations of *indignados* and the more neutral tones of the name preferred by activists – 15M, a reference to the date on which the movement started – involved different social narratives and, by extension, divergent representations. By associating the movement with a negative and reactive passion, the name *indignados* limited its agency and presented it in a potentially violent light, which benefitted the narrative mobilised by the establishment. Indeed, shortly after demonstrations began, a prominent Conservative politician dismissed protesters as 'antisystemic', claiming they 'should run for office in the elections' (El País 2011a) if they wanted to change society. The name 15M, meanwhile, with its strong temporal focus, could be understood as a new beginning or even as a historical landmark, which could also connect with the controversial yet powerful protests of the aforementioned 13M.

Textbox 2.1 (Mis)translating people's 'outrage'

An example of how the name 'indignados' could be politically misleading comes from the Italian book *Conflitto: l'Indignazione può davvero cambiare il mondo?* ('Conflict: can outrage really change the world?'), written by political scientist Pierfranco Pellizzetti in 2013. Pellizzetti takes as his starting point the idea that popular 'outrage' – exemplified by Spanish protesters – is not enough to change a political system. However, this claim would have been easily accepted by most protesters and generally by anyone affected by the 15M climate: 'outrage' was always understood as the first stage towards a transformation of the system based on greater fairness, accountability, and solidarity. By isolating this element, Pellizzetti's book misses a whole aspect of the movement and therefore benefits – intentionally or not – the establishment's interpretation of the 15M.

In what looks like a belated aim at making economic profit from the debate, the book was translated into Spanish in 2019, when the political cycle opened by the 15M and, more generally, the whole 'movement of the squares' was giving clear signs of exhaustion in a global political context that had shifted towards conservative positions. The title chosen by the Spanish publisher (Pellizzetti 2019) was much more provocative and could be interpreted as a rebuttal of the movement: *El fracaso de la indignación* ('The failure of outrage').

Bridging future and past: the resurgence of political books

As noted, the 15M shares its pressing need to find new points of reference with other pro-democracy movements, since a critique of each country's history implies a redefinition of its intellectual and social heritage. At a second level, this intellectual perspective could be placed within a wider range of reappraisals of the past and its connection with political action. On the one hand, Enzo Traverso (2016) has argued that contemporary left-wing movements are overwhelmed by the burden of the utopias and revolutions that were defeated during the 20th century, which implies that they would need to mourn these defeats in order to overcome them and start anew. From a related perspective, Mark Fisher (2012, 2013, 2014) has reflected on the concept of 'hauntology', developed through a particular reading of the work of French philosopher Jacques Derrida (1993). According to Fisher, hauntology is characterised by 'a nostalgia for all the futures that were lost' (Fisher 2013, 45) in the transition from the openness of the post-war period to the ascent of neoliberalism and the triumph of the aforementioned 'capitalist realism'. While the immediate post-war decades were characterised by an imagination of alternative futures, the neoliberal world is defined by a strict pragmatism summed up by the motto 'There is no alternative', which in turn limits 'the capacity to conceive of a world radically different from the one in which we currently live' (Fisher 2012, 16). In this sense, hauntological products and processes are defined by the melancholia – a feeling also evoked by Traverso – and the spectres of these futures that were promised, but never materialised. At the same time, however, they are also characterised by '*a refusal to give up* on the desire for the future' and 'to accommodate to the closed horizons of capitalist realism' (Fisher 2014, 21; my italics), which makes them highly charged in terms of political content – in fact, the hauntological persistence of past struggles has been studied (Gilman-Opalsky 2016) as a shared feature among numerous contemporary protests across the world.

As implied earlier, this concern for lost futures was a characteristic aspect of 15M discourses. While one of the first platforms leading to the movement was called 'Juventud sin Futuro' ('Youth without Future'), one of its most-repeated claims was that this generation 'would be the first to have a worse life than their parents', emphasising how the promise of a better future that was consubstantial to modern European societies had been betrayed. Therefore, it is not coincidental that the 15M is defined by an 'ambiguous' relationship (Kornetis 2014) with the Transition to Democracy, combining both criticism (against the so-called Culture of the Transition) and revindication (of the lost futures that appeared during this period). For a start, an important number of protesters and activists belonged to the generation that grew up during the years of political transformation (roughly 1975–1986, as discussed earlier), and were likely to have vivid memories of the many promises and political experiments taking place during this period (Labrador 2017 offers an insightful overview of the counterculture of the time, as well as a post-15M reading of its spirit). As I argued elsewhere (Fernández 2017, 135–136), the 15M sees the Transition as a double-faced period, since the movement shows a determination to recover certain aspects of this time (popular mobilisation, politicised culture, openness to change, and alternative ways of conceiving society) while expressing a need to repudiate its political and cultural consequences (mostly symbolised through the Culture of the Transition). In this sense, the hauntological side of the 15M and its concern for 'lost futures' is expressed in the revaluation of certain past models, genres, works, and individuals that are perceived to have been unfairly forgotten and undervalued as a result of the pressure from the official narrative of the time (see Fernández 2017 for an analysis in the field of popular music).

Within the publishing field, a crucial example of this tendency is the resurgence of politically committed publishers with a strong interest in translation, reinvigorating a model that had enjoyed centrality during the early years of the Transition to Democracy (Simó Comas 2015). While some of these publishers had a lengthy trajectory before the 15M (Akal, Siglo XXI, Traficantes de Sueños, Virus, Lengua de Trapo), others were created after the crisis began (Capitán Swing, Katakrak, Hoja de Lata, Casus Belli, El Salmón). In both cases, however, it was the beginning of the new political cycle that increased their visibility in the field, in response to a social demand for responses. As a member of the cooperative Traficantes de Sueños ('Dream Traffickers') claims, with the 15M 'more people started to be interested in books on economics and politics, since they wanted to understand how this swindle [*estafa*; i.e. the economic crisis] had taken place' (Beatriz García interviewed in Corroto 2014). Similarly, Lengua de Trapo (literally 'Cloth tongue', an expression used for a person who has difficulties expressing themselves) argues in its catalogue that 'essay-reading sky-rocketed' after the 15M, expressing 'a need of our society to look at itself in the mirror' (Lengua de Trapo 2019).

Like the Anglo-American 'radical publisher' or the French *éditeur engagé* (Noël 2012), these publishing houses are defined by their understanding of publishing as a form of political intervention with a strong historical component. For instance, Virus associates itself directly with the 'social movements and the anti-authoritarian left' that experienced defeat 'in the 1970s–80s [i.e. during the *Transición*]', and expresses its commitment to the 'patient and difficult reconstruction of dissent and alternative culture' at the turn of the 21st century (Virus 2019a). Similarly, Traficantes de Sueños (TdS) and Capitán Swing present themselves by reformulating Michel Foucault's (1974, 1389–1392) notion of books as a 'tool-box' for multiple social uses. While TdS is defined (Traficantes de Sueños 2019a) as a project aiming to provide 'the tool-box that can shape the cycle of struggles in forthcoming decades', Capitán Swing (2019a) – which took its name from a fictional character created by English Luddites (Hobsbawm and Rudé 1969) – claims to offer various 'sets of tools' to enable 'critical reading' and to help readers to 'understand the current state of affairs'.

In line with the hauntological component of the 15M, their connection with the political publishers of the *Transición* is not only expressed through an affinity in terms of editorial models, but also through the reissue of materials that were distributed during this historical period and had been out of print for a long time. For instance, Juanma Agulles, essayist and member of the publishing collective El Salmón, has stated (personal interview, 6 April 2019) that they are interested in 'a certain number of abandoned, forgotten books' published during the *Transición* and no longer reissued, since these works are representative of 'many relevant criticisms that were pushed to the margins' after 'the success of the *Cultura de la Transición*'.

The connection between this type of publisher and the reappraisal of the past was most clearly expressed through the organisation of the independent bookfair Feria del Libro Político de Madrid ('Madrid Political Book Fair'), which has taken place twice at the time of writing (April 2018 and April 2019) and brings together numerous politically committed publishers, such as the ones mentioned earlier. Firstly, the acronym chosen for the fair, FLP(m), was itself an ironic reference to the political atmosphere of the *Transición*. On the one hand, the initials FLP coincide with those of a well-known movement, the Frente de Liberación Popular ('Popular Liberation Front'), a student-led anti-Francoist group that played a central role in the personal and political evolution of many individuals who would go on to become relevant left-wing leaders during the Transition to Democracy (García Alcalá 2001). On the other hand, the use of the abbreviation '(m)' immediately links with the proliferation of political schisms during late Francoism and the *Transición*, which were often expressed through the addition of initials within parentheses to the original name. For instance, the Partido Comunista de España (PCE, Spanish Communist Party) had two major schisms of this kind: the Partido Comunista de España (marxista-leninista), known as the PCE (m-l), and the Partido Comunista de España (reconstituido), known as PCE (r).

To further emphasise this historical reference, the poster for the first edition of the bookfair (see Figure 2.1), which was designed by Emma Gascó, showed a drawing of a young woman walking with determination and carrying a small banner with the acronym FLP(m). Both traits suggest that the character in the poster was on her way to a demonstration. More importantly, the figure wears bell-bottoms, a type of trousers that are strongly associated with the student-movement of the *Transición* in Spain. In this way, the image establishes a strong lineage between past, present, and 'lost future': the bookfair not only places itself in connection with the climate of protest of late Francoism and early democracy, but also makes an appeal to those alternative political projects – expressed through the imaginary 'FLP(m)' – that were not successful in the long term and were replaced by dominant parties.

Translation-as-tradition 39

Figure 2.1 Poster for the 2018 edition of the Feria del Libro Político de Madrid, designed by Emma Gascó.

Textbox 2.2 Translational and hauntological solidarity

In early July 2015, a large piece of graffiti appeared on a wall in Langreo, a former industrial city in Asturias (Northern Spain) with a strong history of working-class struggle, especially connected to coal-mining (Shubert 1987; Vega García 2002a). The mural (see Figure 2.2) was signed by ADEPAVAN – an assembly of unemployed people from the area that was created after the 15M – and expressed support to the winning side in the referendum held in Greece by the ruling party, Syriza. There, citizens voted against accepting the conditions of the bailout proposed by the European Commission, the International Monetary Fund, and the European Central Bank, although, as is known, Syriza would later accept the conditions of the bailout despite the result. With the exception of an old mining lamp, similar to those used in Asturian coalmines, the graffiti was mainly a bilingual text in Greek and Asturian, a Romance language spoken in the region: NON / OXI / HAI UNA LLUZ EN GRECIA QUE CALEZ EUROPA ENTERA / Ζήτω η Ελλάδα / Puxa Grecia ('NO [in Asturian and Greek] / THERE IS A LIGHT IN GREECE THAT WARMS THE WHOLE OF EUROPE [in Asturian] / Long live Greece [in Greek and Asturian]').

Despite the brevity of the message, its complexity in historical, political, and translational aspects draws upon several layers of meaning. The sentence 'Hai una lluz…' is a free translation into Asturian of two verses by singer-songwriter Chicho Sánchez Ferlosio: 'Hay una lumbre en Asturias / que calienta España entera' ('There is a fire in Asturias / that warms the whole of Spain'). Ferlosio's song, which quickly became a hymn of anti-Francoism (Fernández 2017, 137–138), was written during the Asturian mining strikes of 1962, a major event in the evolution of political struggle in late Francoism, since they encouraged other movements of protest within Spain (Vega García 2002a) while raising international awareness and inspiring solidarity in the face of Francoist repression (Vega García 2002b).

By connecting local struggles from the past with foreign struggles from the present, the mural establishes a hauntological and translational relationship of solidarity between them. In the same way that Asturian miners led other Spanish workers in their fight against the Francoist dictatorship, Greek voters could now lead the way for other European citizens in their fight against the imposition of austerity and the 'dictatorship of the markets' (a concept frequently used in Spanish to characterise the non-democratic pressures of the economy upon politics; e.g. Torres 2010). There is a hauntological element in this claim (a 'future lost'), because the individuals looking for political inspiration – the unemployed people around Langreo – could not find it in the present of Asturias or Spain, but had to look back and reclaim a fight from the past (the 1962 mining strikes). At the same time, the direct identification between the Asturian and the Greek context – symbolised not only in the bilingual text, but also in the use of the colours of the Greek flag inside the letter 'o' in both NON and OXI – expressed a commitment to international solidarity that went in line with the alter-globalisation ethos: in a globalised system, activists need to translate between the diversity of their languages and cultures in order to realise that they share similar concerns because they face the same opponent (neoliberalism).

Translating against the 'Cultura de la Transición'

In this context of regeneration, translation occupies a privileged space within the catalogue of politically committed publishing houses, a characteristic that was equally shared by the publishing sector that emerged during the *Transición* (Labrador 2017, 239). This relevance is particularly clear within book series in

Figure 2.2 Mural in support of the 2015 Greek referendum (Langreo, Asturias). Photography shared by ADEPAVAN on their Facebook site (Bakunin 2015).

the fields of politics, economics, and history, which rely heavily on translation. Table 2.1 offers an analysis of figures from January 2011–October 2019 for a choice of politically committed publishers. These include essay series in Akal: *Cuestiones de Antagonismo* ('Matters of Antagonism'; Akal 2019a) and *Pensamiento Crítico* ('Critical Thinking'; Akal 2019b), Traficantes de Sueños (2019b, 2019c, 2019d): *Historia*, *Mapas*, and *Prácticas Constituyentes* ('Constituent Practices'), Siglo XXI's (2019) *Historia*, Virus' (2019b) *Ensayo*, Pepitas de calabaza's (2019) *Ensayo*, Casus Belli's (2019) *Pensamiento Atiempo*, Lengua de Trapo's (2019) *Ensayo*, La Oveja Roja's (2019) *Ensayo*, Capitán Swing's (2019b) *Ensayo*, and Sylone's (2019) *Crítica & alternativa*, as well as the whole catalogue for Katakrak (2019) and El Salmón (2019), which only have one book series.[8]

Firstly, the data reveal that, in most of the series analysed (13 out of 15), translations amounted to at least half of the books published, peaking with *Pensamiento Atiempo* (100%, although with a rather small sample of books), Capitán Swing (96.09%, being the publisher with the largest catalogue in both translations and absolute numbers), Traficantes' *Prácticas constituyentes* (94.73%), and Akal's *Cuestiones de antagonismo* (94.64%). This tendency clearly shows how translation is a pivotal tool for politically committed publishers. At the same time, a few of these series have also given room to books written by authors involved in the 15M climate, either through different forms of activism (social, cultural, or academic, among others) or through their participation in related political projects, such as the coalition around Podemos or the political platform Ahora Madrid. This trend is particularly clear in the case of Akal's *Pensamiento*, since books written by politicians, activists, and fellow travellers constitute a major source of publications for the series: they amount to 35.14% of all books in the series and 76.47% of the books written in Spanish. Another

Table 2.1 Books published by selected series of politically committed publishers: translated books vs. books originally written in Spanish (January 2011 – October 2019)

Series	Translated books	Books in Spanish	% of translations
Pensamiento Atiempo (Casus Belli)	9	0	100
Ensayo (Capitán Swing)	123	5	96.09
Prácticas Constituyentes (TdS)	18	1	94.73
Cuestiones de Antagonismo (Akal)	53	3	94.64
Katakrak	16	2	88.89
Historia (TdS)	11	5	68.75
Ensayo (Virus)	10	6	62.5
Ensayo (Pepitas de calabaza)	60	39	60.61
El Salmón	14	11	56
Mapas (TdS)	16	13	55.17
Pensamiento Crítico (Akal)	40	34	54.05
Historia (Siglo XXI)	33	29	53.23
Crítica y alternativa (Sylone)	5	5	50
Ensayo (La Oveja Roja)	4	7	36.36
Ensayo (Lengua de Trapo)	4	14	22.22

relevant example would be Traficantes' *Mapas*, where they amount to 20.7% of all books and 46.15% of Spanish originals. Finally, the case of Lengua de Trapo – whose owner, Jorge Lago, was a founding member of Podemos – is extremely relevant in this sense: although it is one of the very few examples of a politically committed publisher with a low percentage of translations (22.22%), the largest number of those books originally written in Spanish (71.43%) were authored by individuals who are politically active, through some kind of involvement (direct participation, advising, or public support) with any of the parties that emerged during this period (Podemos, Anticapitalistas, or Más País).

Ultimately, here we can clearly see how political publishers' catalogues are decisively influenced by a political understanding of knowledge that is linked to a strong emphasis on translation – through their own commitment to the book as a political tool, but also through their recourse to politically active authors. Together, they conform to a wider strategy of opposition to the Culture of the Transition. In this regard, we can view the CT as a 'conservative' repertoire, in the sense argued by Itamar Even-Zohar (1990a, 21), that is, as one that is fully established, where every individual product is 'highly predictable' and 'any deviation' is considered 'outrageous'. At this point, the task of politically committed publishers lies precisely in the destabilisation of the repertoire through the introduction of innovative ideas, paradigms, and models, which can either be imported from other systems (translation) or promoted from the peripheral, emerging areas of the system (authors associated with the 15M climate).

Translated books, activist readings: the importance of 'paratexts'

Within the catalogues for these publishers, an important space for interaction between imported books and local activists and politicians consists of the prefaces or epilogues that accompany translations. These types of texts fall within the wider category of the 'paratexts' (Genette 1987) of the book, that is, those elements that shape and bind together the sense of the book, such as its title, cover, and supporting texts. As Batchelor (2018, 142) explains, a paratext is 'a consciously crafted threshold', which has 'the potential to influence the way(s) in which the text is received'. In other words, a paratext always involves an intention to guide the reader towards a certain interpretation of, or reaction to, the text. Echoing the definition of books as a 'toolbox' that some politically committed publishers have adopted, the paratext would be a set of instructions that suggests potential uses for the provided tools. This is especially relevant when the author of the paratext – in our case, an activist or a politician – is better known in the context of reception than the author of the translated book and becomes, in this way, a major point of attraction for potential readers (a matter raised by Batchelor 2018, 39, in the field of literary translation). As discussed earlier in this chapter, this kind of intellectual debate and interpretation is not neutral, especially in a politicised context: while they can contribute decisively to the diffusion and popularisation of a given text, activist and political readings need to be understood within a larger process of 'branding' (*marquage*; Bourdieu 2002, 4), which inscribes new senses and meanings into the translated product. Although in this section I will focus on less problematic cases, in Chapter 6 I return to this question, looking at the case of Podemos in order to outline the potential ambiguities of these processes in the search for 'militant' capital.

A recurrent trope in these activist readings is the notion of 'usefulness', that is, the relevance of the translated text for social and political action. While the trope is far from new, it is relevant in this context for three interrelated reasons: firstly, it underlines the commitment expressed by publishers to generate books that contribute to a transformation of society; secondly, it shows that translations respond to a perceived lack or absence within the cultural context; finally, it marks yet another clear distinction with the ideological system of the 'Cultura de la Transición', where cultural products with a clear political aim were considered unsuitable and of lesser importance (Echevarría 2012).

A first form of the notion of usefulness is that of the book as a tool that can reveal a hidden truth or expose the fallacies of mainstream discourse. An early example of this strategy appears in the Spanish edition of Matt Taibbi's *Griftopia*, a report of the links between super-riches and the American government, which was translated and prefaced by Pablo Bustinduy (an academic who would later become Podemos' representative for International Affairs), and published by Lengua de Trapo. In his introduction to the book, which appeared only a few months after the occupations of the squares (November 2011), Bustinduy explicitly linked it with the aims of Occupy Wall Street and the 15M, claiming it showed 'in full swing [...] the machinery of hellish complexity' that these movements were seeking to dismantle (Bustinduy 2011, 14). In this way, Bustinduy was implicitly setting a task for the new-born movements, based on the idea that they should understand the system they were facing before they could successfully undo it.

A similar strategy of exposure is deployed in the Spanish translation of David Madden and Peter Marcuse's *In Defense of Housing*, which analyses the global housing crisis as a problem created by economic and political interests that have turned housing into a commodity. The translation, published by Capitán Swing, included a foreword by Jaime Palomera, a researcher in urban anthropology who also acts as spokesperson for the Catalan Sindicat de Llogaters ('Tenants Union'). This grassroots collective campaigns for greater protection of tenants, especially against the abuses of corporations and funds that invest in housing for commercial purposes (see Chapter 5 for related discussions). The choice of Palomera – whose name featured prominently on the cover (Capitán Swing 2019c) – as author of the paratext emphasised the publisher's political stance, as in recent years tenant collectives like the Sindicat have been putting pressure on political parties to pass new laws to control rents (Estévez 2018). In his foreword, Palomera (2018, 12) connected the translation to current struggles and stressed that the book was useful 'to debunk the myths that discourses close to the economic and political power have successfully popularised in recent decades'. Translation, therefore, becomes not only a means of exposing mainstream arguments, but also a source of information for the generation of alternative arguments.

A second variant of the 'usefulness' trope, which connects directly to the reappraisal of recent history, is mobilised in the case of reissued translations. Here, authors of paratexts tend to link the political break between the post-15M climate and the recent past with the process of digging for discarded historical references. For instance, in his foreword to a translated anthology of Karl Marx, literary critic and book-publisher Constantino Bértolo refers to the renewed interest in the work of Marx after years of neglect, claiming that this process 'has to be linked to a certain characteristic or specific trait of the current crisis' (Bértolo 2017, 28), which the critic identifies with the increasing dominance of economic jargon within political debate. Therefore, in the context of 'the new political concerns that have emerged around the 15M and Podemos' (29), an increased demand for Marx's texts lies in the need to disentangle the economic aspects of social reality.

When viewed within this line of thought, reissuing a given book can represent yet another form of criticism to the impositions of the Cultura de la Transición, which is either implicitly or explicitly acknowledged in the paratext. The foreword to the new edition of Karl Polanyi's classic work *The Great Transformation*, published by Virus, offers a pertinent example. In this text, historian Emmanuel Rodríguez and sociologist Isidro López, both of whom have been involved in the 15M and in the activist space around the publisher Traficantes de Sueños, open their presentation by praising Ediciones de la Piqueta ('Pick-axe Editions'), the 'small radical publisher' that issued the first Spanish translation of Polanyi in 1989 (Rodríguez and López 2016, 10–11). Due to its publishing activity, Rodríguez and López claim that 'the Spanish intellectual field, always sparing in words' (10), has an unacknowledged debt to La Piqueta, which had to shut down in the early 1990s.

Finally, a third variant of the trope, which has become more frequent with the evolution of the 15M climate, presents the book as a basis for the assessment of recent political action, its achievements, and its shortcomings. This is the case of the foreword written by Yayo Herrero for the Spanish translation of Janet Biehl's *The Politics of Social Ecology*, also published by Virus. Herrero (2018, 11), a well-known ecofeminist involved in a variety of activist projects, proposes the use of Biehl's book 'as a possibility to revise' the Spanish movement known as 'municipalismo' (Rubio-Pueyo 2017), during which a series of citizen platforms and coalitions managed to win local elections in many important Spanish cities (such as Madrid, Barcelona, Santiago, Saragossa, Cádiz, or Corunna, among others), but faced enormous difficulties in transforming their cities under major economic pressures. While acknowledging that 'it might be unfair to assess them in the light of this book', Herrero (2018, 11) posits this analysis as a first step in order to consider 'the difficulties' of these platforms and to present 'a programme for action', as well as for finding 'a mirror in which to look at themselves' and to see their deficiencies.

Textbox 2.3 Appropriating translations for activist purposes

The subordination of translation to political aims is a constant within the 15M climate that is vividly expressed in the brief trajectory of Libros del Marrón (roughly translatable as 'Mess Books'). The creation of the collective was announced in the summer of 2015 (La Haine 2015) and it only published three translations, in a very short timeframe: a selection of texts from historian E.P. Thompson (2015), another from sociologist Pierre Bourdieu (2015), and a chapter co-written by filmmaker Alexander Kluge and philosopher Oskar Negt (Kluge and Negt 2015). These pocketbooks, which imitated the design of some underground political publishers of the *Transición* (simple type font, coarse paper, and lack of inner margins), could only be found within a small network of cooperative and libertarian bookshops.

A first particularity of this publisher is its anonymous character, since no personal name, location, or reference is indicated in the books. This anonymity is clearly linked to the publications' stated activist purpose of collecting money in order to fund legal fees and fines resulting from political struggle. As stated in each translation, 'all earnings from this book' will be 'allocated to alleviate the breach between the universal right to justice and the existence of court agents, public notaries and other workers' with 'surrealistic fees', as well as to allow 'our lawyers to free up time for proceedings' and 'to pay fines derived from collective mobilisation' (Bourdieu 2015, 3). The criminalisation of protest increased dramatically in Spain after the so-called *Ley Mordaza* or 'gagging law', passed by the Conservative government in 2015, which imposed heavy fines for protests and gave enhanced powers to police forces (López-Terra 2017; Amnistía Internacional 2018). Without naming it overtly, the collective behind Libros del Marrón ironically described it in their opening advertisement as a 'law worthy of the clumsiest among despots' (La Haine 2015).

A second, connected particularity lies in the fact that the publishers acknowledge that 'we do not have, nor want, any rights upon the texts', using them 'without permission' in the belief that 'their authors would be proud to see that their work was serving our current aims' (Bourdieu 2015, 3). This opposition to intellectual property rights is not unusual amongst anarchist and libertarian publishers, who privilege the social value of knowledge; the cooperative Calúmnia ('Slander'), for instance, which is based in Majorca, has republished numerous translations of classic works by Rudolf Rocker and Murray Bookchin without acquiring any rights. In the case of Libros del Marrón, this appropriation is linked to the fact that several among these translated texts are out of print or very hard to find (as argued in Thompson 2015, 6; Kluge and Negt 2015, 77) and does not exclude certain forms of attribution: in their accompanying notes, the collective thanks the original translators for their contribution to the advancement of knowledge and, in some cases, names specific practitioners, such as Elena Grau, 'seldom mentioned, who has taken so much effort to make Thompson speak our tongue' (Thompson 2015, 6).

Despite its marginal nature, this set of books brings together a series of key characteristics of translation within the 15M climate: a strong belief in the political role of translation, which nevertheless privileges political aims over translational considerations; a direct connection between book publishing and political action; an awareness of the forgotten and abandoned texts that have been generated over time and the need to reclaim them for new struggles; and a defence of the collective relevance of knowledge, in line with numerous projects with 'free culture' (a topic that will reappear in Chapter 3).

Conclusions and points of reference

This chapter has presented an overview of certain characteristics of the 15M movement that will resonate throughout this book, and which the reader should bear in mind for future analyses. Firstly, I highlighted a break between the 15M and the dominant narratives of recent Spanish history, which has led to an absence of political and cultural references that must be addressed through alternative histories (the hauntological search for 'lost futures'), foreign imports (translation), and activist production. While these strategies are manifested in different actions (such as activist debates or even graffiti, as seen in Textbox 2.2), they coalesce in the resurgence of politically committed publishers that focus on the transformation of society through the generation of translations and the publication of contemporary authors, frequently connected with the political and activist field.

This centrality of translation is equated with a notion of political usefulness, that is, translations are produced with the objective of providing a tool for political action, which reinforces publishers' political commitment. At the same time, this notion of usefulness tends to be mediated by activists and politicians who provide the paratexts to the translations and, therefore, aim to prioritise a certain reading of the text. In this way, this strategy connects with the politicised readings of the 15M generated within the initial years of its appearance and, more generally, with a dispute over the meaning and sense of this historical period.

Subsequently, both areas of analysis contribute to a more nuanced understanding of the ways in which politics and culture interact within the 15M climate, and in particular of the role of translation in the construction of politicised meanings. At the same time, the central role allocated (or self-allocated) within this process to activists, politicians, and other social agents points out the unevenness within this construction that I referred to when discussing the notion of 'expanded translation'. While the process is undoubtedly collective and multiple, the leading position of certain actors can provide decisive turns, as will be discussed in the following chapters.

Notes

1 One of my most vivid impressions of the 15M assembly I attended more frequently – in Granada, a major university city in Southern Spain – was how many members of the crowd experienced the occasion of talking to the assembly as a kind of cathartic process in which they lost their fear and started *enjoying* the feeling of discovering their own voice. This was an impression shared by other attendees I met across different camps, even if their feelings were occasionally mixed: while some celebrated the opportunity that the assembly provided for the process of learning how to develop a political speech, others lamented that this practice often became self-celebratory. In this sense, José Luis Moreno Pestaña (2019, 283), a sociologist and philosopher who was involved in assemblies, has argued that the absence 'of mechanisms for closing deliberation' led to extremely lengthy debates that gradually excluded those attendees who had less time due to family or work commitments.
2 A poster that circulated in the early days of the protest expressed this union between Spanish and Arab protesters through the depiction of a crescent moon within a sun held by a hand. The crescent is a symbol traditionally associated with Arab/Muslim culture, while the sun, in this context, was an obvious reference to *Plaza del Sol* (literally 'Sun Square') in Madrid.
3 On 11 March 2004 (11M), shortly before Spain's general elections, Madrid suffered several train bombings that caused 192 casualties. Despite early findings suggesting the involvement of Islamists in response to Spain's backing of the American invasion of Iraq, the Conservative government of the Partido Popular attributed exclusive responsibility to the Basque terrorist organisation ETA. On 13 March (13M), citizens

48 *Translation-as-tradition*

used SMS to arrange spontaneous protests against the government's perceived duplicity, contributing to the Conservatives' electoral defeat. The motto of this campaign – '¡Pásalo!' ('Pass it on!') – became a symbol of popular activism (Anonymous author 2004).

4 For readers unfamiliar with Spanish history, it is worth highlighting that the first king of the new democratic state, Juan Carlos I, was chosen as heir by General Franco himself.

5 A personal anecdote might be useful to highlight the extent to which these concepts have become part of the intellectual landscape. On October 2017, I was invited to a colloquium at the École Normale Supérieure on the 15M and its consequences. The talk happened to be hosted next to Alain Badiou's office, so I took a photograph of the coincidence and tweeted it. Shortly after, Héctor Tejero – a member of the ecologist network Contra el diluvio (see Chapter 5), who was active in anarchist circles – tweeted back: 'Eso sí que es un "evento"!' ('That's a proper "event"!'), playing on the double sense of the concept.

6 To a great extent, 'multitude' and 'people', like Negri and Laclau themselves, became actual bywords for political programmes and stances. For instance, during a personal interview (15 March 2016), philosopher Germán Cano (a founding member of Podemos) told me ironically that 'only Negrians [i.e. intellectual followers of Negri]' claimed that the 15M was opposed to representation as a political principle.

7 Goutsos and Polymeneas (2017, 192) have criticised the Greek media use of the concept of 'aganaktismenoi' for similar reasons.

8 In the case of Katakrak, I have only taken into account translations into Spanish. Translations into Basque have a specificity in terms of readership that differs greatly from Spanish.

3 The 'commons'
Rethinking collective agency

An important aspect of political struggles is their engagement with the ways in which concepts are defined and used. Disputes over the 'true sense' of concepts (Bourdieu 1992 [1998], 310) are a constant element of confrontation within any social field, something that social movements have made into a central concern across history (Tarrow 2013). Why are names and concepts so important for political struggle? Firstly, as Sydney Tarrow (2013, 12) has argued, words function as 'symbols of contention', that is, they come to represent and to embody a whole struggle; in this way, they can 'mobilise' and 'unite' citizens in a given protest. In Chapter 2, I showed how the Spanish names '15M' and 'indignados' – like 'Occupy', 'Tahrir', and 'the 99%' – served as elements of identification for a wide variety of individuals. These names and concepts, borrowed from 'ordinary speech' or related repertoires (Tarrow 2013, 32), provided a common point of reference for citizens with different backgrounds.

At the same time, concepts are the basis of our understanding of the social world and therefore require a certain degree of consensus on their meaning. In times of 'important political, economic, and cultural shifts', however, 'this consensus falls apart' as 'the taken-for-granted associations between words and things begin to break down' (Fritsch, O'Connor and Thompson 2016, 7). These periods of instability open the way to major conflicts over the right definition of such concepts, 'a sort of semantic civil war' (Gómez Ramos 2016, 15) that is bound up with social struggle. This issue was also raised in Chapter 2 when discussing the way in which a political concept like 'democracy' became a matter of multiple political confrontations, precisely due to a dispute regarding its 'true' meaning. Indeed, Spanish protesters were united against the political system in terms of the need to redefine 'democracy', yet they were in turn divided over the interpretation of its core meaning and functioning.

An important characteristic of the 15M climate has been its constant questioning of language, which relates to its break with mainstream models and repertoires, but also with wider global issues. Recent decades have been characterised by the hollowing out of classical political concepts – 'democracy', 'equality', or 'freedom' would be telling examples – by neoliberal rationality, as they are 'relocated to the economy and recast in an economic idiom' (Brown 2015, 42). In this global moment of 'confusion [...] around language' (Fritsch, O'Connor and Thompson 2016, 20), radical movements must set out to critique and reappropriate existing concepts in order to free them from their neoliberal semantics or to discard them altogether and develop suitable new ones. Within the 15M climate, this transnational tendency has been expressed both through the combination of a critique of existing repertoires and the creation, recuperation, and translation of concepts. Although related analyses will reappear in following chapters, the present chapter focuses exclusively on the interaction between reflection and political practice through a specific concept, the 'commons'. After a brief overview of the historical evolution of the term and its inherent ambiguities, I address its Spanish usages and analyse the difficulties it poses for translation, before looking at three collectives that aim to embody the 'commons' – the politically committed publisher Traficantes de Sueños, the cooperative Guerrilla Translation, and the social centre La Ingobernable – and a political platform (Barcelona en Comú) that has been influenced by existing discourses on the concept.

A brief history of the 'commons'

Over recent decades, the concept of the 'commons' has gained traction in the conceptual framework of many activists, politicians, and collectives across the world (Caffentzis 2016, 96; Subirats and Rendueles 2016, 9–11). Nevertheless, the 'commons' remains a problematic and ambiguous concept, one 'that is both contested and innately political in nature' (Wall 2014, 73) and for which multiple understandings coexist. This has led some researchers to claim that it might be best seen as an 'umbrella' term (Subirats and Rendueles 2016, 9) that covers a variety of definitions. In a similar line of thought, Bollier and Helfrich (2012) have argued that offering a 'unitary perspective on the commons' would be highly problematic, since the concept encompasses both material and immaterial realities, such as social attitudes, worldviews, and intellectual arguments. The following will be a necessarily brief introduction to the 'commons'; a more detailed presentation of current debates in the field can be found in Fernández (2020b).

Historically, the 'commons' can be defined as a wealth or resource that is shared, used, and protected by a community. A key characteristic of this resource is the fluidity of ownership: it can belong to the community as a whole, to a series of members of the community with non-exclusive rights, or even to a third party that allows various forms of communal usage. Although communal use of goods and lands is an ancestral tradition for many cultures (Zubero 2012, 30–32), the term 'commons' stems from 'medieval-era English property law' (Caffentzis 2016, 96), in which it encompassed 'a set of legally recognized assets' (such as meadows, rivers, and forests, to name a few) that either belonged to the King, the Church, or the nobility, and upon which a community had 'customary and collectively managed usage' (*ibid.*).

Between the 16th and the 18th centuries, however, most British commons suffered a process of privatisation resulting in what is known as 'enclosures', which involved fencing off common land in order to allow large landowners to gain profit from it, for instance by using it 'as pasture for increasingly lucrative sheep farming' (Meiksins Wood 2017, 108). Subsequently, enclosures brought about 'the extinction of common and customary use rights on which many people depended for their livelihood' (*ibid.*), as commoners were no longer able to pick wood for fire or to fish in rivers and lakes. Furthermore, since the destruction of the European commons coincided with the beginning of colonialism, the process taking place in the 'Old' World was extended into the 'New'. When European settlers arrived in territories such as America and India, they carried with them a proto-capitalistic understanding of exclusive property that clashed with the communitarian, non-exclusive notions prevalent among many native communities (Cheyfitz 1997, 41–58; Linebaugh 2008, 144–169). From this perspective, colonialism can be understood as a process of enclosure and destruction of the commons on a global scale. Importantly, in the first volume of *Capital*, Karl Marx (1867, section VIII) would subsume both processes within the larger notion of 'primitive accumulation', which allowed the establishment of the social conditions needed for the development of capitalism: when dispossessed commoners and enslaved colonial populations were deprived of their means of subsistence, they became available as workers for the emerging system.

Despite this long historical lineage, neither commons nor enclosures are realities that are limited to the past. Indeed, there are many examples of commons that have been preserved over time (Ostrom 1990), such as the self-managed systems of irrigation that are used in various areas of the world or the many forests that are managed under some type of collective tenure regime (Monterroso, Cronkleton and Larson 2019, 376–377). Equally, the many cases of the privatisation of common resources across the world in recent decades can be understood as processes of enclosure. These include the sale of publicly owned land in Britain (Christophers 2018), the major projects carried out by the Indian State to extract profit from the environment (Roy 2011), and the continuing deforestation of the Amazon for mass-scale agriculture and farming (WWF 2019), among many others.

The strong historical heritage of the 'commons' is not unusual for political language: the concepts deployed in struggles and protests are frequently part of 'a long linguistic narrative' (Tarrow 2013, 12), as concepts generated for past events are resignified or expanded for contemporary realities. However, a decisive factor in the increasing popularity of the concept over recent decades has been its expansion beyond the traditional understanding of the 'natural' commons in order to encompass immaterial fields. The appearance of the 'knowledge commons' (Madison, Frischmann and Strandburg 2019, 77) and, especially, the rapid evolution of the field of information technology – with the rise of the internet, free software, or peer-to-peer (P2P) exchange – has been a major catalyst in this process. Popular examples such as the Creative Commons

(Linksvayer 2012) – a set of licences that allow creators to legally disseminate their creative work while controlling which rights they grant to users – or the online multilingual encyclopaedia Wikipedia are key examples of the dissemination of the concept among citizens and users. However, the dominance of immaterial, digital commons in recent understandings of the concept has been also a contentious point in contemporary debates. For instance, Silvia Federici (2012, 142) has argued that Antonio Negri and Michael Hardt's approach to 'the common' as an immaterial, digital space based upon 'the informatization of production' completely neglects 'the material basis of the digital technology the Internet relies upon', overlooking the fact that computing is heavily reliant on a range of 'economic activities – mining, microchip and rare earth production – that, as currently organized, are extremely destructive, socially and ecologically'.

In this context of revitalisation, the eruption of the global crisis in 2008 saw a notable rise of the commons as a paradigm of political action. Firstly, the wide-ranging processes of expropriation and privatisation – in fields such as public health, schooling, pensions, and state assets, among others – taking place across a number of countries have placed collective property in the spotlight, highlighting the need for certain areas of social life to be preserved from market competition. In this sense, the 'commons' has acquired 'the value of a criticism' (Dardot and Laval 2014, 96) that can be directed at the major processes of accumulation currently taking place. At the same time, mistrust towards governments has given a new momentum to autonomous spaces based upon sharing and collaboration between individuals, which are defining factors of the commons (Federici and Caffentzis 2019, 93–94). Finally, the award of the 2009 Nobel Prize in Economic Sciences to Elinor Ostrom, a major figure in the study of the field, gave the concept a new opportunity to circulate globally (Zubero 2012, 17).

The combination of these factors – opposition to privatisation, defence of collective agency beyond the State, and the increased popularity of the commons – arguably played a major role in the occupation of public spaces that characterised the movement of the squares. As outlined in Chapter 2, these occupations reclaimed a whole set of common goods and values – not only public spaces (the squares), but also symbols (flags) and concepts ('democracy') – in the name of the majority of the population ('the people' or 'the 99%'), and they did so in response to calls and manifestoes 'from below' that were not promoted by political parties or institutions. Moreover, many of these improvised sites and camps started offering basic services – from cleaning, medical and legal services, and food provision to security and sign interpreting (Kadet 2011; Castells 2012, 58–60; Bravo 2014; 15Mpedia 2016a) – that were carried out by the protesters themselves and freely available to any citizen. In this way, they have been characterised as examples of 'urban commons' (Harvey 2012, 73), since citizens effectively reclaimed a public good to put it at the service of the community. In the Spanish context, the renewed relevance of the commons within the 15M climate has been expressed through the emergence of a large variety of community-based projects, which include social centres (Bango 2019), book and publishing cooperatives (La Vorágine 2019), housing co-ops (Lacol and La Ciutat Invisible 2018), banking initiatives (Bank of the Commons 2019), and citizen platforms for the communal use of public spaces (La Lleialtat Santsenca 2019), among others (see Álvarez-Blanco 2019 for an archive of commons-inspired projects).

Translational issues: what do you call the 'commons'?

As briefly explored in the previous section, the 'commons' is a concept with a long and dense history, which inevitably adds further complexity to its definition and usages. For the purposes of this book, it is particularly relevant to focus upon a very specific ambiguity of the 'commons': its linguistic aspects. Even though the reality of the 'commons' is present in a great variety of cultures across the world (Zubero 2012, 30–32), it is a European concept – in its English-speaking form and, to a lesser extent, through cognates in other languages – that has acquired centrality in theoretical discourses, and this could potentially limit our understanding of other conceptualisations. For instance, theorists from Central and Latin America are currently exploring concrete indigenous forms of communal agency such as the *ayni*, the *chuqu* or the *k'ax k'ol* (Gutiérrez and Salazar Lohman 2015, 34–36; Tzul Tzul 2015, 132–134), as they can be more productive for their local political struggles. This tension not only hints at the pervasive hierarchies that dominate linguistic and cultural exchanges (the so-called 'world system of languages and translations'; Heilbron 1999, Sapiro 2009a), but also leads to a related question: the difficulty of translating the 'commons'. In this section, focusing exclusively on the 15M climate, I analyse how translation has contributed to the popularisation of the 'commons' in Spain, while highlighting the conceptual vagueness that characterises its usage.

As other scholars have noted, to date there has been little reflection on the usage of activist and theoretical concepts that, 'although translated into Spanish, involve *a certain degree* of difficulty' (Platero, Rosón and Ortega 2017, 9; italics in the original) in terms of understanding and definition. In the case of the 'commons', a defining particularity of Spanish-speaking terminology is its variety and ambiguity (Subirats and Rendueles 2016, 9): citizens, activists and politicians can refer to 'los bienes comunes', 'los comunales', 'los comunes', 'lo común', and 'el procomún' to denote different aspects of an interrelated reality that is subsumed within the English-speaking concept of 'commons'. Furthermore, the vernacular vocabulary for traditional, natural commons is abundant (Alonso Leal and Sampedro Ortega 2017, 108), locally diverse, and not necessarily related to the lexical range of the 'common'. In the few cases in which a reference to the semantic field of the 'commons' exists, it tends to appear as an adjective, that is, categorising the given resource, as in the case of 'tierra *comunal*' ('common land') or 'monte *comunal*' (a communal hill or forest).

54 *The 'commons'*

At this point, we are compelled to ask how users deal with this ambiguity. On the one hand, translators and activists are frequently called upon to explain and justify their linguistic choices as a way of facilitating communication, even though these strategies might not always be fully successful. For instance, in the Spanish translation of Silvia Federici's *Caliban and the Witch*, which was published by Traficantes de Sueños in 2010 and became a kind of radical 'best-seller', with eight reissues by 2017, the translators include the following footnote:

> La expresión inglesa *commons* ha adquirido, con el uso, la condición de sustantivo. Se refiere a «lo común» o lo «tenido en común», casi siempre con una connotación espacial. Hemos decidido traducirlo, según corresponda, como «tierras comunes» o «lo común».
>
> (Federici 2010, 42)

> [The English expression *commons* has acquired with usage the value of a noun. It refers to 'the common' or to what is 'held in common', most of the time with a spatial connotation. We have decided to translate it, depending on the context, as 'common fields' or as 'the common'.]

Although the explanation helps readers understand the complexity of the concept, its narrow focus on the 'material' and 'spatial' commons occludes pertinent aspects of the concept, such as the focus on practices and relationships between users (as argued by Federici and Caffentzis 2019, 94). Interestingly, this reduction is even more marked in the Catalan translation of *Caliban*, published by Virus in 2018, as the translator always opts to render the 'commons' in the sense of 'common goods' or 'common fields' (Federici 2018, 56, 144, 174, 201).

This process of explanation becomes particularly striking, yet also problematic, in the use of a term that is specific to Spanish political language: 'el procomún'. With the abstract sense of 'common good', its usage has been attested from the late Middle Ages and early Renaissance (Corpus del Nuevo Diccionario Histórico del Español 2019), but it fell into disuse for most of the 20th century, until activists in the field of free culture began to reappropriate the term in the early 2000s. As briefly mentioned in Chapter 2, this movement, which advocates free sharing of culture in various forms (copyleft, open access or free software, among others), has strong intellectual links with the birth of the 15M (Grueso 2012; Fuster, Subirats, Berlinguer, Martínez and Salcedo 2015, 78–79, 190–191). The political relevance of this collective has given additional momentum to 'procomún' as a Spanish translation of 'commons' in specialist circles (Zubero 2012, 23), yet it has not served to clarify the conceptual debate.[1] For instance, the cooperative ColaBoraBora, which focuses on the improvement of social relationships within companies and organisations

(ColaBoraBora 2019a), devotes an introductory section in its website to the 'procomún':

> El 'procomún' (traducción al castellano del 'commons' anglosajón), es un modelo de gobernanza para el bien común. La manera de producir y gestionar en comunidad bienes y recursos, tangibles e intangibles, que nos pertenecen a tod*s, o mejor, que no pertenecen a nadie.
> (ColaBoraBora 2019b)[2]

> ['Procomún' (Spanish translation of the English 'commons') is a governance model for the common good. The way to produce and manage in a community those goods and resources, both material and immaterial, that belong to everyone or, even better, that belong to no one.]

While this definition opens up one side of the issue that was absent from the previous explanation, its focus on a model of 'governance' for the *production and management* of 'goods and resources' is reductionist, as it emphasises the process and the product at the expense of 'the sharing itself and the solidarity bonds produced in the process' (Federici and Caffentzis 2019, 94). At the same time, it risks being politically slippery in a period where financial institutions and national governments are popularising the paradigm of community-based management as a way of 'cheapening the cost' (Federici and Caffentzis 2019, 90) of social services and cushioning the effects of budgetary cuts (De Angelis 2012).

Despite its problematic overtones, this production-oriented understanding of the 'commons' is becoming increasingly popular through the concept of the 'commons economy' ('economía del procomún' in Spanish, 'economia del procomú' in Catalan). According to the Catalan co-op Femprocomuns (2019), this model, which opposes 'market economy' as 'resources are shared instead of being exchanged', has 'the aim of promoting the production of goods (*béns*) that benefit everyone'. As noted earlier, this conceptualisation of 'the commons' can obscure the key aspects of community and the social bonds that generate but also *surpass* the actual resources.

Finally, despite its generalised usage as a technical term for Spanish activists, the popularisation of 'procomún' has not served to reduce the multiplicity of terms that can be used for the translation of the 'commons'. However, certain collectives seem to be trying to develop a more systematic combination of terms that provides coherence within diversity. In this sense, the Spanish version of David Bollier's *Think like a Commoner*, whose translational process will be analysed in the next section, constitutes a very relevant step in this direction. Although the Spanish text, produced by the cooperative Guerrilla Translation, does not include specific footnotes or accompanying commentaries to justify its linguistic choices, in-text analysis shows a three-fold strategy: 'procomún' is used when referring to the 'commons' as an abstract principle; 'comunes' denotes the specific immaterial realities and practices shaped by collective action; and 'comunal' is applied to the

56 *The 'commons'*

traditional resources belonging to a community (see for instance the interplay between these options in Bollier 2016, 11).

Traficantes de Sueños: translating the commons

A central point of reference in defining a Spanish understanding of the commons is the politically committed publisher Traficantes de Sueños, whose editorial activity was briefly discussed in Chapter 2. Functioning as a cooperative, Traficantes is also a founding member of the Fundación de los Comunes ('Foundation of the Commons'), a not-for-profit project created in 2013 that defines itself as a 'laboratory for critical thought from social movements' (Fundación de los Comunes 2015) and involves politically committed publishers (Katakrak, in Pamplona), self-managed centres (Nociones Comunes, in Saragossa, La Casa Invisible, in Málaga, and Ateneu Candela, in Tarrasa), and cultural cooperatives (La Hidra, in Barcelona). In this sense, Traficantes can be understood as both a product of and a contributor to the Spanish process of reception of the commons, as it is based upon the principles of the commons while also contributing to their dissemination.

Firstly, Traficantes shows a commitment to the commons through its books, which are published under a 'Creative Commons' licence that allows free download and non-commercial sharing. Along with information on the licence, the opening pages for every book include an explanation of the publishing house's commitment to open knowledge and links it with the larger aims of the movement for free culture, claiming that Traficantes 'adopts without restrictions freedom of access to knowledge'. This short manifesto concludes with the Latin motto *Omnia sunt communia* ('Everything belongs to everyone'). Traditionally attributed to the German Reformation cleric Thomas Müntzer, this Latin sentence has become a central motif for multiple activists across the world (De Angelis 2017; see Figure 3.1): two former councillors of the 15M-inspired local platform Ahora Madrid – including a member of Traficantes, Pablo Carmona – quoted it in the original Latin when they were sworn in (A. Gil 2015) as an expression of their commitment to the defence of the common good. In this way, Traficantes' books are the embodiment of the principles that they expose, while connecting classical and contemporary understandings of the commons.

However, beyond this concrete commitment to knowledge as a commons, Traficantes has not espoused a specific understanding of the commons; on the contrary, it has channelled a diversity of proposals from multiple perspectives, such as a series of seminars (Nociones Comunes 2013) and a lengthy string of publications. In this section, I will focus on a set of texts published since the beginning of the new political cycle (Madrilonia 2011; Linebaugh 2013; Bollier 2016), which is, in my view, particularly relevant when attempting to trace the dissemination of the commons. As part of this analysis, I will highlight how these texts contribute to a performance of the commons through different processes of translation.

Figure 3.1 The motto 'Omnia Sunt Communia' written on the wall of a university restroom (Universidad Complutense, Madrid). The stickers above it refer to the autonomous social centre La Ingobernable (see below).

Firstly, *La Carta de los Comunes* (*The Charter of the Commons*), a pamphlet signed by Madrilonia (2011), an online collective that contributed to the 15M protests, experiments with the translation of a fundamental genre for contemporary understandings of the commons: the charter. Following a prologue written in the dystopian Madrid of year 2033, where the economic crisis seems not to have receded, the book presents a charter 'of the Metropolitan Commons' (*los Comunales Metropolitanos*) — supposedly written in 2015, yet using an archaising language — that aims to establish the centrality of 'the goods, knowledges, and riches that being common (*comunes*) to all women and men make life in common (*la vida conjunta*) possible' (Madrilonia 2011, 17). The model for Madrilonia's charter is the medieval English *Magna Carta* (1215), to which the book pays homage not only through its content and stylistic features,

Figure 3.2 Detail of the book cover for *La Carta de los Comunes*. Note how one of the English *Charters* has been used as background motif.

but also visually, using an image of the *Carta* on the cover of the book in combination with a drawing of the Madrid square of Callao, an icon of the commercial and marketable character of the city (see Figure 3.2). In this connection between a historical reference and an imagined future, this 'charter of the commons' can be understood, once again, as a hauntological critique of the recent past: at a time when the Spanish Constitution, one of the pillars of the Transition to Democracy, is being heavily criticised for its inadequacies and shortcomings (to the point of scholars referring to a 'constitutional crisis'; see Boix Palop 2019), this charter proposes a new social pact that links contemporary claims with a different historical tradition of struggles for 'common rights'.

The inspiration behind this historical lineage is to be found in the reappraisal of medieval English charters undertaken by historian Peter Linebaugh in *The Magna Carta Manifesto* (originally published in 2008 and translated into Spanish by Traficantes in 2013), which studies how rights granted in these charters have inspired understandings of the commons across the world and, more importantly, how the memory of those struggles has resonated in multiple processes of opposition to privatisation and oppression. In this sense, both Madrilonia's text and Linebaugh's translation can be seen as part of an effort to create an alternative history for contemporary struggles, by honouring and reclaiming a landmark in the history of the commons while establishing links between foreign and national traditions in the search for more productive political tools that can be opposed to the current frameworks (such as the Spanish Constitution). In so doing, the text and its translation take the medieval English charter beyond its actual legal content and transform it into a symbol for a variety of

Figure 3.3 Fragment of a leaflet advertising a course on the commons (La Hidra Cooperativa 2017).

struggles across the world; see for instance the iconic use of the charter to advertise a course on the commons by La Hidra, a Spanish activist collective involved in the Fundación de los Comunes (see Figure 3.3).

Finally, Bollier's (2016) translation can be said to fully perform an understanding of the commons, since the whole translational process was developed upon a model of cooperation. Firstly, it was funded through a crowdfunding campaign (Goteo 2016), where citizens interested in the project could contribute within their means. Secondly, the translation was carried out by the

> **Textbox 3.1 Commoning knowledge**
>
> In the final section of Chapter 2, I referred to the practices of libertarian publishers, such as Calúmnia and Libros del Marrón, which privilege the political usefulness of knowledge over the restrictions of copyright. In the context of the current discussion of the commons and the movement for free culture, these transgressions could be reformulated as a process of 'commoning' knowledge, that is, of making common a collective resource that tends to be 'enclosed', as activists against copyright have frequently argued (Dardot and Laval 2014, 95–100).
>
> A relevant example in this respect is the summarised version of Elinor Ostrom's (1990) main book on the 'commons', which was edited by Ateneo El Acebuche, an anarchist-libertarian centre based in Málaga. This version (Puche 2015) was included within 'Cuadernos de Apoyo Mutuo' ('Booklets for Mutual Aid'), a series within which El Acebuche aims at 'recovering books that have been forgotten, left aside or directly hijacked by the publishing oligopoly' (El Acebuche 2019). The notion of 'mutual aid' is a clear echo of Piotr Kropotkin's anarchist classic, which is linked to the general principle underlying 'the commons' in the introduction (Puche 2015, 8–10). With the stated goal of contributing to the dissemination of Ostrom's work, this brief text constitutes a double 'commoning' of the copyrighted material, as it offers a choice of relevant excerpts from the existing Spanish translation while it is made available for free download under a creative commons licence.

cooperative Guerrilla Translation, which espouses the commons as its ideological underpinning (see next section). Thirdly, it was published by four not-for-profit cooperatives – Traficantes de Sueños in Spain, Sursiendo in Mexico, Cornucopia Editorial in Peru, and Tinta Limón in Argentina – which not only ensures fair conditions of production but also facilitates distribution of the book across Spanish-speaking countries while avoiding 'long distance shipping, which is pricy, inefficient, and environmentally unsustainable' (Goteo 2016). Finally, the product contributes to the promotion of 'free culture', as the e-book version is free for individual users and the book mock-up can be freely reprinted by any not-for-profit publisher. In this way, through a publishing process enshrined in the logics of the commons, Bollier's translation becomes a form of prefiguration (as understood by Maeckelbergh 2011): a text on the commons is transformed into an action towards the commons.

Guerrilla Translation: the 'commons' as paradigm

As already mentioned, Guerrilla Translation is an activist translation collective, created in Spain in 2013. The collective is linked to the free culture movement through two of its founding members (Ann Marie Utratel and Stacco Troncoso), notably with the P2P Foundation – a non-profit organisation 'dedicated to advocacy and research of commons-oriented peer to peer (P2P) dynamics in society' (P2P Foundation 2019) — and The Commons Transition Primer (2019), an online repository of research papers and educational documents on the commons and free culture.

Guerrilla Translation connects translation and the commons in two different ways: through its practice and through the governance that supports it. Firstly, as stated by the collective itself, their main aim is to 'create a plurilingual knowledge commons' (Guerrilla Translation 2019a), in which translation plays a major role. Using the language pair English-Spanish as its main arena, the collective aims to create 'a laboratory to experiment with new ideas' in the face of the current crisis that enables a two-way dialogue between linguistic areas: on the one hand, translating 'very valuable and interesting concepts [that] are coming out of the English-speaking world' (Guerrilla Translation 2019b) so they can be implemented in Spanish-speaking contexts, while, on the other, contributing to the dissemination of concepts generated in Spain whose 'sharing with English speaking countries' has been largely 'dependent on happenstance' (ibid.). The resulting commons is currently built through the bilingual site of the cooperative, where materials are categorised within seven main axes (Activism, Environment, Feminism, Mind, New Economy, P2P/Commons, and Post-Capitalism), as well as a YouTube channel with subtitled videos (Guerrilla Translation 2019c).

Secondly, in order to generate this translational commons, Guerrilla Translation is based on a dual model that differs from previous examples in the field of activist translation. The majority of activist collectives for translation and interpreting, either professional (De Manuel Jerez, López Cortes and Brander de la Iglesia 2004; Baker 2006a, 2013) or non-professional (Pérez-González 2016; Baker 2016b), are based on a strict notion of volunteering: the individual who engages with translational practice generally does it in addition to the rest of their activities and for a limited period of time, since activist engagement constitutes a moral reward in itself that excludes a monetary, economic bond. As Baker (2013, 40) has argued, this can be a particular source of tension for activist translators, who need to navigate between the attacks of professional translators — who frequently portray them as 'a threat to the profession' (ibid.) — and undervaluation by other activist groups, which might 'treat them as low-cost service providers rather than equal players in the political field' (ibid.). In fact, Piróth and Baker (2019) have shown how the logic of volunteerism is exploited by organisations such as Translators Without Borders, which adopts a 'top-down model' that 'reflects a corporate vision of the translation community' (6), as it generates a significant amount of money that is not distributed to, nor invested in, the volunteer translators.

For its part, Guerrilla Translation is based upon the combination of income-generating and not-for-profit translations, which aims to guarantee that members of the collective are paid for their work regardless of its nature (Guerrilla Translation 2019a). They ensure the fairness of the process by following three rules: first, both paid and unpaid jobs are treated equally, in terms of allocating the resources that each project requires; second, paid jobs are charged using a system of pricing that is not based on the complexity of the text, but the financial means of the client (Guerrilla Translation 2019d); third, income generated by the cooperative is distributed according to the translational work conducted by every member for both commercial and non-commercial projects. In this way, the collective moves from the logic of volunteerism (long-term and economic bonds are avoided) to the logic of cooperativism, since sustaining the activity of the community is not detached from the goal of ensuring the livelihood of its members.

La Ingobernable: an 'urban commons'

Another example of politicised collectives that are inspired by the spirit of the commons is autonomous social centres, which activist and former councillor Pablo Carmona has described as 'institutions of the common' (Carmona in Gutiérrez 2017, 118). A social centre is a multi-purpose urban space that is managed, governed, and protected by a community, generally but not exclusively made up of activists. In fact, as Flesher Fominaya (2015a) has shown, a significant number of activists who took part in the 15M occupations had been involved in different social centres across the Spanish State, such as the Patio Maravillas in Madrid (Diagonal 2015) and La Invisible in Málaga (Bango 2019). In turn, the 15M gave new momentum to this social form with the emergence of self-managed spaces such as the CSC Luis Buñuel in Saragossa (CSC Luis Buñuel 2019), el Banc Expropiat de Gràcia in Barcelona (15Mpedia 2016b), and the CSOA La Madreña in Oviedo (15Mpedia 2016c), among many others. A frequent, though not compulsory characteristic of these centres is that they came about as a result of occupying an abandoned and disused building, generally belonging to a public institution or to a corporation, to put it at the service of any citizen.

A notable example of this trend was La Ingobernable ('The Ungovernable'), self-defined as a 'social centre for urban commons' (La Ingobernable 2019a). La Ingobernable was located in an affluent area of Madrid, in a building that had belonged to a public university – the Universidad Nacional de Educación a Distancia (UNED), a distance-learning institution similar to the British Open University – but in 2013 was given over to a private foundation that had close ties with the local government under the rule of the Conservative Partido Popular. In 2017, a group of activists occupied the building, which had been completely abandoned following its concession to the foundation, and 'freed it up to put it at the service of the commons' (La Ingobernable 2019a).

Working upon the principles of the commons, this self-managed centre offered its space for non-profit activities that were open to the local area – lessons, sports, seminars, or conferences, among others – and based upon solidary and voluntary work on behalf of members. Playing on the name of the university that was formerly based at the building (UNED), La Ingobernable also created UNEDI – acronym for 'UNa Escuela De Ingobernables' ('A School for Ungovernable People') – which was defined as 'a space for self-learning, reflection, and critical debate' (La Ingobernable 2019b). Through UNEDI, La Ingobernable hosted a variety of seminars on topics that include the 'urban commons' (La Ingobernable 2018a) as well as debates with international authors such as post-capitalist theorist Paul Mason (La Ingobernable 2018b), feminist thinker Nancy Fraser (2019c), and anti-gentrification analyst Lisa Vollmer (2019e), during which voluntary consecutive interpreting was generally provided.

A major point of controversy regarding La Ingobernable, which highlights the specificity of the commons, was its repeated collusion with local governments. As argued by numerous authors, one of the defining characteristics of the commons is 'autonomy', that is, an ability to self-manage and self-regulate that clearly separates what is 'communal' from what is merely 'public' (Federici and Caffentzis 2019, 96), since the latter is always managed by one of the various administrations that constitute the State and can be subject to encroachment. As seen earlier, these opposing forces were clearly involved in the origins of La Ingobernable: a 'public' asset (the building) was not protected, but privatised without democratic consultation by a local government, until a group of activists gave it a 'communal' use, placing their sense of social justice above the decisions of the state (as Carmona argues, the commons 'tends to break existing laws'; quoted in Gutiérrez 2017, 118). As a consequence of this will for autonomy, La Ingobernable had a tense relationship from the outset with Ahora Madrid, a left-wing platform connected to the movement of the squares that ruled Madrid City Council from 2015 to 2019. In this confrontation, one of the moral arguments raised by La Ingobernable was that Ahora Madrid, which consistently refused to legally grant the use of the building to the collective, was letting down the same social movements that had brought it to power, as it was adopting the restrictive logic of the 'public' instead of supporting a logic of the 'commons'. Although an agreement between both parties seemed feasible in 2019, La Ingobernable turned it down on the grounds that the Council offered them only a 2-year permit with limited autonomy and a reduced share of the space (La Ingobernable 2019d). In May 2019, an alliance of conservative parties with external support from the far-right won the regional elections and immediately committed itself to the eviction of La Ingobernable, which finally took place in November 2019.

Barcelona en Comú: the institutional commons

A telling example of the relevance that the 'commons' have acquired within political terminology after the 15M is the local and regional platform Barcelona en Comú ('Barcelona in Common'), which won the Barcelona City Council elections in 2015 and again in 2019, although with a smaller percentage of the vote. Launched in 2014 as a citizen platform for the local elections, it supported the creation of a coalition with Podemos in 2015 (En Comú Podem) for the general elections and of a second coalition (Catalunya en Comú) for the regional elections in 2016.

The birth of Barcelona en Comú (BeC) was strongly linked to the Catalan section of the Plataforma de Afectados por la Hipoteca (PAH, 'Platform of People Affected by Mortgages'), a grassroots platform that brought together citizens affected by the consequences of the mortgage crisis (see Flesher Fominaya 2015b and Chapter 5). In fact, Ada Colau, spokeswoman for the PAH, immediately became BeC's most visible figure and was elected as their candidate for city council. A second strand that provided a backbone to the platform was a reflection on the commons, through the contribution of activists in the orbit of Fundación de los Comunes and, more importantly, through academics affiliated to the Institut de Govern i Polítiques Públiques (IGOP, 'Institute for Governance and Public Policies'). The IGOP, which is dependent upon the Universitat Autònoma de Barcelona, was created by Joan Subirats in 2009 and has been defined as 'the entrance gate for the *commons* in Catalonia' (Forti and Russo Spena 2019, 37; italics in the original). Subirats, a professor in political science, was a founding member of BeC, became councillor for Culture in 2017 and was re-elected in 2019, running as number two in Colau's list. Finally, another academic who was also involved in the foundation of BeC was Gerardo Pisarello, a specialist in constitutional law, who had lectured extensively on the commons and translated Ugo Mattei's manifesto for its protection and defence (Mattei 2013).

From its very beginning, BeC reclaimed the idea of the 'commons' through a series of discursive features, starting with its own name, which aimed at espousing a defence of Barcelona as a city 'of common goods' (Forti and Russo Spena 2019, 42). Its first political programme was devised through a multi-scale system (Barcelona en Comú 2015a), which involved public consultations in every district of the city as well as a series of committees of experts working on 'thematic axes'. The programme (Barcelona en Comú 2015b) was held together through the notion of action 'in common' ('en comú'), as each section was introduced with this phrasing, from 'la ciutat en comú' ('the city in common') to the individual districts covered. Importantly, the programme devoted a specific section to the relationship between the 'public' and the 'common', a matter of major relevance in a city that has a strong network of cooperatives and self-managed projects (Fernández and Miró 2016).

Under the heading 'Apostar per noves formes de gestió en comú' ('Supporting new ways of management in common'; Barcelona en Comú 2015b, 58), this section of the programme acknowledged the relevance of citizen initiatives that had emerged in Barcelona since the beginning of the crisis, emphasising how they have 'questioned the externalisation of [public] services to companies' and linking their success to the 'bonds of social cooperation' upon which these projects 'have been built'. However, while supporting processes to reinforce 'the sense of belonging and the common' (*allò comú*) and to enable 'democratization regarding decisions on the city's common goods' (*béns comuns*), the programme did not address the thorny question of the potential autonomy of a given common. In this sense, while entailing a major departure from traditional understandings of the relationship between government and society, Barcelona en Comú's approach to the commons remained dominated by the prevailing logic of the 'public'. Nevertheless, other analysts have supported this approach, including academic and activist Vicente Rubio-Pueyo, who has argued that the focus of the municipalist movement and, by extension, of the BeC is not 'the creation of self-sustained communities that form around "pure" commons', but 'the opening of a political struggle oriented towards a "commoning" of the public sphere', which would involve 'turning institutions into infrastructures for the common good' (Rubio-Pueyo 2017, 21).

With their victory at the local elections, Barcelona en Comú had the chance of becoming 'institutional political translators' (to use the terminology of Doerr 2018, 79): through their experience as activists for the commons, the platform could aim at translating popular demands into legislation that puts them into practice. A main step forward in this direction was the approval of a programme for 'citizen heritage in community-based usage and management' ('Programa de patrimoni ciutadà d'ús i gestió comunitàries') in 2017. The programme explicitly addressed the 'urban commons' (*comuns urbans*; Ajuntament de Barcelona 2017, 1), defined as 'responses to needs detected by citizens themselves' and provided 'on a collective basis' by 'groups of citizens' (*ibid.*). Its starting point was the assumption that 'the public' (*allò públic*) could become 'the common' (*allò comú*) thanks to the promotion of 'new forms of interaction between the local public institution and a series of citizen-based communitarian projects' (*ibid.*). In this way, BeC's programme was aiming to establish a continuum of commons-based practices, which would range from the completely autonomous to partnerships between citizens and the local government. Although still in its initial stages at the time of writing, this city-council-driven initiative was the most ambitious programme in this field within the boundaries of the Spanish State.

However, this process of institutional translation does not exclude tensions with commons-based projects. For instance, the theatre project Antic Teatre has criticised the way in which discourse on the commons can contribute to an excessive *institutionalisation* of the commons:

> [Our project] started because we thought, what's going on in this neighbourhood? What are the problems here? Community projects can also be a trend. Now, the new city council wants community projects, everything is about the commons (*procomún*), but then some people are paid, something is absorbed, and that is not a community project.
> (Antic Teatre in Álvarez-Blanco 2019, 296–297)

In other words, the involvement of local governments in the management of community life can lead to the emergence of fictional commons, which are developed by a professional collective that is specifically hired for a set task, instead of being based on cooperation between members of the community who identify a problem and aim at solving it collectively.

> **Textbox 3.2 *Auzolan*, a Basque perspective on 'the commons'**
>
> In 2017, the government of the Basque Country – led by a coalition between the conservative Basque Nationalist Party and the Basque federation of the social-democrat PSOE – proposed a new bilingual motto for its official communications: 'Euskadi, auzolana / Euskadi, bien común' (Boletín Oficial del País Vasco 2017). This choice is not only indicative of the increasing appeal of the language of the 'commons' across the political field, but also provides a glimpse into the conceptual perspectives that derive from local understandings of the commons.
>
> The Basque word 'auzolan' – used in the official motto in the nominative form 'auzolana' – can be loosely translated as 'communal work' or 'work undertaken by neighbours' (Diccionario Elhuyar 2019). In Basque-speaking rural areas, the custom of 'auzolan' involved cooperation between members of the village in order to conduct a given work that required additional help due to its size or complexity (Lopez de Etxezaharreta and Gonzalez Ruiz de Larramendi 2011). This work could be conducted for the benefit of the whole community, but also for smaller groups within it, such as a given family. The premise for this work was reciprocity, as any person or group requiring help would in turn be expected to volunteer for others in the future.
>
> Therefore, 'auzolan' implies a more dynamic perspective than 'bien común' ('common good'), the Spanish equivalent chosen for the Basque motto: while the latter focuses upon the resource ('good'), the former emphasises the process ('work'), which contributes to highlighting how the commons are not a given reality, but one that is actively constructed. At the same time, however, the central role played by 'work' in the 'auzolan' concept, as well as the fact that this work takes place within the community, but not necessarily for the benefit of the whole community, can also support narratives that aim to use the conceptual framework of the 'commons' from a market perspective. To a certain extent, this seems to be the line followed by the Basque government, who argued in their supporting text that 'auzolan' embodies, among notions of 'solidarity' and 'community', the 'collective culture of an entrepreneurial society' (Boletín Oficial del País Vasco 2017).

Conclusions

While presenting a number of ideas I will return to in the following chapters, this chapter simultaneously ties in with a series of previous arguments. Firstly, the analysis has shown a specific case of political renewal through translation, arguing how a translated concept (the 'commons') has been adapted and applied to Spanish reality by a variety of users connected to the climate of the 15M, as part of their search for a new political language that responds to current realities. In doing so, it has been possible to analyse how the political and economic crisis – with its drive towards privatisation of the 'public' – has encouraged activists to search for different forms of collective agency. In this way, therefore, it can be argued that adopting different conceptual languages and frameworks becomes a first step towards an experimentation with new political practices that have an impact on social reality.

Secondly, the study of numerous examples has shown the enormous complexity of the process of reception, which involves a great variety of actors (from translators and activists to organised collectives, institutions, and even political organisations) that promote different linguistic usages and conceptual understandings of a translated concept. In this sense, this chapter has provided a first, in-depth analysis of the process I have previously called expanded translation: in order to trace the adoption of a given translated concept, it is not possible to focus exclusively on a given set of translations, as the construction of meaning around it is greatly influenced by a variety of other textual and political interactions. On the one hand, the process of translation does not start from scratch, but tends to connect with a substratum of previous movements (in this case, free culture and social centres) that contribute to the general debate with their own traditions and internal debates. On the other hand, as I argued in the introduction, this process is always subject to tensions and power imbalances, since the capacity for dissemination varies for different actors: for instance, although Barcelona en Comú's discourse on the commons is indebted to its members' activist pasts and their engagement with other collectives, the platform's access to Barcelona City Council automatically provides it with a larger potential for the construction of a discourse on the 'commons' than any individual activist collective would enjoy. At the same time, those power imbalances can also have a decisive impact on the discourses and practices that shape concepts, as I have addressed in the set of strains and ambiguities that are generated between commons and institutions.

On a related note, the analysis opens the door to another potential conflict as we question whether academic and activist choices can be detrimental to communication with the majority of the population. In previous sections, I explored the way in which a certain activist culture favours the use of the technical term 'procomún' as a translation for the 'commons', even though it is a historical concept that had fallen into disuse and would not be familiar to many citizens. However, other strands of political action (most notably La Ingobernable and Barcelona en Comú) have continued using coinages that are closer to everyday language, such as 'comunes'/'comuns'. This tension highlights the major need for activist language to be adequately addressed and adapted to the collective that is aiming to convince, a question that will certainly resonate in later chapters.

Notes

1 For instance, the multilingual site Remix the Commons has also adopted 'procomún' as the standard translation of the English 'commons' and the French 'communs' (see Ambrosi 2013).
2 In this quote, the use of the asterisk in the word 'tod*s' is one of the many ways in which Spanish activists avoid using a gendered form (Spanish generally has marked gender endings for nouns, adjectives, and pronouns).

4 Towards the care strike
Translation and the rise of the feminist movement

On 8 March 2018, I went to work at Complutense University, in the northern outskirts of Madrid, just like any other normal teaching day. However, a remarkable difference stood out on campus: female students – usually a major cohort among Humanities undergraduates – were largely missing. You could spot one or two, here and there, seemingly walking faster than on an average day, making this general absence even more noticeable. In my classroom, as expected, only a male student showed up. While the global feminist strike of 2017 had a moderate impact in Spain, the overwhelming force of the 2018 strike – a gendered action in which only women were called upon to take part, whereas men were required to continue with their daily tasks while taking on a share of women's work – was condensed in that image: when female students walked out, the university with the largest population in the whole country was suddenly empty.

In the evening, I joined the feminist demonstration with a few friends. The planned route connected Paseo del Prado – the long and leafy boulevard where the Prado Art Museum is located – with the final rally at Gran Vía, a central avenue in the commercial area of the city centre. Way before we approached the tail of the demonstration, both sides of the street were booming with an impressive myriad of women: girls, teenagers, mothers pulling prams, middle-aged and older women; white, black, Latina, and mixed-race; collectives of lesbian and trans women. Our pace became slower and slower as we moved along Paseo del Prado as people started cramming the avenue. As we passed by La Ingobernable – the Madrid headquarters for the feminist movement, whose façade looked directly over the boulevard – a group of activists started hanging a banner from its windows: 'Sin nosotras se para el mundo' ('Without us [women], the world stops'), one of the main slogans of the demonstration. As it was fully unfolded, everyone marching on the street started clapping and shouting in support, until the noise became a roar of celebration.

Even if the success of the 2018 feminist strike – with millions of protesters on the streets and around 120 marches across the country – was uncontested, the scene of the banner had, in my view, a special symbolism. In late May 2011, when the occupation of Sol Square was in full swing, an incident with a similar banner had briefly soured the ambiance, revealing one of the hidden conflicts behind the 15M's image of unity. From one building, a group of protesters had hung a hand-written placard with the message 'La revolución será feminista o no será' ('Revolution will be feminist – or won't be at all'), which was negatively received by the majority of those on the square – especially the male protesters. It was booed and hissed until a young man climbed up to the building and untied the banner to great applause (Sánchez 2018). In 2011, feminism was perceived as a divisive discourse within the 15M (Galcerán 2012, 31), a movement that had 'a patent fear of strong arguments' that could create 'internal rifts' (Rodríguez 2016, 73). By 2018, however, feminism had become a powerful movement with a strong social presence that cut across parties and organisations, turning the date '8M' (8 March) into another key signifier for Spanish activism.

This chapter contributes to a better understanding of the increasing relevance of feminism since the beginning of the new political cycle and the way in which this evolution has been constructed. After an introductory section in which I provide the context of contemporary feminist movements across the Spanish State, the following sections focus upon the role of translation as part of feminist genealogy, paying special attention to the impact of feminism upon the book sector, before analysing the process of translation and reception of the concept of 'care', which played a decisive role in the conception of the feminist strike.

Recent reconstitutions of the feminist movement

At the turn of the 21st century, the field of feminism within the Spanish State was undergoing a period of internal tension. To start with, there was a marked sense of 'dispersion', with the emergence of a multiplicity of new collectives that emphasised 'difference as an inherent condition for political practice' (Gil 2011, 36). In fact, many among these groups and collectives did 'not feel part of the feminist movement, nor take it as a point of reference' (2011, 37). Furthermore, there was an increasing process of co-optation of the movement from various institutions (Gil 2011, 37; Gimeno 2018, 118), especially after the return of the social-democrat PSOE to central government in 2004. During the presidency of Rodríguez Zapatero (2004–2011), the Women's Institute (*Instituto de la Mujer*) was attributed greater relevance within the structure of the government and the first Ministry for Equality (*Ministerio de Igualdad*) was created in 2008, although it was quickly dismantled after the beginning of the economic crisis (Gimeno 2018, 118–119).

The perceived shortcomings of institutional feminism and the transformation of the social context in the face of the global recession opened up a new space for the reconstitution of feminism as a political force. In December 2009, the *Federación de Organizaciones Feministas del Estado Español* ('Federation of Feminist Organisations of the Spanish State') organised a summit in Granada gathering feminist collectives from the whole state, which served to celebrate the 30th anniversary of the first meeting of this kind in Spain (1979). The summit, which had not run since 2000, brought together more than 3,000 women and highlighted two prominent factors that are key to understanding the movement's revitalisation. It was not only intergenerational, bringing together feminists who had started their engagements with political action anywhere from the 1970s to the early 2000s, but it also committed itself to the promotion of 'critical', 'non-institutionalised', and 'autonomous' feminisms (Montero 2009, 878), emphasising its distance from ongoing processes of co-option.

The emergence of the 15M movement in 2011 would turn out to be a contradictory, yet decisive experience for feminists. On the one hand, they faced important disagreements and misunderstandings with other protesters, as briefly discussed earlier. During the early days of the occupations, the absence of an adequate space for feminist debates (Galcerán 2012, 31) and protesters' decision to overlook key feminist issues, such as the 'gendered impact of neoliberalism' in the form of the 'feminisation of poverty' (Bergès 2017, 18), prompted the creation of various collectives that aimed to foreground their concerns, such as Comisión Feminismos Sol ('Sol Committee for Feminisms') in Madrid, Feministes Indignades ('Outraged Feminists') in Barcelona, and Setas Feministas ('Feminist Mushrooms', a reference to the building under which the camp was located) in Seville, among others. For instance, as part of their response to this absence of feminist concerns, activists at Sol adopted a 'pedagogical' approach (Galcerán 2012, 33), arranging sessions on 'feminism for beginners' and establishing a dialogue with other committees to make their issues more visible.

Ultimately, however, feminist involvement at the occupation was deeply harmed by forms of sexism and even sexual harassment. In early June, two weeks after the beginning of the occupation, Feminismos Sol read a document at the general assembly explaining their decision to stop camping at the Square, while remaining an integral part of the debates during the day:

> Nights here at Sol are the source of tension and fear – not being able to rest, having to deal with all sort of violent and unpleasant situations[1]. [...] we have been informed of, and have experienced ourselves, sexual, sexist, and homophobic abuse. We understand as abuse: sexual intimidation, molestation, eyeing and gesticulating, contempt and abuse of power, insults and physical assault, undesired sexual and non-sexual touching, paternalistic attitudes.
>
> (Feminismos Sol 2011)

Without reaching similar levels of contention, Feministes indignades (2011) also denounced 'racist and male-chauvinist attacks' at Catalonia Square in Barcelona, and made an explicit commitment 'not to tolerate' any more events of the kind.

On the other hand, feminist involvement in the 15M occupations became an important laboratory for new momentum within the feminist movement. Firstly, it helped deepen the intergenerational approach of the Granada summit at a local level. In the case of Sol, the 15M brought together three generations of women (Bergès 2017, 19): precarious workers and students in their 20s, who were active in student unions but had no previous political experiences; activists in their 30s, linked to autonomous feminism and anticapitalist movements; and veterans who had been involved in various actions of the 1980s, such as the Asamblea Feminista and the squatter movement. Secondly, it provided an opportunity to reappraise political action, to explore processes of communication to wider audiences, and to experiment with other forms of protest, such as the occupations of public space (Bergès 2017, 22–27).

In the following years, feminist networks constructed at, or reinforced by, the 15M experienced a 'snowball effect', as a feminist activist put it (Jiménez Talavera interviewed in Touton 2019, 243–244): each engagement by the movement attracted more support for future actions. Its first major victory took place in 2014, when the feminist movement antagonised the conservative government of the Partido Popular over a draft for a law restricting the right to legal abortion (Gimeno 2018, 119). The scope of the mobilisations – 30,000 women gathered in Madrid from across the country in February 2014 (Ceballos 2019, 13) – did not only halt the legal reform, but also forced the minister who had put it forward to resign. Importantly, this campaign contributed to the reinforcement of intergenerational links, as many feminists who had been active in the struggles of the *Transición* joined the mobilisations, contributing to a sense of continuity for the movement (Touton 2016, 201–204).

Building upon this momentum, the movement became increasingly involved in the denouncement of sexist and gendered violence, arranging multitudinous demonstrations such as the *Marcha Estatal contra las Violencias Machistas* ('State March against all forms of male-chauvinist violence') in November 2015 and the protest against the lenient sentences given to a group of sexual offenders – popularly known as 'La Manada' ('The Wolf-pack') – in November 2017 (Ceballos 2019, 14–16). In turn, this wave of protests was reinforced by international protests taking place at the time, such as the global #MeToo movement against sexual harassment and the *Ni una menos* ('Not even one [woman] less') protests against gendered violence in Latin America (Gago and Cavallero 2017), which would feed directly into the future success of the feminist strike.

> **Textbox 4.1 The languages of '#MeToo'**
>
> In late 2017, the hashtag #MeToo, which was launched by American film actresses who wanted to denounce cases of sexual harassment and sexual assault in the film industry, became a global trend and prompted many women across the world to share their own experiences. The hashtag was soon translated and adapted across different countries; examples include the French #balancetonporc ('Grass up your pig') (Muller 2017) and the Italian #quellavoltache ('that time when') (Manifestolibri 2018).

In Spain, however, the #MeToo hashtag was less central than a later action: '#Cuéntalo' ('#Tell it'). Started in April 2018 by feminist journalist and writer Cristina Fallarás, it generated three million tweets in ten days, exposing thousands of murders, rapes, and cases of sexual abuse (Aragón 2019). Importantly, Fallarás has claimed that the action was conceived in part against the logic of #MeToo: while the latter 'was vertical and aspirational, not collective', because it had been initiated and dominated by 'powerful or famous women', #Cuéntalo was aimed at 'creating a horizontal narrative' for 'a collective memory that had not been narrated' (Fallarás interviewed in Aragón 2019). In other words, the campaign was not based upon individual reactions to a given case, but rather upon the construction of a community of women that generated a common resource (their shared narrative). In this way, #Cuéntalo enabled a grassroots approach to the conflict that was not dominated by well-known voices and figures, which fitted in with a defence of 'hashtag feminism' as a way to empower and galvanise 'the voiceless' through the emergence of 'intimate publics' that are defined by women themselves (Chen, Pain and Barner 2018, 197–198).

Communal searches for 'genealogy'

From the perspective of the cultural and political repertoire, a major transformation that was caused by the increasing relevance of feminism as a social power has been the generation of a plethora of processes and products – from board games to websites and books – aimed at tracing and reconstructing a feminist 'genealogy'. Building upon Foucault's (1971) understanding of the concept – which emphasised the non-linear, non-essential, radically historical origin of human realities – feminist genealogy questions those ideas that seem 'the most natural, the most hegemonic' in order to critique them by '(re)inscribing power, body, knowledge relationships' (Pillow 2003). In other words, feminist genealogy seeks to historicise what has been constructed as natural, such as the role of men and women in society or even the mere notion of 'man' and 'woman'. By showing the contingent character of these social discourses, feminist genealogy does not aim to unveil a supposed truth; on the contrary, it presents itself as 'an active process of knowledge production' (Gil 2011, 41) that unsettles hegemonic narratives. In the context of this section, I argue that many feminist activists and writers often use the concept of genealogy in a slightly more restricted sense, that is, as the process of discovering and reclaiming a series of female references – mostly hidden, suppressed, or undervalued by patriarchal society – to construct an alternative tradition. In this way, genealogy could be understood as a specific and more concrete form of the wider revaluation of the past that has characterised the 15M climate (see Chapter 2).

An important characteristic of projects and cultural products marked by this genealogical drive is collectiveness in its multiple forms. At a rather evident level, all of them emphasise a sense of collectivity, since they aim at contributing to the (re)construction of a non-patriarchal interpretation of history by illuminating the actions and experiences of past and present women. At a second, practical level, these projects depend decisively on the collective: while many among them have been developed thanks to crowdfunding, they are frequently based upon shared work, either performed by a group or cooperative with relatively stable boundaries or through collaborations between a less-defined, ad-hoc collective. In this sense, it can be argued that many among them are shaped by various understandings of the commons, emphasising the strong bond between feminism and the commons previously posited by Silvia Federici (2012, 142–144), which allows women to 'shape a collective identity' and to 'constitute a counterpower' in the face of capitalist and patriarchal dynamics.

A relevant example of the interaction between translation, feminist genealogy, and the commons is Wikiesfera ('Wikisphere'), a project attempting to reduce the gender gap on the online encyclopaedia Wikipedia, where only 10% of contributors are women. The project was launched by Patricia Horrillo, an activist for free culture who, as a consequence of her involvement with the 15M in Madrid, became one of the founders of 15Mpedia.org, an online encyclopaedia based upon the model of the knowledge commons that aimed to cover and archive any matter associated with the movement (Horrillo 2019). Since its creation in 2015, the Wikiesfera project has been holding weekly sessions in which female participants 'create, edit, and translate content' in order to reduce Wikipedia's gender gap (Barrilero 2018). Equally, Wikiesfera also organises thematic 'editatonas' – a coinage for feminist 'editathons', i.e. intensive sessions devoted to Wikipedia editing – where women generate and translate content for the encyclopaedia from a gender perspective, focusing on a given group of female practitioners (such as photographers or film directors) in each session (Horrillo 2019). In this way, Wikiesfera has generated a horizontal community of user-editors who, relying on their communal work, contribute to the creation of a common of free, accessible knowledge that highlights female experience.

Another relevant example of this triple interaction would be the work of the collective Sangre Fucsia ('Fuchsia blood'), created in early 2013 by a group of women with expertise in radio production (Sangre Fucsia 2019a). Shortly after its foundation, the collective launched their eponymous radio programme, which is recorded at the feminist social centre Eskalera Karakola ('Spiral Staircase') and broadcast by Ágora Sol Radio, an autonomous, self-managed radio station that was set up in late 2011 out of the necessity to provide the 15M with new means of communication. Through a 'horizontal' and 'assembly-based' decision-making process, Sangre Fucsia devotes weekly thematic shows to different topics 'from a feminist perspective' (Sangre Fucsia 2019a), ranging from mountaineering to punk, masonry, and feminist humour (2019b). In 2015, using materials gathered during their first 100 shows, Sangre Fucsia put together the boardgame *Feminismos Reunidos* ('Compiled Feminisms'), which links the collective's understanding of the commons with a feminist genealogy, in a process where translation plays a relevant role.

Firstly, the game's financial setup evidences a non-for-profit, activist ethos at both ends: it was financed through crowdfunding and the economic surplus that it generated – its success prompting several reprints – has been reinvested in other independent feminist projects, such as the magazine *Píkara* (Sangre Fucsia 2017). Secondly, *Feminismos Reunidos* is based upon a revealing process of translation of models – similar to the one I discussed in Chapter 3, analysing Spanish usages of the British Magna Carta – that is combined with feminist appropriation. The game adapts the classical question quiz popularised by the Trivial Pursuit board game, which it follows in its general rules, design, and visual features; in both cases, the games consist of a series of thematic questions that lead to the accumulation of tokens for different areas of knowledge, each of them symbolised by a different colour. However, while Trivial Pursuit emphasises – starting with its own name – a notion of knowledge and general culture as mere depoliticised entertainment, *Feminismos Reunidos* binds together recreation and a political usage of knowledge, stating explicitly how the goal of the game should be simultaneously 'to have fun' and 'to learn something about our own feminist genealogies' (Rule book of the game, page 1). In this way, the Trivial Pursuit model is not simply translated or adapted, but 'hijacked' – a feminist practice consisting of the appropriation of the 'original' in order to make it express the translator's political intentions and aims (Von Flotow 1991, 72–74). Through this 'hijacking' of the model for activist aims, *Feminismos Reunidos* can be placed within a larger tradition of 'critical' games that are 'designed for artistic, political, and social critique or intervention' (Flanagan 2009, 2).[2]

Finally, the game reinforces feminist references and symbols for the movement, as each area of knowledge used in the game is represented by a relevant female figure: Simone de Beauvoir (feminist theory), Angela Davis (social movements and activism), Judith Butler (sexuality, gender, and LGBT), Frida Kahlo (arts and culture), Olympe de Gouges (advancement of women's rights), and Valentina Tereshkova (women's history). Importantly, this choice of references is revealing of the role played by translation in the construction of intellectual icons within the 15M climate discussed in Chapter 2, as the majority of these figures (De Beauvoir, Davis, Butler, and to a lesser extent de Gouges) are authors with a translated work.

This genealogical drive towards the reinforcement and/or recuperation of past references is also expressed in another 'critical' board game, *Herstóricas pioneras* ('Herstoric pioneers'), which was crowdfunded in 2018. The card game, which is mainly designed as a pedagogic tool for children, was developed by the eponymous collective Herstóricas, whose name is a translated neologism based on the concept of 'herstory' (Mills 1989, 118–119), which advocates for a militant feminist reinterpretation of male-dominated, traditional historiography. Through this coinage, the collective aims – in a slightly bombastic way – at 'naming all the women that have preceded us in history' (Verkami 2018a), which is precisely the goal of the game: to popularise the work of a series of Spanish women that stood out across numerous fields (arts, culture, politics,

76 *Towards the care strike*

and science, among others), but have not been properly acknowledged and valued in society.

Genealogy, translation, and the publishing field

The impact of feminism upon book publishing deserves a specific section of its own, as this has arguably been the cultural field upon which the resurgence of the feminist movement has had the most visible impact. While this drive has undoubtedly contributed to wider debates, it is also potentially subject to the ambiguities of the 'publishing boom' that was prompted by the 15M movement (see Chapter 2) and the subsequent search for economic and 'militant remunerations' (Gaxie 1977). As Tables 4.1. and 4.2 show, the publication of books on feminism increased considerably in the 2017–2019 period, both in absolute terms (considering the number of ISBN licenses given in the country) and within the specific sector of politically committed publishers. Following a general trend within this group of publishers, the increase is greatly indebted to translation, which accounts for more than 60% of the books (Table 4.2.). However, feminist authors such as the poet Luna Miguel (2019) and the essayist Carolina León (2019), a member of the cooperative Traficantes de Sueños, have recently criticised the subsequent 'overabundance' of feminist books that, in León's words, 'will not be remembered in six months' time and would not pass the most basic test for rigour' (León 2019).

Beyond the potential ambiguities within this publishing trend, the genealogical motif runs through an important number of books, acquiring a particular relevance in two categories of works: those conceived with a strongly pedagogic and formative character, as well as landmark works that are republished or rediscovered. Two relevant examples of the first category, among others, are the university course *Historia ilustrada de la teoría feminista* ('Illustrated history of feminist theory'; De Miguel and De la Rocha 2018) and the introductory anthology *Feminismos* (Ranea 2019). The first is an

Table 4.1 Number of ISBN licenses for books in Spanish (both originals and translations) under the rubric 'Feminism'

Year	Licenses
2019 (October)	163
2018	168
2017	137
2016	87
2015	72
2014	68
2013	60
2012	79
2011	111

Table 4.2 Number of books (translations into Spanish vs. Spanish originals) on feminist topics published by politically committed publishers*

Year	Translations	Spanish Orig.	Total
2019 (October)	10	9	19
2018	7	6	13
2017	4	3	7
2016	6	1	7
2015	5	0	5
2014	2	1	3
2013	1	0	1
2012	1	1	2
2011	1	0	1
%	63.79%	36.21%	

*Publishers and book series included in this sample are listed in Table 2.1 and discussed in Chapter 2.

illustrated version of the annual course taught at the *Instituto de Investigaciones Feministas* ('Institute for Feminist Research', Complutense University), originally led by Celia Amorós (1993–2004) and later by Ana de Miguel (from 2005 onwards). Playing upon the formatting of class notes (underlining, highlighting key sentences, and using different colours), the book offers a synthetic and historical approach to various feminist topics and theories for a wider audience. Through a collective approach, it provides a space for interaction between 'transnational' thought and 'national' reception, as each theory and movement is introduced by one of the many lecturers teaching on the course. Importantly, the whole project is placed under Amorós' opening statement that women 'need our genealogy', which is presented as a continuous, collective effort, since 'patriarchy is constantly erasing the traces of our genealogy' (De Miguel and De la Rocha 2018, 11–12).

Similarly, the anthology *Feminismos*, compiled by sociologist Beatriz Ranea, states its desire to contribute to 'our genealogy' and to 'the revindication of the struggles' that took place throughout history (Ranea 2019, 10); in this sense, the compiler claims that the book 'is not simply an anthology, but also – or rather – an act of gratitude' (Ranea 2019, 11) to previous generations of feminists. Translated authors – such as Kate Millett, Vandana Shiva, Germaine Greer and bell hooks – constitute a central part of the anthology, although the role and the complexity of translation are not problematised or discussed.

The second category marked by a genealogical approach – revindicated landmark works – is pivotal for the project developed by Ménades, an editorial collective launched in 2019 out of a 'commitment with literature written by women' (Verkami 2018b). Partly supported through crowdfunding, Ménades aims to publish books written by women and/or dealing with their reality. In particular, one of their book series, 'Las olvidadas' ('The forgotten [women]'), is strongly oriented towards genealogy: the collective defines it as an answer to the question 'where were they [*ellas*]?', as it focuses on the recuperation of authors that 'were alien to public recognition and literary movements' (Verkami 2018b). Importantly, translation plays a key role in this series, as the majority of references published so far (seven out of eight books) are translations of English, French, and Greek sources.

Finally, the engagement of independent publisher Katakrak with the work of historian Gerda Lerner represents an example of feminist genealogy in its fullest sense, as it combines the reclaiming of an undervalued figure with a defence of historical reflection as a political tool. In 2017, Katakrak reissued the Spanish translation of Lerner's *The creation of patriarchy*, which had been out of print for several decades, and emphasised its importance as a tool to 'deconstruct [...] history as thought by those high-class, male historians' that have shaped contemporary understandings of society (Lerner 2017, 12). In fact, Nerea Fillat, a member of the collective, claimed that the book could become an important tool for the feminist movement, as it provided 'a paramount material to construct the history of women' (Madrid book presentation, 6 March 2018).[3] In 2019, Katakrak reinforced this claim with the publication of the second volume in Lerner's project, *The creation of feminist consciousness*, which had not previously been translated into Spanish. Reaffirming the need to understand history 'as a tool for political action', the collective claimed that Lerner's book – through offering 'a history of female authors' – provides 'a historical-feminist analysis' against 'the non-existence of a female "subject" in traditional historiography' (Lerner 2019, 12), which has in turn led to 'an accumulation of knowledge produced by men' and 'a dispossession of women's intellectual production' (*ibid.*).

'Care' as a political concept

As discussed in Chapter 3, the exploration and renewal of language and concepts is a key trait within contemporary activism, and Spanish feminism is no exception. Indeed, it has developed thanks to multiple debates taking place not only within the field of feminist theory, but also across related fields such as gender and sexuality studies. In their landmark dictionary for the field of gender and sexuality studies in the Spanish State, Lucas Platero, María Rosón, and Esther Ortega (2017) have studied how feminism, as well as other activist movements, have incorporated a series of translated, adapted, or directly borrowed concepts such as 'agencia' (*agency*), 'empoderamiento' (*empowerment*), 'capacitismo' (*ableism), queer/cuir*, and *cyborg*, among others. In the following sections, I address the Spanish reception of 'care', a concept that is surprisingly absent from Platero, Rosón, and Ortega's dictionary but plays a key role in feminist struggles across the world and has acquired a central position in the political framework for feminists across Spain.

The concept of 'care' embodies the whole set of actions and practices that are needed for the support of daily life, ranging from basic chores – such as cooking and cleaning, but also feeding and washing, in the case of children, the elderly, and the dependent – to more complex social habits, such as engaging with friends and the wider community. In this sense, 'care' is understood by various feminist thinkers – such as Silvia Federici (2012, 65–125) and Nancy Fraser (2017) – as a central element within the larger framework of 'social reproduction', that is, the process that enables the historical sustainability of human life.[4]

While 'care' has been an integral part of human history, feminist scholars argue that it did not exist as an independent area of activity until the Industrial Revolution, as previous societies did not make such a clear cut distinction between activities taking place inside or outside the family and the community (Carrasco, Borderías, and Torns 2011, 17–18). Between the late 18th and the early 19th centuries, the Industrial Revolution created a veritable 'crisis of care' that threatened social reproduction among the lower classes, due to the high demand for manual workers (men, women, and children) and the long shifts in unhealthy, strenuous conditions (Fraser 2017, 26–27). As a response to this threat to their social and economic fabric, Western societies reacted via the progressive reduction of children and women's work, as well as an increase of male workers' salaries (Carrasco, Borderías, and Torns 2011, 19–24). In turn, the combination of these measures led to the creation of the 'unproductive', 'full-time housewife' as a social figure (Folbre 1991; Federici 2018, 69–80) and to the emergence of a discourse that essentialised women's dedication to care, justifying it as part of their supposed 'nature' (Knibiehler 2017, 47–75) and as an expression of their 'love' for their family (Bock and Duden 1980). In this way, a decisive rupture would take place between two forms of work that were previously enmeshed: while productive work at the factory or company will be waged, socially valued, and male-dominated, reproductive work at home will be unpaid, unvalued, and associated with women. What this process involved was not only the submission of one gender to another, but also the concealing of a key economic reality (Dalla Costa and James 1975; Federici 2017b): capitalism extracts enormous benefit from unpaid labour, as the workers who produce for the system are able to do so thanks to the many tasks of 'caring' performed by women at their homes.

While care gradually became a key social reality with the advancement of industrial society, its emergence as a political concept only took place in the 1970s and 1980s (Carrasco, Borderías, and Torns 2011, 31–35) thanks to feminist activism. One of its first exponents was the international campaign Wages for Housework (WfH, 1972–1977). Taking as its starting point the recognition of domestic work as real work that 'was being exploited' (Toupin 2018, 1), a network of feminists across countries such as the United States, Germany, Canada, and Italy – including important thinkers such Mariarosa Dalla Costa, Silvia Federici, and Selma James – demanded a salary for house workers, which would give them greater independence, but also a chance to reject this domestic work as an 'expression of [their] nature' (Federici 2012, 19), as the system had constructed it. Although this demand was seen by other sections of the feminist movement as 'a step backward in the demand for women's equality' and rejected in favour of 'a strategy of "family-job reconciliation"' (Toupin 2018, 3), the movement raised a number of issues such as the centrality of care and the critique of the distinction between paid and unpaid work, which continue to reverberate in the present day, as will be discussed later.

Over recent decades, debates on 'care' have acquired a renewed centrality not only for activism, but also within a variety of academic disciplines (economy, sociology, and governance, among others) due to the emergence of the 'crisis of care', which Nancy Fraser has interpreted as an 'acute expression of *the social-reproductive contradictions of financialized capitalism*' (Fraser 2017, 21–22; italics in the original). In a nutshell, this crisis implies a conflict between capital (i. e. the drive to extract continuous and increasing profit) and the sustainability of life, as the care labour needed to support it can no longer be provided. This conflict is taking place as a result of a combination of ageing populations in Western countries, a programme for global austerity that results in cuts to investment in social welfare, the widespread precarity of jobs, and the breaking down of family and social networks (Pérez Orozco 2009, 713–714), which places the provision of care under enormous strain. At the same time, the increasing incorporation of women into the paid workforce puts an additional burden on their shoulders, as they have to work a 'second shift' (Hochschild and Machung 2012) at home, due to the unequal distribution of care work. In turn, this crisis reinforces dynamics of inequality between countries through the creation of 'global care chains' (Hochschild 2000), as the search for care workers to cover for women joining the paid sector in the global North causes important influxes of migration from poorer regions of the world, frequently breaking up families and destabilising these communities. In consequence, the crisis of care represents a major danger to the quality of human life, but also a major challenge to the 'capitalist realism' that underpins neoliberalism: if Mark Fisher (2009, 16) argued that this 'realism' can only be seriously 'threatened if it is shown to be in some way inconsistent or untenable', the dramatic situation of care points precisely towards the 'unrealistic' premises behind the current system of profit-generation.

'A general strike has never been such': from 'care' to the 'huelga de cuidados'

The concept of care was introduced within Spanish feminist debates at the turn of the 21st century, thanks to the work of anticapitalist economists (Federici 2017a, 22–23; Gimeno 2018, 121) such as Amaia Pérez Orozco and Cristina Carrasco, as well as through the translations, talks, and activist endeavours of Italo-American thinker Silvia Federici, who is highly regarded by Latin American and Spanish feminists (Gutiérrez Aguilar 2019, 39).[5] In a manner similar to the case of several other concepts, the reappraisal of care would fall within a wider 'rediscovery of debates already held by feminists in the 1960s-1980s' (Cámara and Facet 2018, 11) by younger generations of politicised women.

A first characteristic of the reception of care – shared with other concepts discussed in this book – is the difficulty of translation, which leads to a multiplicity of options: 'el cuidado' (singular form of 'care'), 'los cuidados' (plural form), and 'el trabajo de cuidados' ('the work of cares') are the most frequently used options in Spanish. Important scholars in the field – such as Carrasco, Borderías, and Torns (2011, 75) – have labelled them as 'infelicitous translations' and prefer the use of the English term. This tension is not specific to the Spanish-speaking context, however, and French feminists for instance have also debated the difficulties of translating 'care' and the convenience (or otherwise) of adopting the English term as such (see Delphy and Molinier 2012, 305–306 for a debate on 'the surcharge in meaning' of the available concepts and Pouly 2017, 11–13 for a defence of its translation). Yet, despite this, and as I will show in the following pages, the increasing adoption of this constellation of terms by Spanish feminists has naturalised them, especially in the case of 'los cuidados' and related forms in other state languages (the Catalan 'cures' and the Galician 'coidados'), which have been widely used and incorporated across feminist actions.[6]

Before the start of the 15M political cycle, two major events contributed to placing the debate on care in the spotlight. Firstly, the PSOE government's so-called 'dependency law' passed in 2006 (Boletín Oficial del Estado 2006), which aimed at establishing a system of support for dependent people, understood as those who, due to illness or age, were no longer autonomous and needed the help of a carer. While expectations were high for this law, its results were greatly disappointing due to its restricted understanding of dependency, the lack of trained specialists, and its chronic underfunding (Carrasco, Borderías, and Torns 2011, 76–77), further aggravated by the economic crisis of the 2010s. Despite this disappointment, debates surrounding the dependency law contributed to shedding some light upon the hidden reality of care and the precarious conditions of (mostly migrant) women working in the care sector, who started to self-organise in collectives such as *Territorio Doméstico* ('Home Territory'), created in 2016. One of its founders, Rafaela Pimentel, an activist and care worker of Dominican origin who has co-lectured with Federici and Pérez Orozco, defined the association as an attempt to 'make pots and pans political' (Pimentel in Collective authorship 2019, 47), that is, as a way of exposing the political nature of domestic work.

The second major event was the aforementioned 2009 feminist summit in Granada, as the programme was punctuated by multiple debates on care, such as the limits of the dependency law, the experiences of migrant women as 'carers' (*cuidadoras*), the 'crisis of care' ('la crisis de los cuidados'; Pérez Orozco 2009, 713–714), and anticapitalist perspectives on care (Sandra Ezquerra 2009). The event advocated for a reappraisal of care as a central factor for sustainable societies.

The renewed momentum for political action that the 15M provided was yet another catalyst for initiating debates on care (Bergès 2017, 23; Galcerán 2012, 35–36), which began to take centre stage for feminism, prompting a string of new publications (Borderías, Carrasco and Torns 2019, 411), and becoming a 'symbol of contention' (Tarrow 2013, 12) for the whole movement. The year 2012 marked a tipping point, with the first 'huelgas de cuidados' ('care strikes') being held. These were instigated by feminist activists on the occasion of the two general strikes that took place in Spain against a new labour law passed by the conservative government (for an overview and critique of this labour law see ATTAC Madrid 2012). On the day of the first strike (29 March), various collectives across the country defended the need for care to be viewed as part of the field of work in order to make it visible, while denouncing the way in which the feminisation of care and its unpaid character led to precariousness (Colectivo Feministas en Movimiento 2012). For the second strike (14 November), various feminist movements that were closely linked to the 15M movement – such as Feminismos Sol (Madrid), Feministes Indignades (Barcelona), and Setas Feministas (Seville) – supported the call for a 'care strike' (*huelga de cuidados* in Spanish, *vaga de cures* in Catalan) as an integral component of the action. As part of this intervention, Feminismos Sol (2012) issued a pamphlet – titled 'Comando de cuidados' ('Care Commando') – explaining their political stance and denouncing care as invisible, unpaid, and feminised labour (see Figure 4.1). Importantly, the pamphlet translated the basic underpinnings of anticapitalist approaches to the reproduction of labour to a wider audience – ideas developed, for instance, by Federici (2012, 65–125) – arguing that the invisible work performed by women enables the existence of a worker 'who arrives at the workplace fed, cleaned and ironed, ready not to worry about anything other than producing (for the company that benefits the financial system)' (Feminismos Sol 2012, 2).

Building upon these debates, the politicised notion of 'care' as a central, yet invisible component of human work would play a vital role in the process of redefining and enriching the very notion of 'strike'. In 2014, the newly created Catalan movement 'Vaga de totes' ('Strike for all [women]') emphasised how a 'general' strike only addressed 'a waged worker involved in the recognised labour market', and excluded 'many people and many forms of labour' (Vaga de totes 2014). In opposition to this model, the collective advocated for a model of strike that involved all forms of labour – 'productive, reproductive, domestic, sexual, formal or informal' – and expanded into a 'consumption' (*vaga de consum*) and 'care strike' (*vaga de cures*). In a similar line of thought, journalist Isabel Cadenas recalls how at a meeting in preparation for the 2018 feminist strike 'a comrade said: a general strike has never been such, because us women were still in charge of care (*los cuidados*)' (Cadenas in Collective authorship 2019, 28).

All of these lines of political thought coalesced in the manifesto issued by the Madrid-based organising committee ahead of the successful 2018 feminist strike, which was punctuated throughout by the centrality of 'care' and devoted a whole section to the 'care strike' (*huelga de cuidados*). Despite its brevity, this document offers a formidable synthesis of decades of feminist theory and praxis in an accessible and direct language, which bears direct traces of debates on social reproduction, care, and housework. After denouncing the fact that

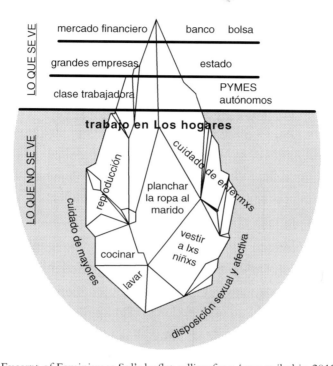

Figure 4.1 Excerpt of Feminismos Sol's leaflet calling for a 'care strike' in 2012. Work is symbolised as an iceberg, of which only a small part is visible – 'care work' constitutes the largest, yet also hidden and invisible part.

women are still in charge of 'domestic and care work' (*el trabajo doméstico y de cuidados*), which is essential 'to ensure the social reproduction of life' (Comisión de Contenidos 2017, 14), the manifesto claims that the strike 'aims at making patent that the economic system would collapse without our daily care work (*trabajo de cuidados*)' (18): a form of work 'that has been made invisible [*invisibilizado*] and devalued [*desvalorizado*] even though the system is supported through the appropriation of care (*los cuidados*) undertaken by us, women' (*ibid.*). The convergence of this analysis with previous feminist movements was made explicit during a talk by Silvia Federici on the contemporary heritage of the Wages for Housework campaign (Madrid, Palacio de la Prensa, 19 March 2019), when a spokeswoman for the organising committee declared that the 'care strike' (*huelga de cuidados*) had been directly influenced by 'Italian feminists' and the WfH movement.

Along with feminist thought, a second major influence on the manifesto was the grounded experience of care workers, which was expressed in the stark denouncement of their conditions of exploitation – 'ranging from precarity to human trade (*trata laboral*)' (Comisión de Contenidos 2017, 14) – as part of 'the global care chain' (*la cadena global de cuidados*). This centrality of domestic and care workers was also manifested in the choice of Rafaela Pimentel, a representative of Territorio Doméstico, as one of the spokeswomen for the Madrid committee. Importantly, by ensuring the visibility of exploited care workers and their concerns, the movement was also articulating a rebuttal of liberal and institutionalised versions of feminism that focus on the achievements of privileged women. Shortly after the strike, *Senda de Cuidados* ('Caring Path') – an association created in 2012 from an alliance between members of Territorio Doméstico, groups of migrants, 15M protesters, house workers, and local Christian activists – provided a clear summary of this stance:

> Although mass media prefer focusing on the demands that affect high-class women (such as the glass ceiling), the feminist movement is slowly putting on the agenda the crucial issue of care (*los cuidados*), which affects each and every woman, but especially those with fewer resources.
>
> (Senda de Cuidados 2018)

Finally, the manifesto put forward a radically innovative demand, aimed at achieving a more egalitarian distribution of work. Acknowledging that 'women stop but care doesn't stop' ('Paramos las mujeres, pero no paran los cuidados'), the feminist movement made a call for the inclusion of 'the provision of care' (Comisión de Contenidos 2017, 18) as part of 'minimum services', something that was ground-breaking in at least two respects. Firstly, minimum services in the event of a strike are only required by the International Labour Office for 'essential services' (those whose interruption 'would endanger the life, personal safety or health of the whole or part of the population') and 'public services of fundamental importance' (ILO 2006, 124). Therefore, by calling for the inclusion of care in the definition of minimum services, the feminist movement was rightly placing the invisible, unpaid, and undervalued work of care at the same level as the key areas that enable the normal functioning of a country. Secondly, in order to facilitate these services, a network of 'caring points' – 'puntos de cuidados' in Spanish, and 'punts de cura' or 'espai de cures' ('care spaces'), in Catalan – was developed, where men voluntarily assumed caring duties in the place of the striking women. The physical spaces were provided by social centres – such as La Canica, Eskalera Karakola, and La Ingobernable, in Madrid, or the Ateneu Popular de Les Corts in Barcelona – and various smaller parties and trade unions (Vaga Feminista 2018; Hacia la huelga feminista 2019). In this way, a meaningful interaction between care and commons took place, which built upon the political potential of both: while the care strike challenged the patriarchal and neoliberal character of contemporary societies, the commons-based provision of care demonstrated the possibilities of citizen cooperation beyond the state and the market.

Textbox 4.2 A multilingual strike

While my discussion in this chapter has mainly focused on Spanish and, to a lesser extent, Catalan texts, the 2018 feminist strike was a truly multilingual event, based upon the diversity of multiple collectives across the Spanish State. The highly innovative character of the strike and the various constituencies involved meant that regional and local committees tailored their messages according to their vision. For instance, the Galician committee (Galegas 8M 2018) devoted part of its call for the 'care strike' (*folga de coidados*) to a concrete, fact-based analysis of the situation of Galician women regarding care work, while also explaining, in a pedagogic manner, the multiple areas it covered: 'coidados de saúde' ('healthcare'), 'coidados ás crianzas' ('childcare'), 'coidados da limpeza' ('care for cleaning'), and 'coidados dos maiores' ('care for the elderly'). For its part, the Aragonese committee released a leaflet in seven languages (Spanish, French, English, Romanian, Arabic, Russian, and Chinese), which posed a series of key questions regarding dedication to care work and an invitation to join the strike or to publicly support it (see Figure 4.2). Although no direct reference was made to the domestic sector, its choice of languages evidenced that the pamphlet was aiming to engage with migrant women, who are disproportionately involved in the 'global care chains'.

Conclusion

Linking with analyses and findings presented in previous sections of the book, this chapter has shown the centrality of translation for the political practice of the feminist movement in Spain, highlighting its commonalities with other forms of political engagement in the 15M 'climate' while also pointing to its divergences. Firstly, I have argued that the rise of feminism as a political agent has made a clear impact upon the cultural field, as happened with the emergence of the 15M movement, and that the interaction between the movement and the book industry could be understood in both positive and negative terms. Secondly, the genealogical drive within the movement was connected to, although not equated with, the wider process of questioning the past espoused by the 15M, as well as to its search for alternative references and models. Finally, the reception of the concept of 'care' (*los cuidados*) and its contribution to the development of the 2018 feminist strike has reinforced other case studies on the process of 'expanded translation' that leads to the formation and dissemination of a political concept. As in the case of the 'commons' studied in Chapter 3, the construction of meaning around a concept proved to be complex, multi-level, and greatly conditioned by the influence of political actors. In fact, whereas the 'commons' still seems marred by a certain terminological instability, the

86 Towards the care strike

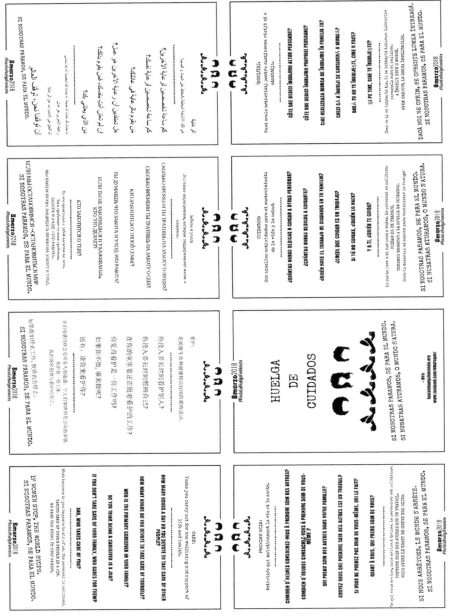

Figure 4.2 Multilingual leaflet produced by the Aragonese 8M committee calling for a 'care strike'.

determined adoption by the feminist movement of 'cuidados' and its related coinages has contributed to a wider dissemination and solidification of the concept.

At a practical level, a major point of difference in the study of the translational practices of the feminist movement has been its strong and fluid imbrication with the paradigm of the commons (an idea already put forward by Silvia Federici), both in genealogical projects (Wikiesfera, Feminismos Reunidos) and in the provision of care ('caring points' for the feminist strike). In this sense, it could be argued that feminism constitutes – in its most concrete and basic practices – the movement that bears a closer and more direct bond with the autonomous and self-managed ethos revived by the emergence of the 15M.

Bearing in mind the clear success of feminism in recent years, we must make one final caveat regarding the potential appearance of new processes of co-option, either aimed at placating certain sectors of the movement or, even worse, at undermining its demands. In fact, the widespread use of 'cuidados' in political parlance over recent years is a telling example of how the success of a concept can lead to its normalisation. For instance, in 2016 Madrid City Council – led at the time by the left-wing platform Ahora Madrid – launched the project 'Madrid Ciudad de los Cuidados' ('Madrid City of Care'), which aimed at 'directing the whole policy of the Council from the perspective of care', in order to 'place people's conditions of life as a priority' (Alcaldía de Madrid 2016). While the purpose in itself was innovative and very welcome, the initial statement also made it clear that the project did not 'have a specific budget for the time being' (*ibid.*). Considering the pervasive exploitation that the feminist concept of 'care' illuminates, a care-based project without specific economic measures would probably remain at the level of cosmetic change.

Textbox 4.3 The expanded translation of 'mansplaining'

Throughout this monograph, I have argued on various occasions that a political concept is rarely translated in a traditional sense, but is rather subject to a process of expanded translation that involves other textual operations (summaries, second-hand references, quotes, or interpolations) as well as moments of opposition and negotiation. The concept of 'mansplaining' – understood as a patronising and condescending explanation (or general utterance) provided by a man to a woman, regardless of the actual knowledge of the topic that both of them have – provides another brief case-study of this process.

The portmanteau word ('man' + 'explaining') is associated with the work of journalist Rebecca Solnit, author of the 2014 book *Men explain things to me*, which inspired the creation of the concept in online circles. Through its great popularity in mass media and social networks (Fortún 2017), it was quickly disseminated among Spanish activists and readers before the translation of Solnit's book. In fact, when the book was released in Spanish (Solnit 2016a, 19) and Catalan (Solnit 2016b, 24), the translators of both versions opted not to translate the concept, arguing that its semantic complexity and extensive diffusion complicated the choice.

Despite the widespread usage of the English calque, however, different suggestions for translations have been offered, showing the ramifications of the process of expanded translation. In 2017, the linguistic foundation Fundéu BBVA proposed the coinage 'machoexplicación' ('machoxplanation'), which was adopted by several press outlets (Fundéu BBVA 2017b). On the back of this, novelist Lara Moreno (2019) proposed on Twitter that it be further tweaked to 'macholección' ('macholesson'). Nevertheless, in my view, the boldest proposal has been made by feminist author and translator Gloria Fortún (2017, 289–290), who has highlighted the overlap between 'mansplaining' and an already existing slang concept in Spanish: 'cuñadismo' ('brother-in-lawism'), which denotes a male form of reasoning based on commonplaces, stereotypes, arrogance, and lack of engagement with the other.

Notes

1 Worryingly, Sharma (2014) identified similar patterns of sexual harassment at night at the Occupy camps in New York.
2 Although *Feminismos Reunidos* is arguably the version of the game that has enjoyed wider visibility, especially thanks to its coincidence with the reinforcement of the feminist movement as a whole, it is worth noting that it was not the first of its kind to appear in Spain. In 2013, a group of Galician activists published a feminist version of the *Trivial Pursuit* model (Observatorio da Mariña pola Igualdade 2013), while in 2015 a similar project was developed in the Basque Country (EFE 2015). Both versions were characterised by a specific focus on the feminist movements of their areas and used the co-official language for each region (Galician in the first case and Basque in the latter). I am indebted to Olga Castro, who was involved in the development of the Galician game, for information on both projects.
3 As the reader might note, this book launch took place just two days before the 2018 feminist strike. Although it was hosted at Traficantes de Sueños, which has a rather large room for similar events (able to cater for more than 100 people), the venue was overcrowded well before the beginning of the talk, highlighting the interaction between political books and the feminist movement.
4 Although this falls beyond the scope of my discussion, it is important to point out that the concept of 'care' is seen as problematic by many activists and scholars in the field of disability, as they consider it to have frequently led to the infantilisation and dehumanisation of disabled individuals (Kelly 2016, 72–74).
5 A member of the self-managed Luis Buñuel social centre in Saragossa recalls how the venue was 'completely packed' when Federici gave a talk there in September 2017: '500 or 600 people came, it was impossible even to count them' (Nociones Comunes 2018).

6 A small, but telling detail of this shift is Carrasco, Borderías, and Torns' book itself, entitled *El trabajo de cuidados*. On the cover of its first edition (published in 2011), the whole construction (*El trabajo de cuidados*) appeared in light blue letters. However, in the expanded reissue, which was published in 2019, only the word 'cuidados' was highlighted in blue, while the rest of the title was printed in black font. This change suggests that the publishers were aware of the growing importance of 'cuidados' as an eye-catcher for readers.

5 Sea, sun, and dissent
Activist critiques of the 'Spanish model'

Asked to define 'Spain' in a few words, most European citizens would probably provide a constellation of cultural and historical stereotypes – from folk music and popular traditions to iconic food – that is likely to include references to good weather and nice beaches. In such an improvised definition, the geography of the country would probably be restricted to a string of seaside cities (Barcelona, Palma, Alicante, or Málaga) and tourist traps (such as Benidorm, Lloret, Salou, and Magaluf), generally based around the country's Mediterranean coast. Like many stereotypes, the conceptualisation of Spain as a holiday destination obscures a major part of its complex reality, but it also contains a grain of truth: more than 80 million people visited the country in 2018 and the sector amounts to 14% of the national GDP. However, these raw data conceal the fact that the centrality of tourism is the consequence of a long series of political choices with undesirable social, urban, and environmental consequences, which critics have subsumed under the 'Spanish model' (López and Rodríguez 2011) of economic development.

In this chapter, I discuss several examples of political and cultural responses to the negative impact of this 'Spanish model'. After a general overview of the evolution of the model and its effects, I focus on the emergence of discourses or 'narratives' (in the sense proposed by Baker 2006a and 2006b) opposing it and undermining it through the articulation of 'alternative stories' (Baker 2006b, 3). The chapter's goal is to survey and analyse how translation contributes to the narratives mobilised by various collectives that fall within three main areas of antagonism to the Spanish model since the emergence of the global crisis: the impact of financial speculation upon housing; the urban and social consequences of mass tourism; and the shift from the Spanish model to the questioning of the global system that fosters it.

The 'Spanish model' and its consequences

As Isidro López and Emmanuel Rodríguez (2011, 6) have argued, the 'Spanish macro-economic model', largely based on 'mass-market tourism' and 'private home-ownership', has its roots 'in the modernization programme of the Franco dictatorship from the late 1950s'. In the absence of a competitive industrial sector, Francoist elites found a key economic engine in mass tourism, which experienced an enormous leap in the final stages of the dictatorship. Indeed, having barely seen half a million tourists visit in 1950, Spain moved up to roughly 30 million per year between 1973 and 1975, a figure that almost matched the population of the country as a whole (Vallejo Pousada 2015, 91). The configuration of Spain as a tourist destination had clear benefits for both the Francoist dictatorship – it contributed to the normalisation of the image of the country abroad (Fuentes Vega 2017) – and for the international economic system, as Spain was integrated as a 'peripheral' country within the emerging 'global' flux of capital and exchanges (Murray 2015, 28).

After Franco's death in 1975, the Transition to Democracy did not alter this economic model substantially, emphasising the country's dependence upon 'tourism, property development, and construction' (López and Rodríguez 2011, 7). In fact, this specialisation was positively sanctioned by the European Economic Community (future European Union): as part of the negotiations for Spain's inclusion within the organisation in the 1980s, the EEC offered 'extremely generous subsidies' in exchange for a wide programme of de-industrialisation (López and Rodríguez 2011, 8). These funds were largely invested in the country's 'infrastructure' (López and Rodríguez 2011, 18) – mostly transport (highways, ports, and airports) and energy – which went on to play key roles in the development of the tourism and construction sectors (Murray 2015, 100–101). Among other long-lasting consequences, the implementation of this model over the following decades would further entrench two dynamics that had started under Francoism: the 'population drain to the coasts and the big cities' at the expense of the rest of the territory (López and Rodríguez 2011, 16; Murray 2015, 30) and an extractivist use of natural resources with important environmental costs (Vallejo Pousada 2015, 94; Murray 2015, 350–363). At a deeper level, the imbrication between the 'Spanish model', European integration, and the process of Transition towards a democratic system contributed to the generation of a discourse that socially legitimised this paradigm of 'modernisation' (Moreno-Caballud 2015, 41–50) and 'growth' (Prádanos 2018, 47–49), protecting it from criticisms and alternatives.

At the turn of the 21st century, the Spanish model became 'an international laboratory' (López and Rodríguez 2011, 10) for new economic practices, based upon transnational investment, private debt, deregulation of credit, and an enormous 'construction boom', popularly known as 'ladrillazo' ('brick whack'). Firstly, the construction of new housing in the country, which increased 'at a higher rate than the population' (Murray 2015, 65), was facilitated by more flexible laws on land, which enabled the transformation of entire neighbourhoods and opened up rural land and natural areas for development (67). Secondly, the availability of new housing developments contributed to the circulation of international flows of money: at the peak of the housing bubble (2001–2006), foreign capital invested 'an average of €7 billion a year in Spanish property assets', mainly 'in second homes or investments for British and German nationals' (López and Rodríguez 2011, 13). On the back of the housing boom, 'new logics of touristic production' (Murray 2015, 69) were developed, as house rentals and sales became a major market for both internal and external tourists and part-time residents (205–206), generating 'strips of continuous urban fabric along the coastline' (López and Rodríguez 2011, 14) that decisively altered landscapes and ecosystems. Finally, removing credit restrictions and implementing tax relief for house purchases enabled banking institutions to launch a programme of financing that made the housing bubble possible through the indebtedness of private households. As housing prices shot up through the combination of increasing investment and demand, the total credit of mortgages jumped from 97 billion euros in 1994 to one trillion in 2007, which went hand in hand with extended repayment periods – from twelve years in 1990 to twenty-seven in 2007 (Murray 2015, 79–80).

Although the global crisis of 2008 burst the housing and credit bubble, it did not put an end to the 'Spanish model' as such. On the contrary, it actually aggravated some of its worst features. Drastic unemployment made many citizens unable to repay their mortgages, causing a wave of evictions and repossessions that had horrific human consequences – although actual figures are unknown, it is estimated that at least fifty people committed suicide because of an eviction (15Mpedia 2018) – and in many cases violated basic human rights to housing, according to the United Nations (2017). This wave of repossessions, along with the bankruptcy of building companies and dubious selling-off of public housing by a number of public administrations, generated a large stock of reclaimed houses that have been acquired by foreign funds (Juste de Ancos 2016; Gabarre 2019, 84–88). At the same time, the borderline between housing and tourism has been further blurred with the popularisation of online platforms for holiday rental of flats and houses, which have become a lucrative area of investment for funds, companies, and other financial instruments due to the lack of regulation (Gil and Sequera 2018). Finally, the aftermath of the various Arab uprisings – which led to heavy-handed repression, instability, and armed conflicts in other areas of the Mediterranean basin – has prompted a greater influx of tourists to Spain, increasing the importance of the sector for the national economy and attracting, once again, the interest of international private funds (Yrigoy 2018). In a context of high unemployment, this revitalisation of tourism has led to greater precarity for workers, as employers try to minimise labour costs in response to pressure from lenders and funds (Cañada 2019, 279–281). Therefore, the combination of these four factors – repossessions, widespread selling-off of properties, touristification of housing, and higher economic dependence on tourism – has transformed the previous housing bubble into a 'renting bubble' (Estévez 2018), as rents have skyrocketed – by an average of 40–50% in cities such as Madrid, Barcelona, Valencia, and Palma (Gabarre 2019, 30) – and tenants have been evicted in order to host tourists or wealthier residents (Medina 2018; Cruz 2019).

The emergence of popular discourses against the 'Spanish model'

As I briefly mentioned in the previous section, the emergence of the 'Spanish model' was accompanied by a discourse of legitimation based upon notions of 'modernisation' and 'growth' that derided any potential criticism and dissonance as ignorance, lack of realism, or a failure to adjust to historical change. For instance, the enormous population drive towards the main cities and the coastline, which has depopulated large areas of the country, was justified through the depiction of the countryside as a backward place inhabited by 'bumpkins' (*catetos*) (Moreno-Caballud 2015, 43–46). Similarly, critiques of the artificially high prices of the housing sector have been dismissed, at very different stages of the economic crisis, as 'tales, legends, fables' by a housing developer (Vila 2007) and as 'seeing ghosts' by a professor of economics (Bernardos 2018). In this sense, it could be argued that discourses of legitimation surrounding the 'Spanish model' constitute a particular form of 'capitalist realism' which aims to discredit alternatives and make them inconceivable.

The first significant cracks in these discourses appeared during the final years of the housing bubble (2003–2007), with the emergence of the movement for decent housing, which was 'both a precursor to and part of the 15-M movement' (Flesher Fominaya 2015b, 466). The main two strands of it were the platform *Movimiento por una Vivienda Digna* ('Movement for decent housing') and *V de Vivienda* ('H for Housing', a wordplay on the dystopian graphic novel and film *V for Vendetta*, which would become a frequent symbol for the movement of the squares; Gerbaudo 2017, 3). Using provocative slogans such as 'No tendrás casa en la puta vida' ('You won't have a house in your fucking life'), they exposed the speculative processes behind the rise of housing prices, highlighting the massive debts caused by mortgages and the abundance of empty and unsold homes across the country (Blanchar 2007; La Vanguardia 2007).

The start of the crisis redefined the goals of this movement, as previous concerns regarding the difficulty of finding a home were abruptly replaced by citizens' inability to repay their mortgages and the subsequent increase in the number of evictions and repossessions. In this context, the *Plataforma de Afectados por la Hipoteca* ('Platform of those affected by mortgages', or simply PAH) was created in 2009. Its continuity with previous platforms was expressed, for instance, by the fact that Ada Colau (see Chapter 3), who had served as a speaker for *V de Vivienda*, became PAH's main spokesperson for several years.

Without any doubt, the PAH represents one of the most visible and vital forms of activism in the early stages of the crisis, combining direct action (stopping or delaying evictions and protesting in front of politicians' homes), moral and legal support to the victims, and wider initiatives to reform Spanish laws (Flesher Fominaya 2015b, 470–475). In particular, the PAH campaigned for the approval of the *dación en pago* ('dation in payment'), a legal figure that frees the mortgage holder of their debt when the bank or lender repossesses the property. This was a key moment in allowing citizens to 'start anew' (Manifiesto ILP 2011), since under Spanish laws the foreclosure of the home does not cancel the debt. In fact, 'any difference between the value the lender receives for the property and the original debt' – which could be significant, as mortgages had been signed according to the high prices of the housing bubble, while properties were reassessed and sold in a new context of crisis – 'is still the responsibility of the defaulter' (Flesher Fominaya 2015b, 469).

In this way, the PAH also contributed to the denunciation of the 'Spanish model' and the exposure of its discourse, mobilising a whole set of ideas and concepts that placed the housing crisis and the political system in a completely different light. The burden of debt was a 'life-time financial sentence' (*condena financiera de por vida*) (PAH 2011c); the main political parties – PSOE and PP – were characterised as 'enemies' that 'had declared war on people affected by mortgages' (PAH 2011a); representatives of the banking sector were labelled 'criminals' at the parliament by Ada Colau (Díez 2013). Finally, just as the 15M had reframed the 'crisis' as a 'swindle', the PAH claimed that suicides caused by evictions were 'financial genocide' (PAH 2012).

Translating concepts for new narratives

For the purposes of this chapter, it is important to note that this first wave of popular opposition to the 'Spanish model' led to the dissemination and consolidation of two translated concepts that provide a critical perspective on urban and housing processes: *derecho a la ciudad* ('right to the city'), and *acumulación por desposesión* ('accumulation by dispossession'). As has happened with other concepts studied in this book, both had built up a lengthy heritage of debates, yet it was the transformation of the social context and the renewal of their usage that consolidated them as part of the political and activist lexicon.

Related to discussions on the 'gentrification' of cities, but also to the struggles against touristic excesses that will be analysed in the following section, the notion of 'derecho a la ciudad' is arguably the most ambiguous of these concepts. For a start, it is an idea invoking a dual tradition: while the actual coinage stems from Henri Lefebvre's book *Le droit à la ville*, published in 1968, reflection on the topic cannot be disentangled from later Anglophone approaches to the 'right to the city' (Martínez 2017, 7). At a deeper level, the popularity of the concept has implied a relative blurring of its sense. In his prologue to the Spanish translation of Lefebvre's book, sociologist Ion Martínez acknowledges its growing level of circulation – 'from the streets to the academia, from residents' association to institutional politics' – while arguing that the excess of meanings attributed to it makes it lose 'its value as a concept' (Martínez 2017, 7). Along a similar line of thought, Marxist geographer David Harvey has argued that 'the right to the city is an empty signifier', which 'depends on who gets to fill it with meaning' (Harvey 2013, xv); therefore, 'the definition of the right is itself an object of struggle' (*ibid.*).

In addressing the ambiguity of the concept, Harvey proposed the model of the 'urban commons' (discussed in Chapter 3 of this monograph) as a potential way of fighting for a new sense of this 'right' (Harvey 2013, 67–88). 'Through political action on the part of citizens and the people' (73), a city based upon cooperation and solidarity can acquire a completely different sense, in opposition to the privatised neoliberal model. In the context of the global crisis, this link between the 'commons' and the 'right to the city' is key to understanding not only the success of these concepts in Spanish activist discourses (Gutiérrez 2017, 35–44), but also the adoption of David Harvey as an intellectual reference for a variety of movements, such as the PAH. In this process of reception, it is important to highlight the role of Barcelona-based activists who would eventually join Barcelona en Comú (BeC), the political platform also discussed in Chapter 3. On the one hand, Gerardo Pisarello translated Harvey's (2003) 'The right to the city', his first text in defence of the 'urban commons' as a way of redefining the ambiguous meaning of this 'right'; the Spanish translation appeared in 2008 in the political online journal *Sin Permiso* (Harvey 2008), a very popular outlet within the activist field. In the same year, the *Observatori DESC* ('DESC Observatory'), a think-tank for human rights that counted Ada Colau, Pisarello, and other militants among its members (França 2015), hosted an open debate with Harvey on the right to the city and the right to housing (Observatori DESC 2008), which featured contributions from urban planners, institutional representatives, and residents' associations. Similarly, in November 2016, Harvey was invited to meet the Barcelona section of the PAH to engage in a debate on the role played by social movements in the redefinition of the 'right to the city' (PAH Barcelona 2016).

The role of the PAH in the reception of Harvey's work and the popularisation of critical concepts can be best understood through the second example addressed in this section: *acumulación por desposesión*, which finds its origin in an article published by Harvey in 2004. Through the idea of 'accumulation by dispossession', Harvey aimed to expand Karl Marx's notion of 'primitive accumulation' (see Chapter 3) in order to stress that the capitalist system requires a persistent use of 'predatory practices' for its survival; these include 'privatization of land', 'conversion of various forms of property rights – common, collective, state, etc. – into exclusive private property rights', 'suppression of rights to the commons', 'appropriation of assets', and 'national debt', among others (Harvey 2004, 74). In this sense, Harvey's reappraisal of Marx – developed along similar lines by Silvia Federici (2004) in her *Caliban and the Witch* – provided a conceptual tool with which to understand contemporary capitalist practices as part of a historical continuum of attacks upon the commons, the State, and civil society, which is arguably one of the reasons why it has resonated with Spanish activists and scholars since the beginning of the crisis.

The concept played an important role in the PAH's analyses as a tool for exposing the hidden interests behind the conditions of the housing market and the reality of foreclosures. The first key usage of the concept appears in a highly symbolic document for the movement: the intervention presented at the subcommittee for the reform of the mortgage system (July 2011), held by the Spanish Parliament as a response to popular protests against the consequences of evictions and debt. This text, which was signed by Ada Colau and Adrià Alemany as representatives of the platform, argued that the banking sector's resistance to the dation in payment proposed by the PAH was rooted in the banks' determination to make greater profit out of evictions, as they could sell the repossessed property while still claiming the remaining debt from the evictee. According to Colau and Alemany, this practice amounted to '*a clear example of accumulation by dispossession*' (PAH 2011b, 3; italics in the original). This explanatory usage of the concept would later reappear in a book co-authored in Catalan by Alemany and Colau on the housing bubble and the anti-eviction movement, where they characterise the current crisis as a process of 'accumulation by dispossession' (*acumulació per despossessió*) in which citizens are 'the weakest link' and therefore the ones who bear the brunt of these transformations (Colau and Alemany 2012, 79–80). Over the following years, the concept – both in its Catalan and its Spanish form – gradually became embedded as a key signifier in the discourse of the PAH and its allies, reappearing across several communiqués (PAHC Sabadell 2014), denouncements (Sorinas 2015), and analyses of the right to housing (PAH Barcelona 2018) or the new renting bubble (Mogo Castro 2018).

Textbox 5.1 Translating the transformation of the city

A third translated concept that has acquired an important role within urban activism is *gentrificación*, a calque of the English 'gentrification'. The concept denotes the process through which the traditional residents of a popular, often neglected area of the city are displaced by new citizens with higher income, especially as the area is renovated and rents increase. As Neil Smith (1996), one of the main scholars in the area, has shown, 'gentrification' occurs through the intervention of private capital investment that aims at maximising profit at the expense of generating social conflict and urban inequality.

In the Spanish context, the coinage 'gentrificación' has gained greater acceptance in recent years (Fundéu BBVA 2013), although this does not exclude contestation and alternative proposals. In 2015, the *Observatorio Metropolitano de Madrid* ('Madrid Metropolitan Observatory') – an activist research group closely linked to Traficantes de Sueños – released an anthology of translated texts on gentrification and neoliberal urbanism (including texts by Smith and other experts), titled *El mercado contra la ciudad* ('Market against the city'). In the foreword to the book, the *Observatorio* noted the increasing usage of the coinage 'gentrificación' in texts 'for academia or cultural and political intervention' (Observatorio Metropolitano de Madrid 2015, 25), while arguing that for the translation to be complete, it 'should not only be literal but also contextual'. In this sense, the

> *Observatorio* claimed that 'gentrificación' posed the difficulty of 'figuring out its etymology' – the social stratum of the 'gentry' was difficult to decipher for citizens unfamiliar with the English language – and mentioned alternative translational attempts such as 'the genuinely popular *pijización* ["poshification"]' and 'the more academic *aburguesamiento* ["bourgeoification"] or *elitización* ["elitisation"]' (25).
>
> Once again, these debates are not specific to the Spanish case, but point towards the intricacies of adapting Anglophone specialised discourses into other languages: for instance, Gaber (2016) has shown in the Egyptian context how translated concepts in urban planning tend to remain arcane for everyday users, which has led him to advocate for the necessity of engaging with vernacular Arabic terminology as a way of unlocking new perspectives.

The 'breaking down of consensus' on the tourist industry

While activist critiques of speculative processes affecting housing began to emerge before the global crisis, an idiosyncratic feature of activism against the tourism industry – the second pillar of the 'Spanish model' – is its direct relationship with the specific *evolution* of the crisis. Although criticisms of the impact of tourism had been mobilised in the past, particularly by academics and environmentalists (Cañadas and Murray 2019, 12–16), popular opposition to its effects is a clear consequence of the major expansion of the sector over the last decade (17), which cannot be disentangled from the appearance of powerful transnational actors searching for high economic benefits (hedge and vulture funds) and the development of online platforms for short-term rental, mostly associated with the Airbnb model (see below). In this sense, it could be argued that the 'touristification' (Milano and Mansilla 2019, 371–375) of social movements – as tourism has become a new trigger of action for existing movements while prompting the creation of other, ad-hoc movements – represents a second wave of opposition to the 'Spanish model', and one that remains strongly connected to the first. In this section, I examine two examples in the Mediterranean area with similar political goals, but rather different translational approaches: the collective around the publication *Tot Inclòs. Danys i conseqüències del turisme a les nostres illes* ('All Inclusive. Damages and consequences of tourism in our islands'), which focuses on the Balearic archipelago, and the *Assemblea de Barris per un Turisme Sostenible* ('Neighbourhoods' Assembly for Sustainable Tourism'), created in Barcelona in 2015 and renamed as *Assemblea de Barris pel Decreixement Turístic* ('Neighbourhoods' Assembly for Tourism Degrowth') in December 2019.

In a manner similar to a number of housing movements, activism in the field of tourism has had to tackle the hegemonic discourse of legitimation that supports the Spanish model, and that presents any alternative or dissent as unrealistic. In the context of the Balearic archipelago, the disproportionate economic weight of tourism – which amounts to around 45% of the region's GDP

(Pallicer and Blàzquez 2017) – has generated a narrative of support that is popularly condensed in the motto 'vivim del turisme' ('We live off tourism'). From its inception in 2014, the journal *Tot Inclòs* positioned itself against this narrative, setting its main goal as an effort to 'break down the social *consensus* created around tourism' (Pallicer and Blàzquez 2017, 88; italics in the original).

The collective formed around the publication has its roots in the *Coordinadora Llibertària de Mallorca* ('Libertarian Coordinating Committee of Majorca'), which positioned itself in the interaction between anarchist-libertarian and environmentalist activism, a form of activism that had been strong in the island since the 1970s (Munar 2017). In the journal's four editions (2014–2017), its network of contributors included critical academics in various disciplines – either based at the University of the Balearic Islands or at the Catalan research centre Alba Sud – as well as activists. The latter were mostly associated with the *Grup Balear d'Ornitologia i Defensa de la Naturalesa* ('Balearic Group for Ornithology and Defence of the Nature') – popularly known as the GOB, the oldest ecologist organisation in Majorca, founded in 1973 (GOB 2019) – and to *Terraferida* ('Woundedland'), an activist group created in 2015 to denounce the impact of housing and tourism upon the territory (Terraferida 2015).

The journal, which was published in print every summer and later uploaded the articles to a digital site, was clearly oriented towards an internal constituency from the outset. Written in Catalan (the traditional language of the islands, co-official along with Spanish) and focusing on the conflicts that tourism created within the archipelago, *Tot Inclòs* firmly followed its stated purpose of 'breaking down consensus' through a critical analysis of the multiple facets of tourism: increasing power of the hotel guild, the impact of holiday rental upon housing prices, pollution from aeroplanes and cruises, job precarity in the sector, the disappearance of agriculture, and the inaction of the regional government, among many others. A certain will towards achieving a wider reach was seen in its final published number (Tot Inclòs 2017, 22–23), where the journal gave space to collectives beyond the Balearics: the aforementioned *Assemblea de Barris per un Turisme Sostenible*, the *Espai Veïnal Cabanyal* (based in Valencia), and the artistic collective Left Hand Rotation, which presented the case of Lisbon. The lack of a specific focus beyond the Balearics had also manifested in the minimal translation statement on the journal site: after providing a link to 'the translations of articles into other languages *that we have been receiving*' (Tot Inclòs 2019a; my italics) – which only comprise a dozen translations into Italian, one into English, and another into German (Tot Inclòs 2019b) – they suggest that the reader could 'try to translate [the rest of the articles] with Google Translate'. In this way, translation is clearly revealed as an afterthought for the journal: a necessity that is only made evident through the actions of readers – who request or, in the best-case scenario, provide translations – and that the editorial collective seems unable or unwilling to address.

A turning point for debates on tourism took place in 2017, coinciding with this final publication. Protests against the excesses of the touristic model had become more widespread in the archipelago (Valdivielso and Moranta 2019,

1879), including a demonstration in their capital, Palma, that gathered three thousand people under the slogan 'Fins aqui hem arribat. Aturem la massificació turística' ('This far, and no further. Let's stop touristic massification'). In this context of contention, *Tot Inclòs* launched a crowdfund to finance a documentary based on the findings and ideas gathered over the journal's four years of existence (Goteo 2017). While aiming at a larger audience, the documentary explicitly continued the journal's agenda of facing up to the legitimation discourse within the touristic sector, defining itself as 'a counter-narrative to the "We-live-off-tourism" discourse' which 'put on the table an uncomfortable reality that a large part of Majorcan society prefers to avoid' (Goteo 2017).

Although translation did not appear within the project costing, the online version of the documentary offered subtitles in eleven languages, which provides a revealing overview of the audiences it was targeting. It included the four co-official languages of the Spanish State (Catalan, Galician, Basque, and Spanish), three international languages associated with the main nationalities of tourists visiting the Balearics (French, German, and English), three languages of countries facing a similar impact from tourism (Portuguese, Italian, and Greek), and Esperanto, a popular language among anarchist and libertarian groups.[1] Furthermore, the subtitling credits reveal a clearly politicised imprint (Tot Inclòs 2019c) through the involvement of anti-gentrification activists (academic Sílvia Suau and Italian architect Fabiana Pavel), ecologists (GOB worker Cécile Parra), members of local platforms (translator and artist Kirsty Duffield), and a self-managed social centre in Athens (Μεταφραστική Ομάδα Aquelarre από την Κατάληψη Σινιάλο, 'Translation team *Witches' Sabbath* from the occupied centre Signal').

While *Tot Inclòs* adopted an extremely detailed approach to the concrete reality of the Balearic Islands, the *Assemblea de Barris* has followed a different tactic, placing the touristic conflicts of Barcelona in a transnational context through the help of translation. Similarly to other networks of activists (Baker 2013, 32), which perform their translational task through their own choice of materials, the *Assemblea* uses its Facebook group and, to a lesser extent, its blog to share articles and images that present the impact of tourism across different territories: pollution caused by holiday cruises in Marseille (Assemblea de Barris pel Decreixement Turístic 2018a), evictions and displacement of residents under the pressure of holiday rental in Lisbon (2018c) and Athens (2019b), gentrification of deprived areas in Naples (2019a), and the precarity of hotel workers in the United States (2018b). The particularity of its approach lies in the fact that it only posts translational snippets. Although in its earlier stages the platform generated lengthier examples of what they call 'adaptation/translation' (Assemblea de Barris per un Turisme Sostenible 2016), that is, a translated synthesis of the most relevant information in a given text, most of their translations – such as the ones mentioned earlier – consist of just a few lines that summarise the key ideas of the article or post shared. In their brevity, these fragments privilege the search for commonality between cities and neighbourhoods – highlighting the existence of shared problems as an incentive for political action – at the expense of omitting the bulk of the information contained in the documents.

Despite its limitations, the communicative efforts of the *Assemblea* reveal a focus on shared transnational issues that was further manifest in its leading role in the creation of the SET network of cities and territories of Southern Europe facing Touristification in 2018 (Milano and Mansilla 2019, 374–375). The majority of SET's nodal points are located across Spain (Barcelona, Valencia, Pamplona, Seville, Palma, Madrid, Málaga, Girona, Camp de Tarragona, San Sebastian, the island of Ibiza, and the archipelago of the Canaries), although it also covers Portugal (Lisbon), Italy (Venice, Florence, Napoli, and Bergamo), and the island of Malta. As Milano and Mansilla (2019, 375) have noted, the importance of this alliance lies precisely in the acknowledgement of a series of similarities driven by the impact of transnational capital and in the development of an appropriate response that avoids the fragmentation of efforts that comes with local dispersion.

Beyond their different strategies, both *Tot Inclòs* and the *Assemblea* have contributed to the translation and popularisation of discourses supporting greater controls on tourism, particularly highlighting the necessity of imposing 'limits' (Ramis 2017) and 'reductions' on it (Assemblea de Barris pel Decreixement Turístic 2019c). As several authors have argued (Cañada 2018; Milano, Novelli and Cheer 2019; Valdivielso and Moranta 2019), recent years have been marked by the proliferation of critical, yet ambiguous concepts that refer to these issues, such as 'sustainable tourism' ('turismo sostenible'), 'overtourism' ('sobreturismo'), and 'tourism degrowth' ('decrecimiento turístico / decreixement turístic'). Therefore, the involvement of activists and citizens in the usage, assessment, and redefinition of these terms is essential for two reasons. On the one hand, their openness and the lack of definition regarding the agency behind these processes makes them amenable to manipulation by policy makers and the tourist industry (Valdivielso and Moranta 2019, 1878–1879). On the other, the notion of a 'limit' or 'cap' on tourism is not a 'factual' measure that can be calculated 'objectively', but rather a 'social construction' that needs to be achieved 'through citizen participation and negotiation, in situations that are conflictual by definition' (Cañada 2018).

Furthermore, these processes are complex and do not exclude the evolution of perspectives over time, nor changes based on processes of collective reflection. As briefly mentioned earlier, the name of the *Assemblea* initially highlighted the concept of 'sustainable tourism', but was later altered in favour of 'tourism degrowth' in December 2019. In its statement regarding the change, the collective argued that the first 'has become an empty concept, corrupted by lobbies and public powers that use it in their standard whitewashings' (Assemblea de Barris pel Decreixement Turístic 2019d), a critique that had been repeatedly mobilised by the *Tot Inclòs* collective (Casamajor 2017; NH3 and Grumer 2017). In this sense, a solid conceptual framework is fundamental not only to enable activists to dispute the sense of social discourses, but also to undermine the negative counter-discourses created by the tourist industry

> **Textbox 5.2 Airbnb as a distortion of the commons**
>
> In Chapter 3, I briefly noted how discourses on the commons and its related values (fluid ownership, autonomy from the state, or cooperation between individuals) have become increasingly appealing for enterprises and administrations. The online platform Airbnb offers an acute example of this tendency, becoming a by-word for a whole market of holiday rental that includes several other sites. In principle, Airbnb offers individuals the ability to contact each other directly – the 'peer-to-peer' (P2P) model that is a characteristic of the field of free culture – and to host others at their properties without the mediation of any agent or company. Along with this espousal of the P2P, Airbnb has mobilised a discourse of legitimation around the notion of the 'sharing economy' (Quaglieri and Sánchez 2019, 345–346), as hosts are supposed to be sharing not only their homes, but also their cities and 'experiences', with visitors. However, several studies have shown (Gil and Sequera 2018; Valdivielso and Moranta 2019, 1879–1880) that there is a really small number of actual individuals who use the site in areas such as Madrid, Barcelona, or the island of Majorca, as the majority of accommodation in these areas is provided by professional agencies, companies, and landlords with large portfolios. Furthermore, their knock-on effects include the rise of rent charges, the gentrification of entire areas, and the subsequent displacement of residents, which means that the company extracts benefit from the radical transformation of traditional neighbourhoods. In this sense, therefore, Airbnb distorts positive values of the commons and puts them at the service of 'platform capitalism' (Srnicek 2017), a growing business model that relies on the activity of people who are not employed by the platform but nevertheless generate benefit for it.

against them, such as the recent coinage 'turismofobia' ('tourismphobia'), quickly popularised in mass media (Fundéu BBVA 2017a), which presented opposition to the excesses of tourism in a negative and violent light.

From the 'Spanish model' to the global system

Despite its strongly localised effects and impact, the 'Spanish model' cannot be disentangled from the evolution of an economic system that functions at a global scale in its search for profit. As noted in Chapter 1, under globalisation nation-states have become 'jurisdictional claims in a unitary world market' (Arrighi, Hopkins and Wallerstein 1989, 6); therefore, an answer to national problems does not only require the development of transnational alliances (as clearly understood by the SET network), but also the placement of these problems within larger frameworks of analysis. In this final section, I explore the work of two groups that aim to develop larger counter-narratives that highlight the necessity of activists moving 'beyond' the Spanish model: the collective

Contra el diluvio ('Against the deluge'), which focuses on climate change, and the editorial committee around the journal *Cul de Sac* and the publishing house El Salmón, which critiques the concept of 'progress' and the role of technology in contemporary society.

Contra el diluvio was created in 2017 with the aim of 'contributing to the movement against climate change and its consequences' (Contra el diluvio 2017). In its founding statement, the collective claimed that climate change 'should be a priority for any social movement', since 'opposing climate change cannot be disentangled from opposing the capitalist society that generates it'. In order to increase social awareness on the matter, *Contra el diluvio* aimed at 'producing and translating written texts', 'arranging talks and debates', and 'compiling information in an accessible but rigorous manner' (*ibid.*).

The group's dissemination activities started with a regular newsletter that contained translated articles, introductions, and brief syntheses of different topics, generally with the goal of raising awareness and fostering debate between readers and their immediate circle. For instance, the newsletter sent in December 2017 offered links to a 'Christmas introduction to climate change' that readers could use in 'conversations on climate change with a relative, friend, or neighbour' during festive dinners and gatherings.[5] Similarly, in June 2018, it offered a visual introduction on '6 things you can do to fight climate change', covered the majority of languages within the Spanish State (Asturian, Catalan, Basque, Galician, Aragonese, and Spanish), along with English and French versions (Contra el diluvio 2018). Adopting a humorous tone that could engage with a younger audience, the leaflet (see Figure 5.1) played on a well-known internet meme by artist KC Green.

A second step in this process of dissemination was the launch of a reading group on climate change, which took place during the academic year 2018–2019 at the Madrid bookstore Enclave, site of the eponymous politically committed publisher. The group relied greatly on translations – either undertaken by the collective or published in journals such as *Sin Permiso* or the Spanish edition of *New Left Review* – of articles on fair political solutions to climate change, the impact of the human diet, the role of urban planning and private transport, and proposals for the reduction of the working week, among other topics. Through these activities, *Contra el diluvio* sought to expand activist narratives for social change by showing how climate issues undercut a variety of social and political choices.

For its part, the collective Cul de Sac / El Salmón was created in 2010 to 'develop a critique of modernity' while contributing to the removal of 'the stigma' that associates this critique with reactionary thought (Juanma Agulles, personal interview, 6 April 2019). In particular, the group felt urged to act in the absence of other activist movements that shared their analyses; their aim, therefore, is the development of a discourse that goes beyond existing alternatives in the Spanish State. As they argued in their founding statement, 'many collectives focus on combatting a given aspect' of the current system, which,

Figure 5.1. Excerpt of a multilingual climate-change leaflet by *Contra el diluvio* (Catalan version).

'although not being useless in itself', places these struggles at risk 'of being co-opted [by the system] without actually affecting the foundations of its regime' (Cul de Sac 2010a, 4). This perspective would eventually place the collective in a conflictual relationship with the 15M, which they criticised in a short pamphlet (Cul de Sac 2016 [2012]) for failing to understand that the economic system and the enormous reach of technological domination had to be dismantled in order to achieve meaningful changes in society.

While having its roots in an anarchist and libertarian milieu, the group decided to undertake its publishing project to 'move beyond the militant ghetto' (Agulles, 6 April 2019) and reach a wider audience. Its first action was the launch of the journal *Cul de Sac*, which devoted its first issue to precisely this critique of the idea of progress and the centrality of production in contemporary society, highlighting how 'the identification between civilization and material progress' has become equal to a 'faith' (Cul de Sac 2010b, 10). Published a year later, its second issue launched a frontal attack on information and communication technologies and the false pretence of freedom that they provide, while neglecting 'the ongoing destruction of nature and social relationships' that they cause (Cul de Sac 2011, 6).

The journal was to provide a blueprint for the second branch of the collective, the publishing imprint El Salmón, created in 2011 and defined as 'a non-professional, but militant' project with 'a political aim' (Salvador Cobo, personal interview, 6 April 2019). Through different thematic approaches, both sides of the project develop a continuum in their catalogue, which is made up of Spanish authors from a libertarian background (such as José Ardillo and Agustín García Calvo) and an important strand of translations of English (E.M. Forster, Thoreau), French (Encyclopédie des Nuisances, Simon Leys), and Italian sources (Pier Paolo Pasolini, Piergiorgio Bellocchio), undertaken by the members of the project. In this way, the editorial project provides a paradigm of the publishing strategy against the 'Culture of the Transition' that I discussed in Chapter 2, whereby non-canonical and politicised Spanish authors are included alongside the search for alternative discourses in other languages.

Finally, through the combined work of the journal and the publishing house, the collective has also aimed at reconstructing a tradition of thought against progress, industrialisation, and technology; as they have claimed, one of their main purposes is to 'unearth the alternative tradition beneath official history' and oppose 'the triumphalist narrative on the advent of industrial civilisation' (Cul de Sac 2019, 5). In this effort, the revindication of Italian thought plays a central role in their work, which culminates in *Cul de Sac*'s sixth volume, a monograph on Italian authors 'against the machine'. In its introduction, the editorial collective claims that the Italian case offers a unique viewpoint on the consequences of modernity due to 'the brief lapse of time' during which 'industrial development' was articulated in the country, 'with an extraordinary violence and intensity' that prompted a great variety of responses from writers and intellectuals (*ibid.*).

Conclusions

This chapter opened with a sketch of stereotypes and a reductive map of Spanish society, established by the institutional and economic hegemony of the 'Spanish model'. After addressing a variety of collectives, however, it has not only shown the crisis that exists within the model, but also how alternative narratives are emerging at the intersection of numerous transnational debates. While the Spanish model privileged a narrative based on notions of 'modernisation' and 'growth' that located alternatives within the realm of unreality, ignorance, and backwardness, the collectives studied in this chapter have managed to circulate alternative narratives that question these official ones. Against the narrative of housing as a commodity mediated by the market, the PAH mobilised a narrative based upon the right to decent housing and the criticism of the role played by parties and banks in the creation of the housing bubble and the lack of proposals on the crisis of evictions. Similarly, against the narrative that identifies tourism with wealth, *Tot Inclòs* and *Assemblea de Barris* have developed their own narrative that shows the negative impact of tourism and advocates degrowth as the only solution. Finally, *Contra el diluvio* and the collective around *Cul de Sac / El Salmón* have aimed at constructing a sort of alternative 'meta-narrative', as they are directed towards the enlargement and reform of existing activist narratives. While *Contra el diluvio* seeks to convince protesters of the necessity of incorporating climate change into their demands, *Cul de Sac / El Salmón* promote the adoption of a larger framework that supersedes specific struggles.

At a second level, it is relevant to note that while all of these movements have incorporated translation into their political practices, the ways in which they have done so have been far from homogeneous, either in their forms or in their strategies. While the PAH has adopted translated concepts as a way of developing a more solid and critical analysis of the current situation, the *Assemblea de Barris* has privileged a utilitarian approach that aims at fostering identification for a political purpose. Meanwhile, despite their thematic innovation, *Contra el diluvio* and *Cul de Sac / El Salmón* adopted more traditional strategies of generating a translated corpus of knowledge that contributes to expanding societal debates. Finally, translation can even emerge as an unplanned necessity and a delayed awareness, as was shown in the evolution of the publications by *Tot Inclòs*.

In a number of ways, this analysis has also helped to confirm and refine questions and findings raised in previous chapters. Firstly, it has reaffirmed that the adoption, resignification, and dissemination of concepts from academic and intellectual discourses constitutes a field of struggle between groups of actors with diverging interests: from the 'right to the city' to the notion of 'degrowth', concepts are subject to disputes over meaning that aim to incorporate them into certain social narratives. In this sense, activists' involvement in these disputes is vital in ensuring that the emancipating role of political concepts persists, these concepts representing a key element in the struggle to reach wider sectors of the population. Furthermore, the transition from the academic and intellectual field to the adoption of a concept as a part of the political lexicon greatly benefits from the active involvement of popular movements rooted in daily practice, as was argued in the case of 'accumulation by dispossession', a highly technical concept that nevertheless found its way into wider discourses thanks to its incorporation by a powerful platform like the PAH.

Finally, this chapter has extended analyses in previous sections that outline the way in which political discourses and activist concepts offer a synthesis of different traditions and various fields, which need to be taken apart for the purpose of study, but that emerge in a more homogeneous fashion within the political and activist field. Notably, the concept of the 'commons', which was discussed at length in Chapter 3, has reappeared as a central element in discussions of feminist strategy (Chapter 4) and in the present analysis of political approaches to the 'right to the city', showing how political concepts are fluid and indebted to a process of mutual interaction.

Notes

1 A similar approach was followed by the platform *Autopista Mai!* ('Never a Highway!'), which was created in 2018 to oppose the development of a new highway between the Majorcan towns of Llucmajor and Campos. While its site was only available in Catalan and Spanish, the manifesto that called for signatures of support against the new infrastructure was also available in English, French, and German (Autopista Mai 2018). Similarly, when the platform staged a protest at FITUR Madrid, the largest tourism fair in the Spanish State, activists carried banners in Spanish, English, and German with ironic references to the environmental impact of the highway (Amics de la Terra 2019).
2 I refer to this document from my own research archive, as it is no longer available online.

6 Podemos
Successes and contradictions of a 'translational' party

Over the previous chapters, my analysis has mainly focused on platforms and collectives that tend to remain outside institutional politics, as is standard within the field of activism. However, as I argued in Chapter 2, the 15M was traversed by two main 'logics' or 'souls', which differed in their approach to the role of institutions. Furthermore, in Chapter 3, I discussed how access to the institutions (looking at the case of Barcelona en Comú) could contribute to the dissemination of activist practices and to the establishment of new areas of overlap between movements and institutions. In this sense, therefore, addressing the role of Podemos within the 15M climate is inescapable.

In this chapter, I analyse Podemos as a translational project, since translation – both as practice and as product – plays a pivotal role in their political praxis. In short, Podemos is a party generated through a complex process of translations, but also a generator of translations with multiple and ambiguous effects. The chapter is divided into four main sections: in the first, I provide a few guiding elements to contextualise the social dynamics that led to the emergence of Podemos; in the second, I reconstruct the birth of the party as the result of various processes of translation, which focused on the political framework of 'hegemony' and 'populism'; moving on to the third, I present different approaches mobilised by members of Podemos, viewing 'translation' as a conceptual tool used to redefine political action and communication; finally, in line with previous studies on the role of translation as a source of capital (Bourdieu 2002; Casanova 2002; Serry 2002), the chapter finishes by tracing the way in which translated texts and authors have been used as a means of generating a 'militant reward' (Gaxie 1977) and a 'cultural capital' (Bourdieu 1979) that compensates for the lack of strong links with traditional agents and institutions.

At this point, I must note one preliminary caveat regarding periodisation and the very meaning of 'Podemos' as a reference. Since late 2016, the main internal currents within the party – one led by Secretary General Pablo Iglesias and a second one led by Íñigo Errejón, who was the party's ideological architect in its early stages – clashed openly over control of the party apparatus. At the party's second general assembly in February 2017, Iglesias' bloc received clear support from party members and won control of the main decision organs, demoting Errejón and his followers to less relevant positions. The subsequent flow of resignations of many party founders culminated in 2019 with Errejón's departure, first through the creation of a regional platform (Más Madrid) and later with a series of alliances for national elections (Más País). Therefore, every claim made in this chapter, which devotes more attention to the early years of the party, when a unitary perspective was more feasible, must be read with the specific time in which it took place in mind and must consider the specific political agents involved.

From 'Sí se puede' to 'Podemos'

As noted, the 15M sided with a global network of popular oppositions to the consequences of the global crisis in their rejection of institutional politics: their criticism of representation and various experiments in 'direct democracy' (Sitrin and Azzellini 2014, 121–150; Della Porta 2015, 157–210) seemed incompatible with parties and elections. However, the repression of uprisings by state actors (notably in Egypt and Greece) and the general inability of movements to become sustainable in the long term soon placed protesters across the world 'at a critical juncture', creating 'a pressing need to engage with state power' and 'representative institutions' (Kioupkiolis and Katsambekis 2014, 9–10). The Alexia (2016) collective named this moment of impasse the '*resaca*' of the squares, playing on the multiple senses of the Spanish word: 'undertow', in the physical context of the sea, but also 'hangover' (as in the aftermath of a celebration) and 'backlash' (the undesired responses to an action).

The 15M was no exception. Between 2012 and 2013, certain social sectors felt increasingly frustrated with the limitations of popular protest (Rendueles and Sola 2015), as movements started reaching a so-called 'glass ceiling' (Rodríguez 2016, 69–72; Fernández-Savater 2019, 29): activists could clearly see their goals, but a barrier (the established institutions) was preventing them from achieving success. Xavier Domènech, activist and former national MP for Catalunya En Comú (2015–2018), summarised this popular feeling with a very graphic anecdote. In 2013, he was gathering signatures for a new political platform when he was confronted by two activists of the PAH, who claimed they were no longer interested in the creation of new extra-parliamentary movements: 'we have gathered a million signatures [for a new anti-eviction law] and they [the Government] have peed on us. So now we need to launch a political party and pee on them' (Domènech 2016, 55).

At the same time, it has been argued that the 15M climate was also facing internal issues during the 2012–2013 period. On the one hand, the great process of renewed political engagement enabled by the 15M was still lacking 'languages, maps or compasses' (Fernández-Savater 2019, 29) to project itself into the future and to transform the country. Certainly, this absence of new languages and their subsequent, painstaking generation is one of the key points of this monograph; as has been seen at various stages, it is a lengthy and complex process, and clearly less straightforward than would be needed to face the fast-paced developments of the political field since the beginning of the crisis. On the other hand, as briefly mentioned in other chapters, the 15M had 'a patent fear of strong arguments' that could create 'internal rifts', as well as of 'the conflicts and oppositions that are inherent to political antagonism' (Rodríguez 2016, 73). The enormous diversity within the movement could only be held together through general claims and abstract signifiers (such as 'democracy' or the 'people') that avoided the specific strategies to be implemented in order to achieve social transformation. To a great extent, this explains why the collectives emerging after the 15M have tended to be sectorial and cause-based, from the feminist movement to platforms on housing, tourism, or climate-change.

Therefore, the emergence of Podemos in early 2014 must be understood within a changing global context, but also as a response to a moment of clear impasse for social movements in Spain. From its inception, Podemos stood in a complex relationship with the 15M: although party leaders did not claim to represent the movement, they acknowledged that the 15M was both an inspiration and the decisive event that made their political irruption possible (Guedán 2016, 21–33). In fact, future Secretary General Pablo Iglesias stated at Podemos' launch event that their goal was to turn the people's 'outrage' (*indignación*) into 'change' (EFE 2014), which could be interpreted as a direct criticism of the limits of protest. Even its name hinted at a combination of affinity and distance: Podemos ('We Can') is a direct reference to a well-known slogan of the 15M, 'Sí Se Puede' ('Yes, it's possible/it can be done'), but encompassed a key grammatical change – from the impersonality of the 15M motto to the first person plural – that could also be read as a shift in political subjects – from the open, undefined multitude to an organisation with clearer boundaries.

Translating Latin American 'populism'

The project behind Podemos had been in the making for several years (Rivero 2015, 115–150), led by a core team of activists, political scientists, and academics with substantial experience as political advisors for left-wing organisations. Some of its most visible figures in the early days of the project, like Pablo Iglesias, Íñigo Errejón, and Juan Carlos Monedero, came from an academic background and shared an understanding of the university as a politically-committed field characterised by 'an undoubted vocation for [social] transformation' (Guedán 2016, 35). Before launching Podemos, this core team had been working together for many years on a variety of projects, such as advising Latin American governments through the left-wing foundation Centro de Estudios Políticos y Sociales (CEPS; Rivero 2015, 73–76) or producing the political TV shows *La Tuerka* and *Fort Apache*.

Working in Latin America was a decisive experience for future Podemos leaders, a fact acknowledged by Pablo Iglesias (Podemos' Secretary General since 2014) and Íñigo Errejón (Political Secretary from 2014 to 2017) in particular. From Iglesias' and Errejón's writings and reflections, which provided the basis for Podemos' initial political strategy, it is evident that their exposure to Latin American movements and processes led them to consider the benefits and difficulties that would be involved in any potential transfer of political knowledge and practices to the Spanish context. As I show in this section, both have frequently conceptualised this experience in translational terms, and this was to have a decisive impact on the early stages of Podemos' existence.

As has often been the case with politicians of his generation (such as Ada Colau or Gemma Ubasart), Iglesias' personal trajectory as an activist links the two 'waves' of opposition to globalisation (Wolfson and Funke 2016, 62). In the early 2000s, he contributed actively to anti-globalisation protests before writing his PhD thesis on the Italian activist groups *Tute Bianche* and *Disobbedienti* (Iglesias 2008, 2011).[1] However, his time as an advisor in Bolivia and Venezuela showed him the limitations of Western protest movements. Already in 2007, Iglesias would advocate an *indianización* ('indianisation') of the European Left, that is, an unprejudiced opening up of the latter to the political processes taking place in numerous Latin American countries (Iglesias 2007, 279–281). In fact, in his study of the Italian anti-globalisation group *Tute Bianche* ('White Overalls'), who were inspired by the Mexican EZLN, Iglesias highlights their attempt to 'translate the symbols and political praxis of Neozapatism in a politically viable way to the European context' (Iglesias 2011, 365) as one of their main innovations. This process involved a reappraisal of communication as a key aspect of politics and the establishment of a strong leadership for the movement, based around spokespeople with a high degree of media exposure (365–366). This stance garnered criticism of the *Tute Bianche* from other leftist movements, but also allowed them to carve out their own space in mass media. Although Iglesias does not go on to discuss these aspects in further detail, the relationship between translation, communication, and strong leadership is presented as an important thread throughout his understanding of politics, one which would play a key role in the development of Podemos' media strategy.

Alongside Iglesias, the other primary factor behind Podemos' political discourse and strategy was Íñigo Errejón's experience in Bolivia, where he held various political roles for governmental institutions before writing his PhD thesis on President Evo Morales' party *Movimiento al Socialismo* (MAS; Errejón 2011b, 2012). In his writings, Errejón analyses the political success of the MAS within a complex framework that owes much to translation and foregrounds the concept of 'hegemony'. Although this concept is generally associated with Antonio Gramsci, the 'fragmentary and posthumous character' of Gramsci's writings means that his theoretical insights 'had to be actively constructed by his successors through a labour of assembly, rearrangement, annotation and (outside Italy) translation' (Forgacs 1989, 71). In fact, in his understanding of 'hegemony', Errejón follows the reading of Gramsci proposed by Ernesto Laclau and Chantal Mouffe, who retained a substantial part of Gramsci's conceptual structure but reworked it from a post-structuralist perspective.

While Gramsci understood 'hegemony' as the moral and social leadership of one given class above the rest, insofar as this hegemonic class manages to achieve an equilibrium between its interests and those of the subordinated classes (Gramsci 1988, 189–221), Laclau and Mouffe (1985, 120) went beyond the fixed category of class to understand hegemony as a type of political relationship based on 'discursive' and 'articulatory practices' that produce partial and temporary political identities. In a post-industrial context where traditional political subjects (the working classes) lose centrality while others (such as groups advocating identity politics) gain it, Laclau and Mouffe's understanding of 'hegemony' as a process that is based on the articulation of identities paved the way for Laclau's (2005) defence of 'populist politics'. Going beyond traditional social and political categories, populism involves the 'construction of a people' by establishing a new division between 'those below' and 'those above', between 'the people' and 'the elites'. Errejón (2011b, 126–136) identified this strategy in MAS' successful 2005 campaign, whereby the party managed to construct a populist political identity opposing the indigenous popular classes and 'the white elites' who had 'sold off the homeland (*patria*)' (130).

Errejón's experience in Bolivia, and the Gramscian-Laclauian framework he developed in response to it, provided him with a series of political categories that he would eventually start translating for the Spanish context. Indeed, he was well aware that these categories 'were only valid if they were translated', as he went on to explain in a documentary on the birth of Podemos (León de Aranoa 2016, 29'10"–29'30"). Although Errejón's frequent usage of his notion of 'translation' is not supported by a definition, his writings suggest an understanding of the phenomenon as a process that is both highly dependent on context and involves an element of struggle and creativity. Shortly after the 15M, Errejón (2011a) claimed that the Spanish crisis shared important features with the neoliberal crises that had enabled the rise of populist governments in Latin America. These similarities opened the possibility for a populist movement, which Errejón (2011a, 17) tentatively identifies with the 15M and its opposition to the elites by reclaiming and resignifying central concepts like 'democracy' (*democracia*) and 'people' (*pueblo*).

This similarity of factors between crises and their associated potential was made more explicit in Errejón's (2014) obituary for Laclau, who died a few months after the launch of Podemos. According to Errejón, Laclau's reappraisal of populism had acquired a new relevance due to the 'latinamericanisation' (*latinoamericanización*) of Southern Europe, which involved an increasing power of 'the oligarchies' that dismissed the demands of the 'impoverished' popular groups. This levelling between contexts is perceived by Errejón in positive tones, as it gave the European Left a unique opportunity 'not to copy, but to translate […] the wealth of concepts and examples' (Errejón 2014) generated in Latin America. Revealingly, Errejón's opposition between 'copy' and 'translation' not only challenges widespread popular understandings of translation as a straightforward, mimetic activity, but also recalls a famous line by the Peruvian socialist José Carlos Mariátegui, who in 1928 claimed that Latin American socialism should be 'neither replica, nor copy' (*calco y copia*), but rather a 'heroic creation' (Mariátegui 1928, 2) of the masses. This conscious echo of Mariátegui (also elaborated in Errejón and Mouffe 2015, 77) reaffirms Errejón's awareness of political translation as an unpredictable, creative activity that cannot be dominated by a mimetic or reverential approach to its sources, but rather needs to take context into account to achieve its purposes.

A telling example of this translational process was the introduction of the word 'casta' ('caste'), a concept denoting 'Spain's political and economic establishment' (Iglesias 2015a, 17) beyond the traditional categories of Left and Right. 'Casta', a product of translation between languages and political systems, was a highly effective coinage that contributed to Podemos' initial media success. While the term had its origin in Italian politics (Rivero 2014, 30), it aimed to provide a concept denoting 'the elites' against which a populist strategy could be constructed, translating Laclau's theoretical model into the Spanish context. With its hereditary and hierarchical overtones, 'casta' became a useful tool within Podemos' discourse: it depicted Spanish elites as a unified and closed group that existed beyond political accountability. As Errejón explains in his prologue to the Spanish translation of the book that popularised the concept of 'casta' in Italy (Rizzo and Stella 2015), its success was down to its potential 'to make a complex situation intelligible' (Errejón 2015a, 7): the progressive reduction of differences between members of the political elite and its increasing distance from their voters. A measure of its success was its rapid acceptance within political jargon: for instance, the Spanish translation of Owen Jones' (2015) book on the British establishment bore the subtitle 'La casta al desnudo' ('Caste stripped bare').

However, not every translation strategy has been so successful. A key example of this is Errejón's attempts to translate Gramsci's notion of the *nazionale-popolare* or 'national-popular', which denotes the construction of a new national identity led by the popular masses in a progressive direction (Durante 2004). According to Errejón (2015b), this translation was particularly complex: due to the particularities of the Spanish state – formed by various communities, among which some claim their right to be considered nations, such as Catalonia or the Basque Country – the 'national-popular' has to be constructed as 'plurinational'. At the same time, this complexity implies that Spain lacks a set of shared popular 'symbols, myths, references, and leaderships' (Errejón 2015b) to support the construction of the 'national-popular'. In line with this reflection, for the 2015 and 2016 general elections, Podemos aimed at intervening in this area by proposing an interpretation from below of the concept *patria* ('fatherland', 'homeland'): *La patria eres tú* ('you're the homeland') and *La patria es la gente* ('People are the homeland'). However, Isidro López (2016), former regional MP with Podemos, claimed that this strategy completely missed its target: in the Spanish context, *patria* is heavily charged with conservative and reactionary overtones that complicate its reappropriation and ultimately alienated the liberal voters it expected to attract. In this sense, it could be argued that this translation failed precisely because it neglected one of the key aspects of the translational process: the needs of its intended audience. In López's (2016) words, 'it was an arbitrary signifier that [did] not answer to almost anyone's demands'.

At this stage, the escalation of the conflict between the Spanish State and the Catalan pro-independence movement since late 2017 and Errejón's departure from Podemos in 2019 might mean that this debate on the national question will be put on hold for the time being. However, this should not obscure the fact that it represents an ongoing preoccupation for other leaders of the party, including Pablo Iglesias. During a 2017 TV interview with pro-independence Catalan politician Anna Gabriel, Iglesias claimed that the lack of a 'homeland' (*patria*) was 'one of the traditional contradictions of the Spanish Left', and acknowledged Podemos' long-standing interest in the political processes taking place in Catalonia and the Basque Country, as Podemos' leaders had always wanted 'to try and translate those elements into a different national reality' (La Tuerka 2017a).

From this analysis, it is evident that Errejón's (and, to a lesser extent, Iglesias') writings, which provided an initial framework for Podemos' strategy, constitute a highly complex translational space in which processes of translation between languages (Gramsci, Laclau and Mouffe's texts translated into Spanish), theoretical paradigms (Gramsci's concepts translated into Laclau and Mouffe's theory), and political systems (the Latin American experiences translated to Spain) coexist. In this sense, it can be argued that an important part of Podemos' initial discourse and strategy emerged as the result of multiple translation processes.

Textbox 6.1 Disputing the meaning of 'populism'

In recent years, 'populism' has become a major concept within Spanish political discourses, to the extent of being chosen as 'word of the year' in 2016 by the linguistic foundation Fundéu BBVA. In the justification of their choice, the Fundéu highlighted the pervasiveness of the concept while remarking on a 'process of expansion and change in meaning' (Fundéu BBVA 2016).

Academic debates on 'populism' have represented an important tradition in Spain since the beginning of the 21st century (López Alós 2017, 149–150), with a vital hub at Universidad Complutense (Villacañas 2015; Villacañas and Ruiz Sanjuán 2018), a public university in Madrid to which several founders of Podemos were affiliated. It is therefore no coincidence that the popularisation of the concept is closely linked with the emergence of Podemos, which reclaimed the term in its early stages, as discussed in the previous section. From the perspective of the book industry, this can be seen clearly in ISBN figures: while in the five years before the creation of Podemos (2010–2014) only ten books were published on the topic – mostly from a historical perspective or in connection with the Latin American context – 38 publications appeared in the five years following the party's foundation

(2015–2019), peaking in 2017 with 12 items. Furthermore, when the book *Populism*, written by Cas Mudde and Cristóbal Rovira Kaltwasser for Oxford's popular 'Very Short Introduction' series, was translated into Spanish, the authors included a foreword to remark upon 'the particularity of populism in present-day Spain' (Mudde and Rovira Kaltwasser 2019, 14), highlighting how Podemos 'is one of the very few examples of a political party that does not only declare itself openly populist, but also tries to give the concept a positive overtone' (24; my back-translation).

However, the close association between Podemos and the concept, combined with an increasingly negative discourse surrounding it, quickly turned 'populism' into a political weapon in mainstream media, leading the party to phase out the use of the term. At a conference organised at Complutense on the work of Chantal Mouffe and Ernesto Laclau (June 18, 2018), Errejón argued retrospectively that populism 'had become increasingly overcharged [with negative nuances]', which turned into 'practical problems' for the action of the party.

The strategy of deactivating 'populism' as a positive signifier conflated a great variety of political projects under the same label, across the whole political spectrum, emphasising the presence of nationalistic and authoritarian figures. For instance, a collective book on populism (Rivero, Zarzalejos, and del Palacio 2018), funded by the right-wing think tank FAES (closely linked to the conservative Partido Popular), combined a number of caricatures of supposedly 'populist' leaders on its cover – from Donald Trump and Silvio Berlusconi to Marine Le Pen and Vladimir Putin – and included Pablo Iglesias. Although published in an academic imprint (Tecnos) with a sizeable back catalogue in philosophy, the book's opening pages reveal its nature as political propaganda, including Podemos' logo alongside the quote 'A populist government in Spain would be much more than an archaeological anachronism: it would be suicidal' (Rivero, Zarzalejos and del Palacio 2018, 21).

One consequence of this use of 'populism' as an overarching signifier is the blurring of differences between political projects. This criticism was levelled against Fundéu BBVA (2018) when it suggested translating the concept 'alt-right' – denoting the xenophobic, white nationalist movement associated with the rise of Donald Trump – as 'nacionalpopulismo' ('nationalpopulism'). Soon after the publication of this recommendation, social media users criticised what they perceived as an ideological bias: while Piedra Papel Libros – a politically committed book publisher – replied on Twitter to the foundation's statement claiming it was 'a crappy recommendation if you [the foundation] get rid of any reference to the political right' (Fundéu BBVA 2018), linguist Elena Álvarez Mellado (2018) considered the replacement of 'right' ('derecha') by 'populism' to be 'ideologically problematic'.

Political communication as a 'task of translation'

A key characteristic of Podemos' swift rise was its savvy use of alternative TV channels. From 2010 onwards, many future members of Podemos – such as Iglesias, Errejón, Monedero, or future MEP Miguel Urbán – were working together on the production of the TV show *La Tuerka* (*The Screw* or, reflecting the Spanish punk-inspired spelling, *The Skrew*), aired by local stations within the province of Madrid. The show's success saw it move to a digital platform (PublicoTV) and allowed the creation of another show in 2012, *Fort Apache*, which was aired in Spain and Latin America by HispanTV. Assuming that television is the 'fundamental terrain of ideological production' and a major producer of political arguments as well as 'social imaginaries' (Iglesias 2015a, 14–16), the group understood their TV shows as a 'counter-hegemonic' project in which they could 'spread the ideas of the Left in a language geared toward the common sense of the social majority' (Rendueles and Sola 2015). As Errejón would put it – in military terms that seem indebted to Gramsci's definition of the quest for hegemony as a 'war of position' (Gramsci 1988, 222–230) – *La Tuerka* aimed at 'distributing ammunition for those frequent and important daily battles that people fight at the workplace, on the bus, at the pub' (La Tuerka 2013).

As the presenter of both *La Tuerka* and *Fort Apache*, Pablo Iglesias quickly acquired important 'media capital' (Guedán 2016, 128), which gave him the opportunity to eventually become a well-known talk-show host for mainstream channels from 2013 onwards (Rivero 2014, 94–95). Iglesias' successful 'self-made pop persona' (Juliana 2015, 20) was a central asset for Podemos in its initial stages, as he deployed an extensive cultural capital (Bourdieu 1979) against conservative politicians and journalists while embodying 'a kind of post-15M everyman' (Toscano 2015). As a well-trained professional on a part-time university contract, Iglesias could claim to be, like Errejón and others (Juliana 2015, 13), the epitome of anti-austerity protesters (Della Porta 2015, 51–52): young, middle-class individuals who felt frustrated by the dissonance between their high level of educational attainment and their lack of professional opportunities. In this section, I address how, thanks to his involvement in mass media, Pablo Iglesias has reflected extensively on his political practice and, by extension, on political communication as a process of translation. While rarely acknowledged, his reflections are linked to a long heritage of thought, which I contextualise in the final part of this section.

According to Iglesias, many left-wing academics and activists missed their opportunity to play a central role at the 15M protests due to their inability to communicate with 'the common people' (Iglesias and Nega 2013, 93–95), who were not familiar with technical jargon. In his view, this highlighted a traditional shortcoming of the European Left:

> Communication is a pivotal work of translation [*un trabajo fundamental de traducción*]: to transform your diagnosis into a discourse that people can

understand, using words that are useful to explain things. This is one of the fundamental problems with the Left: producing diagnoses so obscure that people think you're speaking a different language.

(Iglesias interviewed in Guedán 2016, 120)

Along these lines, Iglesias praised the 15M motto, 'It is not a crisis, it's a swindle' (*No es una crisis, es una estafa*), as an example of a successful translation: 'it is the political translation [of a complex reality] into a language people understand. Translating *crisis* as *swindle* brings the key class dimension in: the rich are swindling us' (Iglesias and Nega 2013, 12). From his perspective, similar strategies are key to the 'translational work' (Iglesias and Nega 2013, 13) that is required in order to bring the realities behind 'recessions and crises' into 'people's everyday life'.

This notion of translation as an intralingual practice that, on the one hand, avoids the limitations of political jargon and, on the other, reveals and exposes the reality behind official discourses was also supported by other founders of the party, such as Errejón and philosopher Germán Cano.[2] Errejón has claimed that his Bolivian experience helped him understand that an intellectual 'is not a curmudgeon [*un tipo rancio*] who only reads unintelligible stuff, but eminently a translator' who 'has the duty and the ability to take abstract concepts and translate them, making them operational' (Errejón interviewed in Soto-Trillo 2015).[3] Meanwhile, for Cano (2015, 196), Iglesias' ability to translate 'technocratic jargon' into 'a more simple' language that is accessible to everyone allows citizens to critique the actual content of these proposals, while also showing how this 'elitist discourse' has aimed at creating an 'abyss' that isolates experts from the rest of society.

At a second level, Iglesias has reflected on 'translation' as a practice that enables communication between a diversity of political actors. Already in 2011, Iglesias argued that the 15M, through the multiple assemblies and gatherings that were taking place, had started a 'task of translation' (Iglesias and Monedero 2011, 100) that would be central for ensuring understanding between collectives and, eventually, for the construction of a wider front: only through translation would 'movements talk to each other, and movements talk to parties, and parties to each other' (Iglesias and Monedero 2011, 100). With the emergence of Podemos, Iglesias started mobilising the concept in a slightly different manner, arguing that the party did not represent social movements, but translated them. For instance, in a collective interview published on the fifth anniversary of the occupations, Iglesias claimed that 'Podemos does not represent the 15M, no one can represent a movement, but Podemos has arguably implied the fullest electoral translation [*la traducción electoral más completa*] of the 15M' (Ortiz 2016). A year later, in a lengthy interview with *El Salto*, a monthly magazine closely linked to social movements, Iglesias further developed this idea, claiming that:

> We [Podemos' representatives] are truly useful when we somehow enable the most valuable social intelligence in this country, which is to be found

in the organisations of civil society, to have institutional translations. This does not imply making them responsible, but it does imply using all of that capital, all of that value. This could provide concrete translations in the form of parliamentary measures, for instance saying 'we want to translate the PAH 5 [the five housing measures proposed in 2016 by the PAH] into a housing law'

(Iglesias in Martínez López and Elorduy 2017)

Through this reappraisal of the concept, Iglesias was aiming to perform a sensitive and complex task: establishing a relationship between party and movements that was not plagued by the hierarchical notion of 'representation' – strongly repudiated by activists after the 15M – while at the same time acknowledging the inevitable differences between the institutional and the activist fields, which makes a strict continuity between both impossible and requires a certain degree of transformation (the 'translation'). In this way, Iglesias was actively claiming that Podemos' representatives were 'institutional political translators', as conceptualised by Doerr (2018, 79–97): simultaneously being members of the political community and their agents in the political field – with limitations that I discuss in detail later on.

Therefore, we can posit that Iglesias understands translation as a threefold instrument which affords political actors the possibility of going beyond the limitations imposed by political systems, uncovering ideological nuances behind official messages, and fostering potential dialogue between a diversity of collectives. While retaining a certain degree of originality, this complex and variegated understanding of political communication as translation is indebted to the work of various philosophers and political theorists whose conceptualisations bear explicit, although unacknowledged similarities with Podemos' usages. A central reference for this tradition would again be Antonio Gramsci, who devoted part of his prison writings to the historical misunderstandings caused by the inability of many philosophers and politicians to translate messages between different systems and disciplines (Boothman 2010, 108–114). At the same time, Gramsci emphasised the importance of translation for Marxist praxis: since hegemony is achieved by consent, and not exclusively by imposition or mere force, translation is essential in the construction of hegemony, as it allows the emergence of a new, shared political language that builds on the various theories and models that exist within a given society (Lacorte 2010, 218–221). Although Gramsci is not quoted in Podemos' references to translation, Germán Cano acknowledged his influence on this specific approach during a personal interview (15 March 2016).

More recently, Zygmunt Bauman (1987, 127–148) has claimed that postmodernity brought with it a key change regarding the role of the intellectual, who is no longer conceived of as a 'legislator' – that is, a provider of rules and norms that need to be followed – but rather as an 'interpreter', as a specialist 'in translation between cultural traditions' (143) who must facilitate communication between different communities through a dialogue based on mutual respect. Similarly, Judith Butler has claimed – in a formulation that seems to be echoed by Iglesias and Monedero (2011, 100), quoted earlier – that a central task for the Left is one 'of establishing *practices of translation* [...] to see what basis of commonality there might be among existing movements' (Butler 2000, 143; italics in the original). In other words, from a Butlerian perspective, contemporary political actors have the task of finding the common ground shared by multiple groups competing within the political field. This idea of translation is equally close to Boaventura de Sousa Santos' approach to the World Social Forum and his defence of translation as 'the procedure that allows for mutual intelligibility' among multiple experiences of the world, 'without jeopardizing their identity and autonomy' or 'reducing them to homogeneous entities' (Santos 2006, 131–132), an issue I briefly discussed in Chapter 1.

Within this tradition of thought, Iglesias' major innovation lies in his ability to incorporate this notion of translation into his political practice, in which he aims to make technical information understandable with the help of various translated authors. In this way, this strategy of political translation constitutes a source of counter-expertise, as his academic and political knowledge is used to deconstruct and criticise mainstream narratives. This practice was central to Iglesias' introductory reflections to his TV shows, in which he briefly outlined the topic at hand from his political angle. For instance, when the Spanish conservative government started a campaign in 2012 to criminalise and repress popular protests (Zaldua 2012) by labelling them as 'anti-systemic', Iglesias introduced one of La Tuerka's (2012) debates by explaining Immanuel Wallerstein's theory of anti-systemic movements (Arrighi, Hopkins and Wallerstein 1989). Following Wallerstein, Iglesias highlighted that the movements traditionally considered 'anti-systemic' due to their opposition to the capitalist, nation-state system – such as the workers' movement and national liberation movements – are precisely those that had brought about key progressive measures, freedoms, and rights. In this way, with the help of both intra- and interlingual translation, Iglesias turns the derogatory, mainstream use of 'anti-systemic' on its head and reappraises it as a positive concept for his audience: being labelled as 'anti-systemic' is the logical consequence of opposing an unfair political system.

Textbox 6.2 Translation as exposure

The trope of translation as a practice that reveals a hidden ideological reality, evoked earlier by Iglesias and Cano, reappears in numerous political expressions from the period, generated by both politicians and non-politicians. This suggests a shared perception of the political role of translation as a tool for political exposure, which could open interesting pathways for further study.

One of the forms this trope takes concerns the usage of concepts generated by market discourse to mask an undesired reality. The debate on this issue has peaked in recent years with the emergence of numerous neologisms for new working conditions. For example, after the coinage of the word 'trabacaciones' – a portmanteau of 'trabajo' ('work') and 'vacaciones' ('holidays') that aimed to translate the English neologism *workcation* – many Twitter users, such as Jorge(r) (2018), claimed it should actually be translated as 'exploitation of labour'. With similar purposes, the trade-union Comisiones Obreras (2018) launched *Precaripedia*, a website 'translating concepts that sweeten up precarious work' (La Vanguardia 2018), such as 'freelance', 'gig economy', 'minijob', or the already mentioned 'trabacaciones'.

Beyond these ironic usages of the trope, online debates regarding this lexical area tend to highlight the importance of translation in order to illuminate what the original conceals. For instance, an interesting Twitter exchange took place when Pablo Elorduy (2019), editor of *El Salto*, asked users how they would translate 'gig economy', an extremely flexible and controversial form of employment in which employees are treated as independent contractors and paid only for each time they are given a task. Independently from their actual choices, responders in the thread emphasised the necessity of using a concept that would make the precarity of this kind of work clear, proposing coinages such as 'jornalerismo digital' ('digital day labour'), 'destajo digital' ('digital piecework'), and 'economía de las chapuzas' ('hack job economy').

A second form of the trope is applied by citizens in the face of institutional discourses, emphasising the generalised mistrust towards mainstream politics. For instance, in the context of the ongoing conflict between the Spanish state and the Catalan pro-independence movement, the trope has been used repeatedly by journalist Guillem Martínez (2017a and 2017b), who has taken up a critical stance against the actual reach of pro-independence plans. Similarly, in late 2018, a series of Twitter users responded to negotiations between the Spanish and the Catalan governments by using this trope to highlight their disbelief regarding the institutions' future plans (JM 2018; Gibert 2018). In response to a comment from Catalan vice-president Pere Aragonès, who requested a consensual resolution to the conflict that would lead to a future referendum, pro-independence Lluís Gibert (2018) tweeted: 'I translate (*tradueixo*): we will keep doing autonomism [i.e. governing Catalonia as an autonomous community within the Spanish State] to ensure we get a nice salary with the excuse of finding consensus to lay out impossible things'.

Finally, a third form of the trope – partially related to the previous one – assumes a fully parodic character, as a consequence of open ideological disagreement. Through this practice, the signifier 'translation' does not seek to reveal a concrete truth, but rather to expose the speaker's bias in a crude and mocking manner. One example is the reaction of feminist writer Laura Marcos (2018) to an article published by Javier Marías, a novelist associated with the peak of the *Cultura de la Transición*. Marías' (2018) article was a

> critique of a certain number of contemporary words 'that made it impossible [for him] to carry on reading'. The particularity lay in the fact that all of these words were associated with the 15M climate and other social movements, such as the feminist concepts 'empoderar' ('empower') and 'heteropatriarcado' ('heteropatriarchy') or the derogatory coinage 'cipotudo' ('bellendish', used to criticise a male-chauvinist form of writing). Sharing Marías' article with a linguistics Facebook group, Marcos wrote (in Asturian): 'Translation: I am an old man, I'm becoming a whingeing geezer, stop making up new stuff, for god's sake! (Especially new ideas that can question my privilege)'. Here, what Marcos sought to highlight was not a specific purpose to mislead an audience, but Marías' lack of awareness of his own prejudices.

Translation as capital

In previous chapters, I have shown how translation can become the source of innovative political ideas and a practice for communication across different constituencies and social strata. A third element, which cannot be disentangled from the previous two, is how translation contributes to processes of accumulation of cultural and economic capital (Bourdieu 2002, Casanova 2002) and to the generation of a 'militant capital' (Gaxie 1977). This is particularly relevant for new entrants to conservative fields, where the distribution of resources is highly unequal and fixed, allowing translation to become a source of capital for those lacking 'a tradition' (Serry 2002, 71). As I have argued, the role of translation-as-tradition is particularly noteworthy in the Spanish context, due to the ongoing critique and revision of the Spanish past, which means that any post-15M political project, like Podemos, needs to address this issue as part of its process of self-construction.

In the early stages of its existence (2014–2015), Podemos adopted a political strategy that privileged the use of the foreign as a substitute for the national. Unlike established Spanish parties, which have enjoyed links to other sources of power and prestige (such as financial or cultural institutions), Podemos had to build these networks in consonance with the post-15M ethos that involved a systematic critique of the Culture of the Transition. As such, the party sought an initial source of capital within the transnational networks of many of Podemos' founders in the fields of academia and political advising (Rivero 2015, 115–150). This was particularly marked in the case of Pablo Iglesias, who explicitly drew upon his international experiences, such as his postgraduate studies in Political Communication at the European Graduate School, where he was taught by intellectual figures of the left including Slavoj Žižek, Giorgio Agamben, and Judith Butler, a fact highlighted in biographical notes within his books (e.g. Iglesias 2011, 2014). Although these credentials would seem almost irrelevant to the political field, they contributed to the presentation of Iglesias as a 'counter-expert' (Sapiro

2009b, 26) in the image of his tutors, who are known precisely for their capacity to bridge the gap between the academic and the political. In fact, shortly after the European Parliament Election of 2014, in which Podemos made its political breakthrough by gaining five MEPs (including Iglesias), a group of international thinkers and academics – such as Butler and Žižek, former tutors of Iglesias, and other authors associated with the academic left and well-known within activist circles, like Chantal Mouffe, Noam Chomsky, Antonio Negri, and Jacques Rancière – signed a letter of support to the party, encouraging transnational change across Europe and expressing their desire for 'the message of hope expressed by PODEMOS' to spread 'across all our countries' (Apoyo Internacional a Podemos 2014).

Through a strong commitment to internationalism, Iglesias actively placed himself within the heritage of the journal *New Left Review* (NLR), which was founded in 1960 and is considered a fundamental pillar in the birth of Cultural Studies and the evolution of contemporary Socialist thought (Dworkin 1997, 109–140 *passim*), and its sister imprint Verso Books, where authors like Žižek, Butler, or Mouffe regularly publish. Iglesias' engagement with this tradition allowed him to establish a two-way flow of capital through the means of translation, which contributed to further highlighting Podemos' internationalist stance and locating political struggle at a European level instead of restricting it to the national arena, where the party lacked institutional power until late 2015.

Firstly, during his tenure at the European Parliament, Iglesias enhanced his international credentials by becoming a translated author with NLR/Verso. In June 2015, a few weeks before Spain's regional and local elections, *New Left Review* published an English translation of Iglesias' first article-length reflection on Podemos' origins and strategy (Iglesias 2015a), which was later followed by the release of a translated book with Verso (Iglesias 2015b). By addressing a transnational audience through the means of translation, Iglesias' texts generated greater awareness than they would have received at a national level – including unconfirmed rumours that his article in the NLR was being widely forwarded among London City Bankers (I. Gil 2015) – and forced Spanish conservative journalists, who were generally dismissive of Podemos, to address its publication and impact (Oneto 2015; Soriano and Muro 2015; Sainz Borgo 2015).[4]

At the same time, Iglesias has frequently relied on the use of translated materials from the intellectual repertoire of the left to develop a public image based on his 'cultural capital' (Bourdieu 1979), which gives him a series of resources to differentiate himself from other politicians and to foster identification with many anti-austerity protesters. From the beginning, Iglesias was perfectly aware of the keen interest this media usage of translated resources had among viewers and how it contributed to enhancing his role as an intellectual influencer:

> after recommending a book on *La Tuerka*, some publishers and booksellers would ring to tell us we had increased their sales, things like 'you talked

about Nanni Balestrini's *Los invisibles* [*Gli invisibili*] and plenty of youngsters have stopped by to buy it, you quote I don't know which book by [David] Harvey and people ask for it'. That's fantastic.

(Guedán 2016, 124)

Certainly, this accumulation of references can also be mobilised as an element of distinction or self-differentiation (one of the key characteristics of 'cultural capital', thanks to its 'scarcity'; Bourdieu 1979, 4) between Iglesias (and, by extension, Podemos) and other political agents. For instance, in an interview with a major Spanish newspaper (*El País*) during the 2015 general election campaign, Iglesias recommended the Spanish translation of a book by Perry Anderson (2012), founder and editor of the *New Left Review*, to Albert Rivera, the candidate for the emerging centre-right and pro-business party Ciudadanos. Supporting his recommendation, Iglesias claimed that he 'saw him [Rivera] as a bit weak (*flojo*) in international politics' and 'the book would help him understand Europe' (Manetto 2015). Rather than a witty remark levelled against a political rival, this gesture must be understood at a deeper political level. In their early stages, both Podemos and Ciudadanos were associated with a sense of novelty and a lack of links with the perceived corruption of the political system; in many areas of Spain, they subsequently competed for overlapping fractions of young voters with university degrees (Electomania 2018). In this context, Iglesias' erudite attack against Rivera aimed at mobilising his own capital as a means of positing a difference with his competitor, displacing the debate from shared characteristics (youth or novelty) and showing that he was better equipped than his rival on key political issues.

This ambiguity between the dissemination of knowledge and the capture of capital is also present in other media interactions, such as Iglesias' active use of Twitter, where he posts excerpts of books he is reading, including a translated anthology of Italian Marxist Mario Tronti (Iglesias 2016) and the Spanish translation of Eric Hobsbawm's *The Age of Extremes* (Iglesias 2017). While this practice establishes a potential channel of dialogue with his audience – in line with the discourse of transparency, openness, and participation that characterises new parties in the digital era (Gerbaudo 2019) – it also contributes to the wider construction of Iglesias' persona as a public intellectual through the display of capital. In particular, the fact that these excerpts are heavily underlined emphasises the central element of 'embodiment' (Bourdieu 1979, 3–4), which cements the respectability of cultural capital. Unlike other types of 'wealth', cultural capital requires 'personal work' (4) and a 'cost of time' – notably scarce in the case of a politician – that is signalled to observers by Iglesias' underlining of chosen excerpts. Similarly, another material symbol of the effort required by the embodiment of cultural resources was employed during Iglesias' televised conversation with Perry Anderson (La Tuerka 2017b), as a large pile of Anderson's books in Spanish translation was clearly visible on the coffee table between the two speakers.

The limits of translation

As I have shown in this chapter, Podemos can be understood as a political entity based upon multiple processes of interlingual, intralingual, and intersystemic translation. In its early stages, its discourse and conceptual framework were the result of a complex process of translation, largely based on Íñigo Errejón's writings from a Gramscian-Laclauian perspective, while its international presence was fostered through connection with foreign traditions, mostly through the activity of Iglesias as both translated author and media translator. At the same time, communication to citizens relied on practices of translation across a variety of media, which in turn were the source for Iglesias' distinctive political capital. Therefore, it could be convincingly argued that many of Podemos' most significant contributions to Spanish politics have been achieved through translation: a new terminology with a strong Gramscian-Laclauian imprint ('casta', 'hegemonía', and 'populismo'), an openness of the political field to foreign traditions, and a conception of political thought that emphasises everyday usefulness. While acknowledging these successes, however, in this concluding section I argue that many among Podemos' potential limitations and pitfalls are also tied to their usage and understanding of translation.

Translational appropriation as a closure of the intellectual field

Podemos' use of translated authors and concepts has held an important political potential, as it disseminated and popularised certain references while contributing to the 'destabilising' effect (Even-Zohar 1990a, 20–22) of adding new content to the predictable repertoire of the Culture of the Transition. However, its increasing power as a political project enhanced its capacity for appropriating texts and influencing their potential reception, in a clear expression of what Bourdieu (2002, 4) called 'branding' (*marquage*), that is, the process of inscribing new senses and meanings into a translated product within the field of reception. In this way, Podemos has 'branded' certain references to the point of placing any potential debate on the topic under the shadow of the party; for instance, the aforementioned concept of 'populism' – that eventually backfired, forcing the party to abandon it – or the work of Antonio Gramsci. The latter is especially pertinent due to its intensity, which even included a spot for La Tuerka (2014) in which Iglesias advertised a translated anthology of Gramsci, claiming his work was 'the answer' to their whole collective project. While providing an increase in popularity for the Italian thinker, this branding has also discouraged alternative readings, as individuals interested in Gramsci might want to dissociate themselves from Podemos. For instance, activist and philosopher Amador Fernández-Savater – who had reflected on the evolution of the 15M using Gramscian concepts (Fernández-Savater 2012b and 2013b) – told me during a personal interview (16 March 2016) that, since the emergence of Podemos, he would 'not even consider' the idea of quoting Gramsci, as a preventive measure to avoid being associated with internal party debates.

124 *Podemos*

Therefore, Podemos' appropriation of certain translated authors and concepts can ultimately become counterproductive: after the initial period of interest in the given references, their excessive association with the party, as well as the overexposure inherent to mass media, can lead to a closure of debates instead of a productive, long-term renewal.

Cultural capital as a class marker

Similarly, the disproportionate use of cultural capital as a source of political capital is proving to be detrimental for the long-term prospects of the project. From the very beginning, electoral surveys showed that Podemos had an important following among both university students and university graduates (Llaneras 2016), which in principle reinforced the pertinence of using cultural capital as a way of connecting with a core of 15M protesters with a high educational capital (Della Porta 2015, 51–52). However, rather than being a basis for a larger majority, this constituency of citizens with advanced levels of education has become Podemos' core voters (Bayón 2018; Blanco 2018), and the party has struggled to reach beyond them. This strong association between voters and a high level of education and left-wing parties is certainly not exclusive to Podemos: as Thomas Piketty (2018) has noted, political cleavages across many countries have been realigning along this trend, leading to the emergence of what he calls a 'brahmin left'. Nevertheless, the case of Podemos has the additional particularity of its strongly academic background, which has served to alienate other voters. Several analysts and thinkers have identified the 'excess of theory' (Villacañas 2018) that marks Iglesias' and his colleagues' political discourse as a negative factor which has led to an inability to extend their message to other social groups in the long run (Hernández 2018).

This overvaluation of cultural capital is not specific to Podemos, and could be seen as a characteristic of other post-15M platforms. For instance, during the final week of the campaign leading up to the 2019 local elections, Barcelona en Comú distributed a letter in support of Ada Colau that was signed by a lengthy list of international figures, including several academics and intellectuals like Boaventura de Sousa Santos, Chantal Mouffe, Antonio Negri, Judith Butler, and Owen Jones, among many others (Barcelona en Comú 2019). While this attests to the strong international networks of the party, as did the letter used by Podemos in 2014, it once again constitutes a limiting device, since it only addresses a fraction of voters with similar educational profiles to the party representatives. When sharing the letter on his public Facebook account, Raimundo Viejo – an academic, former councillor, and former national MP with BeC – provided a blatant example of this misunderstanding in his supporting statement: referring to the important cohort of authors and thinkers supporting the platform, he wrote 'Who does your book collection vote for? Mine votes Colau!' (Viejo 2019). Such an intellectualised gaze actively excludes a whole set of citizens – those precarious workers, for instance, who do not even have a 'book collection' due to lack of time, training, or means – that a party with a transformative vision should be addressing.

Translation as subordination

Finally, in the conceptual analyses of 'translation' as a communicative practice, I have shown how Podemos' leaders have repeatedly claimed that intellectuals and political representatives have the central role of translating for the citizens: they need to speak a language that people 'can understand', to expose a hidden truth behind complex technocratic jargon, to provide voters with useful concepts, and to mediate between different movements, among other translational tasks. If pursued to its end, this conception implies that intellectuals and political leaders are the ones who 'know', the ones who 'understand' the languages and systems at hand, which makes them the only ones who are able to translate between them, while a majority of citizens are presented as passive receptors who eventually react to these translations, but do not generate them. This conception of the political divide between a privileged minority of 'intellectuals' and the great majority of 'the people' was criticised by Ellen Meiksins Wood in the 1980s as one of the main characteristics of 'New "True" Socialism', a contemporary current of thought to which she ascribed thinkers such as Ernesto Laclau. In terms that immediately remind us of Podemos' discourse, Meiksins Wood (1986, 6) condemned the way in which these theorists assigned intellectuals the central task of 'the construction of "social agents" by means of ideology or discourse', which left 'the inchoate mass that constitutes the bulk of the "people" [...] without a collective identity, except what it receives from its intellectual leaders'.

This foregrounding of intellectuals and politicians within the structure of Podemos contradicts an important strand of thought within the 15M that favoured a more open, non-hierarchical, and collective understanding of knowledge (Anonymous 2012). In opposition to the picture of a mass of citizens that needs to be provided with languages and concepts, as it is unable to generate its own, many radically democratic strands within the 15M claimed that 'non-experts' can also 'trust in their own abilities to collaboratively construct the knowledge they need in any given situation and to generate effective answers to the problems that confront them' (Moreno-Caballud 2015, 3). In consequence, any political party looking to build upon the achievements of the 15M must be one that ensures an alliance between the forms of knowledge enjoyed by intellectuals as counter-experts as well as those constructed by ordinary citizens through cooperation based on their own experience. Such a party would then be in a position to enact the Butlerian understanding of translation that Iglesias and Monedero (2011, 100) briefly hinted at during the mass mobilisations of the 15M: an open party-movement where practices of translation were not restricted to a top-bottom direction, but instead took place in multiple directions, contributing to the articulation of the alliance between a variety of actors and collectives. Iglesias' later reformulations, such as his claims that Podemos should translate proposals from the social movements (Iglesias in Martínez López and Elorduy 2017), reveal a unidirectional flow, as it is the party – with its specific cadres, biases, values, and interpretations of the process – who ultimately would decide what to translate and how.

This is even more disappointing when considering that the original Podemos project was well placed to undertake this process. The party's implementation of the *círculos* ('circles'), autonomous assemblies that could be kickstarted by any citizen, offered a unique tool to develop this process, as individuals could spontaneously engage in political dialogue and submit their proposals, demands, and criticisms to the party. The impressive response to this call – approximately 1,000 *círculos* were created in less than a year (El País 2014) – attested to people's determination to bring the 15M's democratic potential into the new party. Within this structure, the party cadres could have chosen to become institutional translators for the assemblies, placing their cultural capital at their service, enabling a translational alliance between the multiple collectives that were coming together. The path taken, however, was very different, with an increasing isolation of the party organs, which cut 'the flux of information and power' (López 2016) that circulated between the different sections of the organisation. In this way, therefore, Podemos cut its ties with the democratic translational potential of the 15M and had to confront the limits of a strictly institutional project.

> **Textbox 6.3 Owen Jones: a translated ally?**
>
> The complex interactions between the innovative role of translation, the generation of a tradition, the transfer of cultural capital, and the limits of political appropriation find a pertinent example in the reception of English author and political activist Owen Jones, and his later cooptation by Podemos.
>
> Jones gained popularity in Spain at the beginning of the 15M cycle, when Capitán Swing published the translation of *Chavs* (Jones 2012; originally released in English by Verso in 2011), an analysis of the changing image of the working classes in Britain and their vilification by mass media and politicians. Although initially considered 'very British' by the Spanish translator, who opted not to translate the title, in agreement with the publisher (personal conversation with Íñigo Jáuregui, 6 October 2014), the book quickly prompted widespread debate on the changing structure of Spanish society (see Capitán Swing 2019d for a sample of press clips) and has been considered a unique 'representative of the contemporary transformation in the writing, publishing, and reception of essays' (Rendueles 2016).
>
> From the perspective of the cultural repertoire (Even-Zohar 1990a, 21–22), it can be argued that *Chavs* owed its impact to its disruptive potential, since it provided a conceptual framework for understanding a social reality that

was previously lacking one. This is not only shown by the rapid incorporation of the concept *chav* into Spanish political terminology (Villacañas de Castro 2013), but also through the direct inspiration it has provided for books on the relevance of culture in class conflict (Lenore 2014), the conditions of life in the outskirts of Madrid (Embid 2016), and the lack of visibility of the working class (Romero and Tirado 2016).

Eventually, Jones' increase of capital within the Spanish cultural field resulted in his crossover to the political field. During the general election campaigns of 2015 and 2016, he was invited to speak at different rallies supporting Podemos and its allies, in which he featured in a visually prominent place (see various examples of posters in Esquerra Unida i Alternativa 2015; N'Asturies Podemos 2016). In the absence of national figures of similar popularity, Jones exemplified the dual role of the 'critical intellectual' (Sapiro 2009b, 15–17) who can eventually transform his cultural capital into political capital by putting it at the service of a certain cause. In doing so, however, his work underwent the process of 'branding' (Bourdieu 2002, 4) mentioned earlier, as it was inserted within a new reading context. Although it was his lack of association with any existing intellectual or political blocs in Spain that allowed him to be perceived as innovative, Jones' support of Podemos opened the door to a more restricted understanding of his work, as new readers and observers will tend to approach it with reference to this engagement. For instance, when interviewed during the 2016 EU Referendum campaign in the United Kingdom, a Spanish conservative journal ironically described him in the headline as 'Podemos' British guru' (Postico 2016).

Finally, as in other cases discussed in this chapter, this political involvement inevitably has to face up to its potential limitations. Given Jones' lack of familiarity with Spanish politics – as shown, among other cases, by his sweeping foreword to Romero and Tirado's book or his self-avowed uncertainty during post-election negotiations (Ruiz Marull 2016) – his support could only exert a symbolic role among a small minority of Spanish voters. Indeed, only those who were already acquainted with his work would be influenced by it, not the majority of the population that a political party aims to attract. In this sense, while Jones' translated work was of decisive importance to the 15M climate, it is debatable whether his translated role contributed to a party that was already characterised by its highly intellectual profile.

Notes

1 Within this field, Iglesias has also shown an interest in the practical aspects of translation and interpreting, volunteering as an interpreter during the First European Social Forum in Florence (Iglesias 2008: 397) and translating a chapter of Balestrini and Moroni's (2006, 361–394) book on revolutionary movements in 1960–70s Italy.
2 Cano, a member of Errejón's circle, was stripped of his party responsibilities after the 2017 assembly.

3 Adopting a different, yet related approach to intralingual and intersystemic translation, activist Mark Bray claims that Occupy Wall Street was 'a vehicle for translating anarchy to a society that was generally receptive to many anarchist ideas but wary of its ideological trappings' (Bray 2013, 5).
4 As translator of Iglesias' article for the *New Left Review*, I could sense the interest that this publication created among Spanish readers, even generating shocking reactions. After sharing the English text on Twitter, a self-acknowledged voter of the PSOE publicly asked me to upload the Spanish original; when I refused to do so, he aggressively accused me of hiding sensitive information from Spanish voters who were not fluent in English.

7 Conclusion
The ongoing task of translation

As I conclude this monograph, more than a decade has passed since the beginning of the global 'crisis' that opened the current cycle of conflicts. The constellation of protests that formed the movement of the squares seems a distant memory, as their countries have seen the persistence of dictatorship (Egypt), a descent into civil war (Libya, Syria, Yemen) or internal repression (Turkey), the return to power of traditional establishment parties (Greece) or the advent of nationalistic and xenophobic movements (United States, Brazil).

In this context, Spain offers a fraught and complex picture. In the field of activism, as this book has shown, the climate of politicised action that the 15M opened still seems lively and productive, with the emergence of multiple grassroots platforms across various fields of engagement. Social issues and problems, however, have not improved, as precarity in employment has increased (according to unions, approximately half of working people have part-time and/or fixed term contracts; EFE 2019), birth rates are among the lowest in Europe, and skyrocketing rents continue to severely limit access to housing (Gabarre 2019). The territorial crisis, meanwhile, which has been mainly but not exclusively symbolised in the pro-independence Catalan movement, has added a new layer to internal conflicts. Furthermore, institutional politics have repeatedly shown the limits of transformative projects. The 'municipalist' platforms that made substantial advances in 2015 (Rubio-Pueyo 2017) were almost wiped off the map in 2019, losing most councils (with the notable exception of Barcelona and Cadiz). After its peak in 2015, Podemos has been constantly losing votes at every election, becoming a secondary force in parliament. In early 2020, however, it became the minor partner in a coalition government with the social-democrat PSOE, an unexpected move that has been seen by many members of the anticapitalistic branch of Podemos as a major mistake that will put the party in a subservient position within a government largely dominated by the PSOE, historically linked to the Spanish establishment (Munárriz 2019; López 2019). Finally, the far right, which had not played a political role since the beginning of the 15M cycle, has made major breakthroughs, as VOX became the third largest party in parliament – surpassing Podemos by half a million votes and seventeen MPs.

130 *Conclusion*

In this context, it is not surprising that many activists are claiming that the 15M cycle is over or, at the very least, that it is mutating into a different political phase (Fundación de los Comunes 2018, 11) – a perception made even more patent in the light of the economic crash that is likely to follow the ongoing COVID-19 pandemic. As such, this conclusion places itself at this point of conjuncture, aiming to highlight both successes and limitations of activist and political action since the 15M in order to contribute to a collective process of reflection. In the following pages, I address three translational strands – translation at the global and national interface, translation as political renewal, and translation in the search for commonality – in order to draw provisional conclusions as well as to illuminate potential ways forward.

Translation at the global and national interface

Since its emergence, the movement of the squares was placed on a sort of dual scale, as protests had both a national and international dimension (Gerbaudo 2017, 29–59): on the one hand, they aimed to transform the unfair distribution of power within their countries; on the other, they attacked the transnational networks and systems that made these inequalities possible, an opposition that took a more concrete form in the case of the Arab uprisings (the various dictatorships in the area) and a more abstract and diffuse one in the West (the markets, the banks, or the transnational institutions). In both cases, protests showed an awareness of the globalised nature of political struggle and the necessity of engaging with both levels, paying great attention to the dissemination of their actions – a process in which, as has been argued, translation played a truly enabling role, inspiring new movements across several countries. The interplay between the two levels was certainly an asset for the movements, as protests could learn from each other while simultaneously creating a sense of unpredictability, as it was difficult to forecast where the next conflict was going to emerge.

However, as noted in Chapters 1 and 6, the period following the movement of the squares saw both a backlash of repression and a new wave of protest movements, generally leaning towards the right-wing. In Europe and the Americas, the combination of both factors opened a new phase in the crisis, which has been more intensely focused upon the nation-state than on the transnational agenda. Loosely building upon Laclau and Mouffe's theories (Laclau and Mouffe 1985; Laclau 2005; Mouffe 2018), I define this phase as a translation of the consequences of the global crisis into a national framework, which has subsequently re-orientated the conflict. In this process, some of the most perceptive and powerful analyses of the movement of the squares – such as the reappraisal of democracy, the critique of the elites, the oppressive role of transnational agreements, and the necessity of changes in the political system – have been appropriated and placed at the service of other political projects. The success of the Brexit narrative among voters in post-industrial areas affected by globalisation and austerity provides a clear example of this trend: mobilising a well-argued anti-systemic discourse (loss of national sovereignty, pressure on the welfare system, and voters' disaffection), it contributed to the empowerment of members of the same elite who had promoted globalisation and austerity in the first place.

In the Spanish context, the translation of the crisis into a national framework assumed a particular character, taking place through the ongoing conflict between the Spanish central government and the pro-independence movement in Catalonia. As Josep Maria Antentas (2018, 17–18) has noted, the Catalan movement was galvanised by the crisis and espoused a strong democratic potential that resonated with other movements across the State. However, it has failed to present a coherent political project due to paying excessive attention to the national question as opposed to other social and political concerns (Antentas 2018, 18–22, 40–42), preferring to gain the favour of conservative regional elites rather than to engage with the anti-austerity protests started by the 15M. In turn, the central government and the judiciary have reacted against the pro-independence challenge by reinforcing the criminalisation of protest following the occupations and demonstrations of 2011–12 (López-Terra 2017), in a drive that has been strongly criticised by the Spanish branch of Amnesty International (Amnistía Internacional 2019), among others.

Beyond the obvious differences between a repressive and a non-violent movement, both projects shared the aim of translating the social and economic crisis into a strictly political crisis, which would be resolved through the return to the status quo defined by the Spanish Constitution (in the case of pro-centralist narratives) or the emergence of a new state (in the pro-independence case). In their constant clashes over recent years, the dual national framework has obscured and distorted many of the claims put forward by the 15M and limited other translations of the crisis, which were unable to mobilise alternative narratives to return the focus to social and economic issues. Furthermore, as discussed in Chapter 6, attempts by Podemos to generate new national narratives through the means of translation have been largely unsuccessful. Therefore, an open task for activists and political actors is to rebuild a collective narrative from below in order to reopen the debates that these national translations of the crisis have stalled.

Translating as political renewal

In his reappraisal of radical culture and politics during the *Transición*, Germán Labrador (2017, 239–253) shows how numerous artists aimed to 'embody' the literature they read to the extent of completely embracing a new lifestyle – frequently with devastating consequences, such as reproducing the alcoholism and drug-addiction of their literary role-models. Since most of these texts were translations, it could be argued that the *embodiment of translation* opened a door to the (destructive) transformation of their selves. In my view, this practice posits yet another continuity between the radical currents within the *Transición* and the 15M climate, albeit transforming its originally negative character into more positive contours. As discussed across several sections of this book, Spanish citizens have developed political action through the embodiment of translated knowledge and its incarnation in their daily practice: commons-based collectives and cooperatives, politically committed publishers, the care strike, and the platforms for the right to the city and against tourist excesses are vivid examples of the ways in which translation can contribute to renewal. In this way, as in other cultures experiencing 'crises' and 'vacuums' (Even-Zohar 1990b, 47), post-15M Spain is living through a period in which translation 'maintains a central position' in its system, since it 'participates actively in shaping' (Even-Zohar 1990b, 46) the centre of this (political) culture through various engagements and experiments.

While this drive towards renewal is undeniable, I would raise three potential queries as topics of future research and political debate. The first relates to the necessity of understanding that the effects of translation tend to be 'potentially contradictory' (Venuti 1998, 46). As argued in my introduction, ideas, concepts, and models do not circulate according to the seemingly frictionless model of 'diffusion' that is frequently used in Social Movements Studies. Quite the opposite, they are subject to a whole set of 'social operations' (Bourdieu 2002, 4) that place them within relevant debates and struggles in the receiving field. As I have demonstrated, a tension between collective transformation and personal benefit, between dissemination and appropriation, between dialogue and remuneration runs throughout many translational issues across this cycle. While some translations have contributed to political renewal through their activist embodiment (as experiments with the 'commons' and 'care' attest), others were limited in their reach and provided unsatisfactory answers or even contributed to a distortion of the social reality at hand, like the discussions surrounding the 'indignación' in Chapter 2. Similarly, forms of knowledge that have been nurtured by activists and movements have also been subject to market and institutional co-optation, as evidenced for instance in the increasing appeal of the 'commons' (Chapters 3 and 5) or the feminist 'trend' in the publishing sector (Chapter 4). Furthermore, translations can even perform a double function and exert a double effect, as seen in the case of Podemos' and Pablo Iglesias' engagement with political repertoires (*New Left Review*, Verso Books, populism theory, Antonio Gramsci, Owen Jones). With regard to its function, this engagement must be understood as simultaneously the vindication of an alternative tradition and a capture of capital that sought to improve the position of both party and leader. With regard to its effect, meanwhile, this accumulation of cultural capital is an ambivalent resource that appeals to certain voters with high educational capital while alienating others. In consequence, translation cannot be conceived simply as a beneficial contribution to political transformation, but rather as a complex and unpredictable process that is subject to multiple 'partisan' engagements (Tymoczko 2000, 24). The notion of expanded translation discussed across the book has aimed to encompass these tensions, showing how power imbalances in their various forms influence the way in which translations are produced, used, and received.

Closely related to the first point and to the process of expanded translation, my second query for reflection concerns the complex and problematic process of translating political concepts. As was briefly raised across various chapters, many of the coinages and ideas that run through the activist lexicon proved impenetrable to many citizens (as in the case of *procomún* or *gentrificación*), while more accessible ones – such as *cuidados* or *derecho a la ciudad* – are subject to interpretations and appropriations from various groups and collectives, which potentially blur their meaning. In this sense, a process of true renewal requires that the adoption of new concepts goes hand in hand with a determined opposition to any conceptual fetishism; in other words, the concept is not a fixed reality that has to be preserved at all costs, but one that needs to respond to the materiality and evolution of practice. A highly successful demonstration such as the feminist care strike contributed to the popularisation of the *cuidados* as a lens for social reality because it displayed an ability to firmly root it in the daily life of many people. Similarly, critical concepts mobilised by pro-housing platforms had a lasting presence thanks to their acceptance within an activist community. Conversely, this implies that concepts should be discarded when they are no longer operational, especially in the face of their hollowing-out by other actors, as was argued in relation to the Assamblea de Barris' decision to ditch the notion of *turisme sostenible* in favour of *decreixement turístic* and Podemos' disavowal of *populismo*.

Finally, my third point concerns the relationship between translations and texts originally written in Spanish (or in other languages within the Spanish State). As I have argued, both forms of writing respond to a perceived lack or absence within the 15M climate and to the need to oppose discourses associated with the previously dominant 'Culture of the Transition'. In my view, however, it is worth asking ourselves whether the centrality of book translation overcompensates for the relative absence of production in local languages. Whereas translation works from pre-existing materials, which allows for relatively ready access, local production of texts is unpredictable and subject to potential developments that might not take place. In this sense, during my fieldwork I have noticed how some publishers manifested a certain degree of ambiguity towards the actual role of translation. For instance, Salvador Cobo and Juanma Agulles, members of El Salmón, complained (personal interview, 6 April 2019) that they were still not visible as a publishing collective to 'likeminded' writers and activists, but they hoped that their catalogue of translations would become a way of attracting new authors who 'engaged in the conflicts we have here, in our context'. Similarly, Daniel Álvarez, co-editor at Hoja de Lata, argued (personal interview, 20 December 2019) that 'translated books do not always work out well' and claimed that the publishing house had started considering whether they should 'invest in books written specifically for our essay series'. Therefore, the current centrality of book and text translation for political action in Spain must be viewed as part of a concrete set of historical circumstances, which means that the drive towards renewal could transform itself and take on a different shape in future years.

Translation in the search for commonality

As discussed in Chapter 6, the role of translation as a practice that seeks common ground between different movements and constituencies has been addressed from different perspectives by thinkers as diverse as Judith Butler (2000), Boaventura de Sousa Santos (2006, 131–147), and Antonio Negri and Michael Hardt (2009, 340–351). The need for translation was fully recognised by several founders of Podemos and, more particularly, by Pablo Iglesias, who has reflected on this practice from his position as 'institutional political translator'. Nevertheless, Iglesias' understanding of translation revealed a hierarchical and extractivist conception of politics, in which party leader and cadres have a decisive position in choosing what and how to translate from the proposals of extra-parliamentary movements.

The limits of this specific route, however, should not obscure the continued need to search for commonality within the 15M climate. Throughout this book, I have shown how individuals and collectives have resorted to translation, or reacted to it, thanks to its potential for eliciting shared issues, strengths, and problems: from the unemployed Asturians who found inspiration in the Greek opposition to austerity to the citizens in Barcelona who see their city ravaged by the same tourist sector that exploits Marseille or Naples; from the activists who occupy a privatised building in Madrid inspired by a concept borrowed from rural tenancy to the migrant women who feel engaged by the discourse of 1970s Italian feminists; or the users who spontaneously engage on social networks to render euphemistic jargon into politicised language. Translation occurs precisely because it manages to illuminate aspects that are shared between struggles, cultures, and periods. Therefore, translation is always a potential practice for commonality.

In the light of the findings in this book, how could political translation evolve beyond the 15M cycle? In my view, the starting point should be the assumption that both activist collectives and political groupings have limitations. On the one hand, collectives and movements find difficulties in long-term sustainability, clash with the pressures from conservative institutions, and struggle to take their demands to the next level. On the other, parties and political platforms tend to lose sight of their origins and become trapped in networks of power, frequently adopting the *esprit de corps* of the very institutions they were seeking to transform. Therefore, any dilemma that is framed in terms of 'either'/'or' is doomed to remain within these confines. Indeed, Antonio Negri and Michael Hardt, who are well known for their defence of horizontal movements, have recently argued that we must move beyond this dichotomy in order to investigate the dual (and extremely complex) task of 'construct[ing] organization without hierarchy' and 'creat[ing] institutions without centralization' (Negri and Hardt 2017, 14).

The practice of translation could play a crucial role in this process of renewal, yet only if decisive changes are implemented. To start with, translation cannot be a privilege afforded only to leadership or the political avant-garde. As

Jacques Rancière (2009, 22) brilliantly put it, 'an emancipated community is a community of narrators and translators', one in which each member shares the power of being able to tell their own story and to translate their own experience and perceptions into words. Joining the political community involves both the right *and* the responsibility of contributing to this process of translation. At the same time, however, this requires learning from recent experiences regarding class composition and the role of intellectuals. As discussed in this book, the 15M was marred by class- and education-based divides that limited its social reach (Rodríguez 2016) and in turn led to an overrepresentation of this social type within new political platforms, symbolised by academics and intellectuals. In his defence of democracy as an 'anti-oligarchic principle', Moreno Pestaña (2019, 284–286) has rightly argued that democratic communities cannot manage without specialists in various fields, but they should reclaim the right of choosing which problems they should be consulted on, and how they should be brought into the movement. As we well know, it is far too often the case that a specialist or an academic becomes the self-crowned spokesperson for a community because their intellectual and cultural capital gives them an advantage over others. Against this model, an emancipated community would need to recruit and elect their own 'political translators', in the sense discussed by Nicole Doerr (2018, 4–5): individuals who challenge the cultural and linguistic imbalances and the marginalisation that exist in any deliberative democracy. Instead of using their capital to affirm and reaffirm their positions, these translators – always subject to rotation, accountability, and potential deselection – would distribute it to counter social inequalities, ensuring that every member of the community exerts their right and responsibility to translate.

A closing plea for future research paths

As I noted in the Introduction and in Chapter 1, the disciplines of Translation Studies and Social Movements Studies have not engaged yet in a systematic dialogue, despite their many areas of unison and a promising body of interdisciplinary research. This monograph has also sought to advocate for the potential of more meaningful engagement between them. On the one hand, Translation Studies would certainly benefit from going beyond its self-imposed niche, in terms of approaches, traditions, and concepts. I cannot remember how many times I have been told by peer-reviewers and scholars at conferences that many matters I study 'are not translation' or that my research 'does not engage sufficiently with translation scholarship'. To those among my colleagues, I would like to pose the following question: how can it be that political and activist practices and discourses are decisively impregnated by translation, and yet Translation Studies remains largely unaware of their existence? Furthermore, why is it that political reflection on translation keeps increasing, but seldom engages with scholarship in Translation Studies? I am afraid the answer has already been provided by Siri Nergaard and Stefano Arduini (2011, 8–9) in their manifesto for 'post-translation studies': 'new and enriching thinking on translation', they claimed, frequently takes place 'outside the traditional discipline of translation studies'. Refusing to engage with other concepts and practices of translation, as well as with other theoretical and critical traditions, is a risk that no discipline would run if it wants to be intellectually and socially meaningful.

For its part, Social Movements Studies has so far shown little awareness of the translational processes taking place within their objects of study. As argued earlier, the models of 'diffusion' and 'brokerage' have side-lined important aspects of social and political reality that reflection on translation could help to uncover. Concepts, strategies, and repertoires that feature strongly within the field are not simply the consequence of a smooth and unrestricted adoption, but the result of numerous actions conditioned by biases, differences, and diverging agendas. As discussed in Chapter 1, the emerging wave of scholarly research that aims to connect activism, social movements, and translation offers a first step in overcoming this gap. Comparative by nature and well-placed to explain events beyond the linguistic and cultural limits of the nation-state, translation could become a pivotal element in our understanding of political praxis and thought, tracing the heritage and afterlife of movements, questioning the communicative processes that shape political communities, or exploring the transmission and appropriation of repertoires and ideologies. Breaking new ground is a promising and much-needed task, but we must be willing to take up the challenge.

Bibliography

15Mpedia. 2016a. 'Acampada Sol. Organización'. *15Mpedia.* https://15mpedia.org/wiki/Acampada_Sol#Organizaci.C3.B3n.
15Mpedia. 2016b. 'Banc Expropiat de Gràcia'. *15Mpedia.* https://15mpedia.org/wiki/Banc_Expropiat_de_Gr%C3%A0cia.
15Mpedia. 2016c. 'CSOA La Madreña'. *15Mpedia.* https://15mpedia.org/wiki/CSOA_La_Madre%C3%B1a.
15Mpedia. 2018. 'Lista de suicidios relacionados con desahucios'. *15Mpedia*https://15mpedia.org/wiki/Lista_de_suicidios_relacionados_con_desahucios.
Ajuntament de Barcelona. 2017. *Programa de Patrimoni Ciutadà d'ús i gestió comunitàries.* https://ajuntament.barcelona.cat/participaciociutadana/sites/default/files/documents/comunsurbans_doc_sm_0.pdf.
Akal. 2019a. 'Cuestiones de antagonismo'. *Akal.* https://www.akal.com/coleccion/cuestiones-de-antagonismo/.
Akal. 2019b. 'Pensamiento crítico'. *Akal.* https://www.akal.com/coleccion/pensamiento-critico/.
Alcaldía de Madrid. 2016. 'Madrid Ciudad [de] los Cuidados: un plan para mejorar la vida de quienes habitamos esta ciudad'. *Diario de Madrid,* 15 March. https://tinyurl.com/yhmu3445.
Alejos Escarpe, Luis. 2018. 'El movimiento de pensionistas, fenómeno singular de largo alcance'. *Lan Harremanak,* 40: 31–48.
Alemán, Jorge. 2018. *Lacan y el capitalismo.* Granada: Universidad de Granada.
Alexia. 2016. "De Tahrir a Nuit Debout: la resaca de las plazas" *Revista Alexia,* 8 November. http://revistaalexia.es/de-tahrir-a-nuit-debout-la-resaca-de-las-plazas/.
Alonso Leal, Nuria, and Sampedro Ortega, Yolanda. 2017. 'Lo que los bienes comunales cuentan'. In Comunaria (eds.), *Rebeldías en común.* Madrid: Libros en Acción.
Alvaredo, Facundo, Chance, Lucas, Piketty, Thomas, Saez, Emmanuel, and Zucman, Gabriel. 2018. 'World Inequality Report 2018: Executive Summary'. *World Inequality Lab,* available online: https://wir2018.wid.world/files/download/wir2018-summary-english.pdf.
Álvarez Mellado, Elena. 2018. '¿Soy yo, o que en la traducción que propone Fundéu a "alt-right" desaparezca el término "derecha" y en cambio aparezca "populismo" es, digamos, ideológicamente problemático?'. *Twitter,* 11 October. https://twitter.com/lirondos/status/1050436515770318849.
Álvarez-Blanco, Palmar. 2019. *En ruta con el Común. Archivo y memoria de una posible constelación.* Santander: La Vorágine.

Bibliography

Ambrosi, Alain. 2013. 'Définir les communs – Enric Senabre Hidalgo'. *Remix the Commons*, 21 October. https://www.remixthecommons.org/?fiche=definir-les-communs-enric-senabre-hidalgo.

Amics de la Terra. 2019. 'Activistas #antiautopista parodian en Fitur Madrid la promoción turística del Govern de les Illes Balears'. *Facebook*, 24 January. https://tinyurl.com/rs2zshu.

Amnistía Internacional. 2018. 'Una media de 80 multas diarias contra la libertad de expresión'. *Amnistía Internacional*, 5 November. https://www.es.amnesty.org/en-que-estamos/noticias/noticia/articulo/espanaley-mordaza-una-media-de-80-multas-diarias-contra-la-libertad-de-expresion/.

Amnistía Internacional. 2019. 'La condena por sedición a Jordi Sànchez y Jordi Cuixart, una amenaza a los derechos a la libertad de expresión y de reunión pacífica'. *Amnistía Internacional*, 19 November. https://www.es.amnesty.org/en-que-estamos/noticias/noticia/articulo/espana-la-condena-por-sedicion-a-jordi-sanchez-y-jordi-cuixart-una-amenaza-a-los-derechos-a-la-liber/.

Anderson, Perry. 2012. *El Nuevo Viejo Mundo*. Translated by Jaime Blasco. Madrid: Akal.

André-Bazzana, Bénédicte. 2006. *Mitos y mentiras de la Transición*. Barcelona: El Viejo Topo.

Anonymous. 2004. *¡Pásalo! Relatos y análisis sobre el 11-M y los días que le siguieron*. Madrid: Traficantes de Sueños.

Anonymous. 2012. 'Intelectuales. Cuerpo y (des)aparición en el 15M'. In Ernesto Castro and Fernando Castro (eds.), *El arte de la indignación*. Salamanca: Delirio, 25–44.

Antentas, Josep Maria. 2017. 'Spain: from the indignados rebellion to regime crisis (2011–2016)'. *Labor History* 58 (1): 2–26.

Antentas, Josep Maria. 2018. *Espectros de Octubre. Perturbaciones y paradojas del independentismo catalán*. Madrid: Sylone.

Apoyo Internacional a Podemos. 2014. https://apoyointernacionalapodemos.wordpress.com/11-2/.

Appleton, Timothy. 2011. '¿Es el 15M un 'acontecimiento'?'. *Cruce. Arte y Pensamiento Contemporáneo*, June. Translated by Ana López Ruiz. https://crucecontemporaneo.files.wordpress.com/2011/06/es-el-15-m-un-acontecimiento-por-timothy-appleton1.pdf.

Aragón, Paula. 2019. 'Cristina Fallarás: El problema del #Metoo es que era aspiracional'. *Fashion & Arts*, February 13. https://www.magazinefa.com/24-7/cristina-fallaras-el-problema-del-metoo-es-que-era-aspiracional/.

Arrighi, Giovanni, Hopkins, Terence, and Wallerstein, Immanuel. 1989. *Anti-systemic movements*. London: Verso.

Assemblea de Barris pel Decreixement Turístic. 2018a. 'No vull que els creuers em matin: Marsella lluita contra la polució dels creuers'. *Facebook*, 8 July. https://tinyurl.com/svqjowm.

Assemblea de Barris pel Decreixement Turístic. 2018b. 'Hotel Workers Branch'. *Facebook*, 13 October. https://tinyurl.com/vmmjuvr.

Assemblea de Barris pel Decreixement Turístic. 2018c. 'Por cada 100 residentes hay entre 184 y 197 turistas durmiendo en estos barrios'. *Facebook*, 7 December.

Assemblea de Barris pel Decreixement Turístic. 2019a. 'Gran Hotel Napoli, la política y la ciudad rebelde'. *Facebook*, 1 February. https://tinyurl.com/w479eg4.

Assemblea de Barris pel Decreixement Turístic. 2019b. 'Atenes: desnoneu airbnb, no pas okupes!'. *Facebook*, 23 September. https://tinyurl.com/u6v9622.

Bibliography 139

Assemblea de Barris pel Decreixement Turístic. 2019c. 'Comunicat'. https://assemblea barris.wordpress.com/2019/09/26/comunicat-a-barcelona-no-hi-haura-reduccio-demissions-real-sense-decreixement-turistic/.

Assemblea de Barris pel Decreixement Turístic. 2019d. '[Comunicat] Assemblea de Barris pel Decreixement Turístic: de l'ABTS a l'ABDT'. https://assembleabarris.wordpress.com/2019/12/03/comunicat-assemblea-de-barris-pel-decreixement-turistic-de-labts-a-labdt/.

Assemblea de Barris per un Turisme Sostenible. 2016. 'La fàbrica flotant més gran del mon amarra a Bcn'. https://assembleabarris.wordpress.com/2016/05/23/la-fabrica-flotant-mes-gran-del-mon-amarra-a-bcn/.

ATTAC Madrid. 2012. 'Reforma laboral D.L. 3/2012: análisis y crítica'. https://www.attacmadrid.org/wp/wp-content/uploads/REFORMA_LABORAL_RD_2012.pdf.

Autonomedia. 1994. *Zapatistas! Documents of the New Mexican Revolution*. New York: Autonomedia.

Autopista Mai. 2018. 'Manifest'. https://autopistamai.org/manifest/.

Babels. 2015. 'Communiqué: Babels ne participera pas au FSM 2015'. *Babels*, available online: http://www.babels.org/spip.php?article565.

Babels. 2016. 'Babels will not participate in WSF 2016: notification letter to IC & OC of WSF 2016'. *Babels*, available online: http://www.babels.org/spip.php?article568.

Babels. n.d. 'Babels founding charter'. *Babels*, available online: www.babels.org/IMG/pdf/charter_en.pdf.

Badiou, Alain. 1999. *El ser y el acontecimiento*. Translated by Raúl Cerdeiras. Buenos Aires: Continuum.

Baker, Mona 2006a. 'Translation and activism. Emerging patterns of narrative community'. *The Massachusetts Review*, 47 (3): 462–484.

Baker, Mona 2006b. *Translation and conflict. A narrative account*. Abingdon: Routledge.

Baker, Mona 2013. 'Translation as an alternative space for political action', *Social Movement Studies*, 12 (1): 23–47.

Baker, Mona (ed.) 2016a. *Translating dissent: Voices from and with the Egyptian revolution*. London: Routledge.

Baker, Mona. 2016b. "Beyond the spectacle: Translation and solidarity in contemporary protest movements". In Mona Baker (ed.), *Translating dissent: Voices from and with the Egyptian revolution*. London and New York: Routledge, 1–18.

Baker, Mona. 2016c. 'The prefigurative politics of translation in place-based movements of protest: Subtitling in the Egyptian revolution'. *The Translator* 22 (1): 1–21.

Baker, Mona. 2018. 'Audiovisual translation and activism'. In Luis Pérez-González (ed.), *The Routledge handbook of audiovisual translation*. Abingdon: Routledge, 453–467.

Baker, Mona, and Blaagaard, Bolette. 2016. 'Reconceptualizing citizen media: A preliminary charting of a complex domain'. In Mona Baker and Bolette Blaagard (eds.), *Citizen media and public spaces. Diverse expressions of citizenship and dissent*. Abingdon: Routledge, 1–22.

Bakunin, Mijail [Facebook username]. 2015. Untitled Photograph. *Facebook*, 5 July. https://www.facebook.com/photo.php?fbid=686575241474111&set=a.204825309649109&type=3&theater.

Balestrini, Nanni, and Moroni, Primo. 2006. 'Los grupos extraparlamentarios'. Chap. 7 in *La horda de oro (1968–1977)*. Madrid: Traficantes de Sueños.

Bango, Estela. 2019. 'Las otras "ingobernables": los espacios autogestionados surgidos con el espíritu del 15M'. *InfoLibre*, 7 October. https://www.infolibre.es/noticias/p

olitica/2019/10/24/espacios_autogestionados_incrementan_desde_15m_las_alterna tivas_politicas_sociales_culturales_99008_1012.html.
Bank of the Commons. 2019. 'Quiénes somos'. https://bankofthecommons.coop/es/quienes-somos/.
Barcelona en Comú. 2015a. 'Un programa en común'. https://barcelonaencomu.cat/es/programa.
Barcelona en Comú. 2015b. 'Programa electoral. Municipals 2015'. https://barcelonaencomu.cat/sites/default/files/programaencomu_cat.pdf.
Barcelona en Comú. 2019. 'Carta de suport internacional'. *Ada 2019*, 18 May. https://ada2019.barcelona/ca/carta-de-suport-internacional.
Barrilero, Irene. 2018. '"Editatona" por una Wikipedia sin ausencias'. *Píkara*, February 2. https://www.pikaramagazine.com/2018/02/editatona-por-una-wikipedia-sin-ausencias/.
Batchelor, Kathryn. 2018. *Translations and paratexts*. Abingdon: Routledge.
Bauman, Zygmunt. 1987. *Legislators and interpreters. On modernity, post-modernity, and intellectuals*. Cambridge: Polity Press.
Bauman, Zygmunt. 2017. *Retrotopia*. Cambridge: Polity Press.
Baumgarten, Britta. 2013. 'Geração à Rasca and beyond: Mobilizations in Portugal after 12 March 2011'. *Current Sociology* 61 (4): 457–473.
Bayón, Edu. 2018. '#CIS: Voto según el nivel de estudios'. *Twitter*, 8 May. https://twitter.com/edubayon_/status/993810229317001216.
Bennett, Karen and Queiroz de Barros, Rita. 2017. 'International English: its current status and implications for translation'. *The Translator*, 23 (4): 363–370.
Berardi, Franco (Bifo). 2011. *After the future*. Edited by Gary Genosko and Nicholas Thoburn. Oakland: AK Press.
Bergès, Karine. 2017. '¡*La revolución será feminista o no será!:* recomposition des féminismes autonomes dans l'espagne en crise des années 2000'. *Nouvelles Questions Féministes*, 36 (1): 16–31.
Bernardos, Gonzalo. 2018. '¿Por qué no existe hoy una burbuja inmobiliaria en España?' *Crónica Global*, May 2018. https://cronicaglobal.elespanol.com/pensamiento/no-existe-hoy-burbuja-inmobiliaria_144728_102.html.
Bértolo, Constantino. 2017. 'El misterio Marx'. In Karl Marx, *Llamando a las puertas de la revolución*. Madrid: Penguin, 17–122.
Blanchar, Clara. 2007. 'Hay que actuar como héroes para tener una vivienda digna'. *El País*, 27 May. https://elpais.com/diario/2007/05/27/catalunya/1180228044_850215.html.
Blanco, Adrián. 2018. "Cs y Podemos captan a los trabajadores; el bipartidismo, a los jubilados". *El Confidencial*, 5 March. https://www.elconfidencial.com/espana/2018-03-05/panelconfidencial-ciudadanos-podemos-trabajadores-activos-bipartidismo-pensionistas-panel_1529734/.
Blumczynski, Piotr. 2016. *Ubiquitous translation*. Abingdon: Routledge.
Bock, Gisela, and Duden, Barbara. 1980. 'Labor of love – Love as labor: On the genesis of housework in capitalism'. In Edith Hoshino Alback (ed.), *From feminism to liberation*. Cambridge: Schenkman Publishing, 153–192.
Boéri, Julie. 2008. 'A narrative account of the Babels vs. Naumann controversy', *The Translator*, 14 (1): 21–50.
Boéri, Julie. 2012). 'Translation/interpreting politics and praxis. The impact of political principles on Babels' interpreting practice'. *The Translator*, 18 (2): 269–290.

Boix Palop, Andrés. 2019. 'Porosidad democrática y crisis constitucional en España'. In Jorge Cagiao and Isabelle Touton (eds.), *España después del 15M*. Madrid: La Catarata, 109–134.
Boletín Oficial del Estado. 2006. 'Ley 39/2006, de 14 de diciembre, de Promoción de la Autonomía Personal y Atención a las personas en situación de dependencia'. *BOE*, 299, 15 December. https://www.boe.es/buscar/act.php?id=BOE-A-2006-21990.
Boletín Oficial del País Vasco. 2017. 'Otras disposiciones'. *Boletín Oficial del País Vasco*, 12 April. https://www.euskadi.eus/y22-bopv/es/bopv2/datos/2017/04/1701888a.shtml.
Bollier, David. 2016. *Pensar desde los comunes* [orig. *Think like a commoner*]. Translated by Guerrilla Translation. Madrid: Traficantes de Sueños.
Bollier, David, and Helfrich, Silke. 2012. 'Introduction: The commons as a transformative vision'. In David Bollier and Silke Helfrich (eds.), *The wealth of the commons. A world beyond market & state*. Amherst: Levellers Press. http://wealthofthecommons.org/essay/introduction-commons-transformative-vision.
Boothman, Derek. 2010. 'Translation and translatability: Renewal of the Marxist paradigm'. In Peter Ives and Rocco Lacorte (eds.), *Gramsci, Language, and Translation*, . Maryland: Lexington Books, 107–133.
Borderías, Cristina, Carrasco, Cristina, and Torns, Teresa. 2019. 'Epílogo'. In Cristina Carrasco, Cristina Borderías and Teresa Torns (eds.), *El trabajo de cuidados. Historia, teoría y políticas*. Second expanded edition. Madrid: La Catarata, 411–437.
Bourdieu, Pierre. 1979. 'Les trois états du capital culturel'. *Actes de la recherche en sciences sociales* 30: 3–6.
Bourdieu, Pierre. 1992. *Les règles de l'art. Genèse et structure du champ littéraire*. Revised edition [1998]. Paris: Éditions du Seuil.
Bourdieu, Pierre. 2002. 'Les conditions sociales de la circulation internationale des idées'. *Actes de la recherche en sciences sociales* 145: 3–8.
Bourdieu, Pierre. 2015. *Los espíritus de estado y otros textos sobre el poder*. No place: Libros del Marrón.
Bravo, David. 2014. 'Occupy Gezi'. *Public Space*. https://www.publicspace.org/works/-/project/h312-occupy-gezi.
Bray, Mark. 2013. *Translating anarchy: The anarchism of Occupy Wall Street*. London: Zero Books.
Brown, Wendy. 2015. *Undoing the demos*. Paperback edition [2017]. Cambridge MA: MIT Press.
Brownlie, Siobhan. 2010. 'Committed approaches and activism in Translation Studies research'. In Yves Gambier and Luc van Doorslaer (eds.), *Handbook of Translation Studies*, Vol. I. Amsterdam, Philadelphia: John Benjamins Publishing Company, 45–48.
Bustinduy, Pablo. 2011. 'Líneas de situación desde Wall Street'. In Matt Taibi (ed.), *Cleptopía. Fabricantes de burbujas y vampiros financieros en la Era de la Estafa*. Madrid: Lengua de Trapo, 9–14.
Bustinduy, Pablo, and Jorge Lago, eds. 2013. *Lugares comunes. Trece voces sobre la crisis*. Madrid: Lengua de Trapo.
Butler, Judith. 2000. 'Competing universalities'. In Judith Butler, Ernesto Laclau and Slavoj Zizek (eds.), *Contingency, hegemony, universality. Contemporary dialogues on the Left*. London: Verso Books, 136–181.
Cabré, María Ángeles. 2015. 'Judith Butler en Barcelona: contra la subordinación'. *El País*, 20 November. https://elpais.com/elpais/2015/11/20/mujeres/1447995720_144799.html.

Bibliography

Caffentzis, George. 2016. 'Commons'. In Kelly Fritsch, Clare O'Connor, and AK Thompson (eds.), *Keywords for radicals. The contested vocabulary of late-capitalist struggle*. Oakland: AK Press, 95–101.

Cagiao, Jorge, and Touton, Isabelle, eds. 2019. *España después del 15M*. Madrid: La Catarata.

Cámara, Julia, and Facet, Laia. 2018. 'Prólogo'. In Cinzia Arruzza and Lidia Cirillo (eds.), *Dos siglos de feminismos*. Translated by Santiago Morán and Andreu Coll. Madrid: Sylone.

Cañada, Ernest. 2018. 'Overtourism: un concepte en construcció'. *Alba Sud*, 5 November. http://www.albasud.org/blog/ca/1070/overtourism-un-concepto-en-construcci-n.

Cañada, Ernest. 2019. 'Trabajo turístico y precariedad'. In Ernest Cañada and Ivan Murray (eds.), *Turistificación global. Perspectivas críticas en turismo*. Barcelona: Icaria, 267–287.

Cañada, Ernest, and Murray, Ivan. 2019. 'Introducción: perspectivas críticas en turismo'. In Ernest Cañada and Ivan Murray (eds.), *Turistificación global. Perspectivas críticas en turismo*. Barcelona: Icaria, 7–34.

Cano, Germán. 2015. *Fuerzas de flaqueza. Nuevas gramáticas políticas*. Madrid: Los Libros de la Catarata.

Capitán Swing. 2019a. 'La editorial'. http://capitanswing.com/editorial/.

Capitán Swing. 2019b. 'Ensayo'. http://capitanswing.com/libros/ensayo/.

Capitán Swing. 2019c. 'En defensa de la vivienda'. https://capitanswing.com/libros/en-defensa-de-la-vivienda/.

Capitán Swing. 2019d. 'Chavs'. https://capitanswing.com/?s=chavs.

Carcelén-Estrada, Antonia. 2018. 'Translation and activism'. In Fruela Fernández and Jonathan Evans (eds.), *The Routledge Handbook of Translation and Politics*. Abingdon: Routledge, 254–269.

Carrasco, Cristina, Borderías, Cristina, and Torns, Teresa. 2011. 'El trabajo de cuidados: antecedentes históricos y debates actuales'. In Cristina Carrasco, Cristina Borderías and Teresa Torns (eds.), *El trabajo de cuidados. Historia, teoría y políticas*. Madrid: La Catarata, 13–95.

Casamajor, Eliseu. 2017. 'L'abracadabra de la sostenibilitat'. *Tot Inclòs*, 4: 10.

Casanova, Pascale. 2002. 'Consécration et accumulation de capital littéraire. La traduction comme échange inégal'. *Actes de la recherche en sciences sociales* 144: 7–20.

Cassin, Barbara. 2004. *Vocabulaire Européen des Philosophies*. Expanded edition [2019]. Paris: Seuil / Le Robert.

Castells, Manuel. 2000. *The Rise of the Network Society*. Cambridge, MA: Blackwell.

Castells, Manuel. 2012. *Networks of outrage and hope: Social movements in the internet age*. Cambridge: Polity.

Casus Belli. 2019. 'Pensamiento'. http://casusbelli-ediciones.com/pensamiento.html.

Ceballos, Antonia. 2019. 'Nous n'avons plus peur: Chronique des mobilisations contre les violences sexuelles en Espagne (2017–2019)'. *Mouvements*, 99: 12–21.

Chen, Gina, Pain, Paromita, and Barner, Briana. 2018. '"Hashtag Feminism": Activism or Slacktivism?'. In Dustin Harp, Jaime Loke and Ingrid Bachmann (eds.), *Feminist approaches to media theory and research*. London: Palgrave Macmillan.

Cheung, Martha. 2010. 'Rethinking activism: The power and dynamics of translation in China during the Late Qing period (1840–1911)'. In Mona Baker, Maeve Olohan and María Calzada Pérez (eds.), *Text and context: Essays on translation and interpreting in honour of Ian Mason*. Manchester: St. Jerome, 237–258.

Cheyfitz, Eric. 1997. *The poetics of imperialism. Translation and colonization from The Tempest to Tarzan*. Expanded edition. Philadelphia: University of Pennsylvania.
Christophers, Brett. 2018. *The new enclosure. The appropriation of public land in neoliberal Britain*. London: Verso.
Cleaver, Harry. 1998. 'The Zapatistas and the electronic fabric of struggle'. *Texas Liberal Arts*. Available online: https://la.utexas.edu/users/hcleaver/zaps.html#29.
ColaBoraBora. 2019a. '¿Qué es ColaBoraBora?'. https://www.colaborabora.org/colaborabora/que-es/.
ColaBoraBora. 2019b. 'Sobre el procomún'. https://www.colaborabora.org/colaborabora/sobre-el-procomun/.
Colau, Ada, and Alemany, Adrià. 2012. *Vides hipotecades. De la bombolla immobiliària al dret a l'habitatge*. Barcelona: Angle.
Colectivo Feministas en Movimiento. 2012. '#29M: Huelga de cuidados'. https://colectivofeministasenmovimiento.wordpress.com/2012/03/24/227/.
Collective authorship. 2019. *Aquí estamos. Puzzle de un momento feminista*. Madrid: Akal.
Comisión de Contenidos. 2017. 'Argumentario'. *Hacia la huelga feminista*, December. http://hacialahuelgafeminista.org/argumentario/.
Comisiones Obreras. 2018. 'Precaripedia'. https://precaritywar.es/precaripedia/.
Contra el diluvio. 2017. 'Contra el diluvio. Cambio climático en red'. *Todo por hacer*, November. https://www.todoporhacer.org/diluvio-cambio-climatico-red/.
Contra el diluvio. 2018. 'Infografía "6 cosas que puedes hacer contra el cambio climático" [Varios idiomas]'. *Contra el diluvio*, May 26. https://contraeldiluvio.es/2018/05/26/infografia-6-cosas-que-puedes-hacer-contra-el-cambio-climatico-varios-idiomas/.
Corpus del Nuevo Diccionario Histórico del Español. 2019. 'procomún'. Corpus del Nuevo Diccionario Histórico del Español.
Corroto, Paula. 2014. 'La editorial Planeta, a la caza del ensayo de izquierdas'. *Eldiario.es*, 21 December. http://www.eldiario.es/cultura/libros/editorial-Planeta-caza-ensayo-marxista_0_335967135.html.
Court, Carl. 2011. 'A poster with the words Tahrir Square'. *Getty Images*, 17 October. http://www.gettyimages.co.uk/pictures/poster-with-the-words-tahrir-square-is-placed-by-protestors-news-photo-129436870.
Crouch, Colin. 2004. *Post-democracy*. Cambridge: Polity Press.
CRUCE. 2011. 'Rancière y el 15M'. *CRUCE*, 21 December. https://crucecontemporaneo.wordpress.com/2011/12/21/ranciere-y-el-15m-dialogo-entre-jose-enrique-ema-y-amador-fdez-savater/.
Cruz, Laura. 2019. 'Desahucios por alquiler, los desahucios más silenciosos'. *El Salto*, 10 June. https://www.elsaltodiario.com/vivienda/desahucios-alquiler-silenciosos-aumentando.
CSC Luis Buñuel. 2019. 'Inicio'. http://centroluisbunuel.org/.
Cué, Carlos, and Díez, Anabel. 2011. 'Zapatero sobre el 15-M: "Hay que escuchar, hay que ser sensibles"'. *El País*, 19 May.
Cul de Sac. 2010a. 'Presentación'. *Cul de Sac* 1: 4–5.
Cul de Sac. 2010b. 'Apuntes para una crítica de la idea de progreso'. *Cul de Sac* 1: 7–21.
Cul de Sac. 2011. 'Editorial'. *Cul de Sac* 2: 5–21.
Cul de Sac. 2016. *15M. Obedecer bajo la forma de rebelión*. Revised and expanded edition. Alicante: El Salmón.
Cul de Sac. 2019. 'Editorial'. *Cul de Sac* 6: 5–21.
Dalla Costa, Mariarosa, and James, Selma. 1975. *The power of women and the subversion of the community*. Bristol: Falling Wall Press.

144 Bibliography

Dardot, Pierre, and Laval, Christian. 2009. *La nouvelle raison du monde*. Paris: La Découverte.
Dardot, Pierre, and Laval, Christian. 2014. *Commun. Essai sur la révolution aux XXe siècle*. Paris: La Découverte.
De Angelis, Massimo. 2012. 'Crises, Capital, and Co-optation: does Capital need a Commons Fix?'. In David Bollier and Silke Helfrich (eds.), *The wealth of the commons. A world beyond market & state*. Amherst: Levellers Press. http://wealthofthecommons.org/essay/crises-capital-and-co-optation-does-capital-need-commons-fix.
De Angelis, Massimo. 2017. *Omnia sunt communia*. London: Zed Books.
De Manuel Jerez, Jesús, López Cortés, Juan, and Brander de la Iglesia, María. 2004. 'Traducción e interpretación, voluntariado y compromiso social', *Puentes*, 4: 65–72.
De Miguel, Ana, and De la Rocha, Marta. 2018. *Historia ilustrada de la teoría feminista*. Santa Cruz de Tenerife: Melusina.
Dean, Jodi. 2017. 'Introduction: the Manifesto of the Communist Party for us'. In Karl Marx and Friedrich Engels, *The Communist Manifesto*. London: Zed Books, 1–46.
Delclós, Carlos. 2015. *Hope is a promise. From the Indignados to the rise of Podemos in Spain*. London: Zed Books.
Della Porta, Donatella (ed.). 2007. *The global justice movement: Cross-national and transnational perspectives*. Boulder: Paradigm Publishers.
Della Porta, Donatella. 2015. *Social Movements in times of austerity*. Cambridge: Polity Press.
Delphy, Christine, and Molinier, Pascale. 2012. 'Genre à la française?'. *Sociologie*, 3 (3): 299–316.
Democracia Real Ya. 2011. 'Propuestas'. In *La rebelión de los indignados. Movimiento 15M: Democracia real, ¡ya!*. Madrid: Editorial Popular, 87–92.
Derrida, Jacques. 1993. *Spectres de Marx: l'état de la dette, le travail du deuil et la nouvelle Internationale*. Paris: Galilée.
Diagonal. 2015. 'Doce razones por las que el Patio Maravillas es importante'. *Diagonal*, 11 June. https://www.diagonalperiodico.net/movimientos/27019-la-importancia-del-patio-maravillas-doce-puntos.html.
Díaz de Quijano, Fernando. 2011. 'Escritura urgente para indignados'. *El Cultural*, 11 July.
Diccionario Elhuyar. 2019. 'auzolan'. *Diccionario Elhuyar*. https://www.euskadi.eus/ab34aElhuyarHiztegiaWar/ab34ahiztegia/auzolan★/E/Heu020144_0.
Díez, Anabel. 2013. 'Ada Colau: "Este señor es un criminal y como tal deberían ustedes tratarlo"'. *El País*, 5 February. https://elpais.com/politica/2013/02/05/actualidad/1360099627_064949.html.
Doerr, Nicole. 2012. 'Translating democracy: how activists in the European Social Forum practice multilingual deliberation'. *European Political Science Review*, 4 (3): 361–384.
Doerr, Nicole. 2018. *Political translation. How social movement democracies survive*. Cambridge: Cambridge University Press.
Domènech, Xavier. 2011. 'Dos lógicas de un movimiento: una lectura del 15-M y sus libros'. *Sin Permiso*, 1 August. http://www.sinpermiso.info/textos/dos-lgicas-de-un-movimiento-una-lectura-del-15-m-y-sus-libros.
Domènech, Xavier. 2016. *Camins per l'hegemonia. Pensant històricament el present i el futur de Catalunya*. Barcelona: Icaria.
Douzinas, Costas. 2013. *Philosophy and resistance in the crisis*. Cambridge: Polity Press.

Durante, Lea. 2004. 'Nazionale-popolare'. In Fabio Frosini and Guido Liguori (eds.), *Le parole di Gramsci*. Rome: Carocci, 150–169.

Dworkin, Dennis. 1997. *Cultural Marxism in postwar Britain. History, the New Left, and the origins of cultural studies*. Durham: Duke University Press.

Echevarría, Ignacio. 2012. 'La CT: un cambio de paradigma'. In Guillem Martínez (ed.), *CT o la Cultura de la Transición. Crítica a 35 años de cultura española*. Barcelona: Mondadori, 25–36.

EFE. 2014. 'Podemos, nuevo proyecto político para "convertir la indignación en cambio"'. *El Mundo*, 17 January. http://www.elmundo.es/espana/2014/01/17/52d92f6e268e3e965b8b4575.html.

EFE. 2015. 'Crean una aplicación con un trivial feminista en euskera'. *El País*, 6 March. https://elpais.com/ccaa/2015/03/06/paisvasco/1425673389_969656.html.

EFE. 2019. 'Más de la mitad del empleo asalariado en España es precario'. *Público*, 20 August. https://www.publico.es/economia/precariedad-mitad-asalariado-espana-precario.html.

El Acebuche. 2019. 'Ediciones El Acebuche Libertario'. *El Acebuche – Ateneo Libertario*. https://ateneoelacebuche.wordpress.com/ediciones-el-acebuche-libertario/.

El País. 2011a. 'Entrevista con Esperanza Aguirre'. *El País*, 16 May.

El País. 2011b. 'El espíritu de la acampada de Sol se reproduce por las ciudades españolas'. *El País*, 20 May. https://elpais.com/elpais/2011/05/20/actualidad/1305879417_850215.html.

El País. 2011c. 'Aznar califica el Movimiento 15-M como "extrema izquierda marginal antisistema"'. *El País*, 16 October. https://elpais.com/politica/2011/10/16/actualidad/1318772866_993949.html.

El País. 2014. 'La cuadratura de los círculos'. *El País*, 25 November. https://elpais.com/politica/2014/11/25/actualidad/1416910135_495498.html.

El Salmón. 2019. 'Ediciones El Salmón'. https://edicioneselsalmon.com/catalogo/ediciones-el-salmon/.

Electomania. 2018. 'La influencia del nivel de estudios en el voto'. *Electomania*, 14 May. http://electomania.es/cisestudios/.

Elorduy, Pablo. 2019. '¿Cómo traducimos gig economy?'. *Twitter*, 25 November. https://twitter.com/pelorduy/status/1198919119988494341.

Embid, Julio. 2016. *Hijos del hormigón. ¿Cómo vivimos en la periferia sur de Madrid?* Barcelona: Edicions Els Llums.

Emmerich, Karen. 2015. 'Greek journalism and literature in days of crisis'. *Huffington Post*, 29 January. http://www.huffingtonpost.com/karen-emmerich/greek-journalism-and-literature_b_6565218.html.

Errejón, Íñigo. 2011a. 'El 15M pateando el tablero'. *GrundMagazine* 1: 14–17.

Errejón, Íñigo. 2011b. 'Evo Pueblo. La hegemonía del MAS'. In Íñigo Errejón and Alfredo Serrano (eds.), *¡Ahora es cuando, carajo! Del asalto a la transformación del Estado en Bolivia*. Madrid: El Viejo Topo, 111–142.

Errejón, Íñigo. 2012. 'La lucha por la hegemonía durante el primer gobierno del MAS en Bolivia (2006–2009): un análisis discursivo'. PhD diss, Universidad Complutense de Madrid.

Errejón, Íñigo. 2013. 'Régimen'. In Pablo Bustinduy and Jorge Lago (eds.), *Lugares comunes. Trece voces sobre la crisis*. Madrid: Lengua de Trapo, 175–196.

Errejón, Íñigo. 2014. 'Muere Ernesto Laclau, teórico de la hegemonía'. *Público*, 14 April. http://www.publico.es/actualidad/muere-ernesto-laclau-teorico-hegemonia.html.

Bibliography

Errejón, Íñigo. 2015a. 'Prólogo'. In Sergio Rizzo and Gian Stella, *La casta. De cómo los políticos se volvieron intocables*. Barcelona: Capitán Swing, 7–9.

Errejón, Íñigo. 2015b. '¿Por qué Podemos? Algunas razones de la remontada'. *Eldiario.es*, 27 November. http://www.eldiario.es/tribunaabierta/Traduciendo-nacional-popular-razones-remontada_6_456764365.html.

Errejón, Íñigo, and Mouffe, Chantal. 2015. *Constuir pueblo. Hegemonía y radicalización de la democracia*. Barcelona: Icaria.

Esquerra Unida i Alternativa. 2015. 'Acte d'En Comú Podem "Trencar amb l'establishment" a Barcelona amb Owen Jones'. http://www.euia.cat/pagina.php?idp=10871.

Estévez, Marina. 2018. 'Si el PSOE no toma medidas valientes, la burbuja del alquiler desembocará en otra burbuja hipotecaria'. *ElDiario.es*, 7 October. https://www.eldiario.es/economia/PSOE-ceja-modelo-vivienda-propiedad_0_820668652.html.

Europa Press. 2011a. 'González Pons vincula a parte de "Democracia Real Ya" con la "extrema izquierda del PSOE"'. *20 Minutos*, 17 May. https://www.20minutos.es/noticia/1052657/0/pons/democraciareal/extrema-izquierda/.

Europa Press. 2011b. 'Cayo Lara recuerda al 15M que debe cumplir la ley y recurrir a las instituciones si quiere cambiarla'. *Europa Press*, 12 May.https://www.europapress.es/nacional/noticia-cayo-lara-recuerda-15m-debe-cumplir-ley-recurrir-instituciones-si-quiere-cambiarla-20150512132042.html.

Evans, Jonathan, and Fernández, Fruela. 2018. 'Introduction: Emancipation, secret histories, and the language of hegemony'. In Fruela Fernández and Jonathan Evans (eds.), *The Routledge handbook of translation and politics*. Abingdon: Routledge.

Even-Zohar, Itamar. 1978. *Papers in historical poetics*. Tel Aviv: The Porter Institute for Poetics and Semiotics.

Even-Zohar, Itamar. 1990a. 'Polysystem theory'. *Poetics Today* 11 (1): 9–26.

Even-Zohar, Itamar. 1990b. 'The position of translated literature within the literary polysystem'. *Poetics Today* 11 (1): 45–51.

Expósito, Marcelo. 2019. *Discursos plebeyos. La toma de la palabra y de las instituciones por la gente común*. Barcelona: Icaria.

Ezquerra, Sandra. 2009. 'Transformar el cuidado para transformar la sociedad y viceversa: reflexiones y propuestas desde un feminismo anticapitalista'. In *Treinta años después: aquí y ahora. Jornadas Feministas Estatales*. Granada: Asamblea de Mujeres de Granada / Federación de Organizaciones Feministas del Estado Español, 733–736.

Federici, Silvia. 2004. *Caliban and the witch: Women, the body and primitive accumulation*. New York: Autonomedia.

Federici, Silvia. 2010. *Calibán y la bruja. Mujeres, cuerpo y acumulación originaria*. Translated by Verónica Hendel and Leopoldo Sebastián Touza. Madrid: Traficantes de Sueños.

Federici, Silvia. 2012. *Revolution at point zero: Housework, reproduction, and feminist struggle*. Oakland and New York: PM Press.

Federici, Silvia. 2017a. 'Economía feminista entre movimientos e instituciones: posibilidades, límites, contradicciones'. In Cristina Carrasco and Carme Díaz (eds.), *Economía feminista*. Barcelona: Entrepueblos, 21–28.

Federici, Silvia. 2017b. 'Capital and Gender'. In Ingo Schmidt and Carlo Fanelli (eds.), *Reading Capital Today: Marx after 150 Years*. London: Pluto Press, 79–96.

Federici, Silvia. 2018. *El patriarcado del salario*. Translated by María Catalán Altuna and Scriptorium. Madrid: Traficantes de Sueños.

Federici, Silvia, and Caffentzis, George. 2019. 'Commons against and beyond capitalism'. In Silvia Federici, *Re-enchanting the World. Feminism and the Politics of the Commons*. Oakland and New York: PM Press/Autonomedia, 85–98.

Feminismos Sol. 2011. 'Comunicado Comisión Feminismos Sol'. *e-mujeres.net*. https://e-mujeres.net/comunicado-comision-feminismos-sol/.
Feminismos Sol. 2012. 'Comando de cuidados'. *Feministas.org*. http://www.feministas.org/IMG/pdf/Comando-de-cuidados.pdf.
Feministes indignades. 2011. 'Intervenció de Feministes Indignades a l'Assemblea de diumenge 29 de maig'. *Feministes indignades*, 31 May. http://feministesindignades.blogspot.com/2011/05/intervencio-de-feministes-indignades.html.
Femprocomuns. 2019. 'Economia del procomú, el joc'. https://femprocomuns.coop/economia-del-procomu-el-joc/.
Feria del Libro Político de Madrid. 2019. 'Ediciones anteriores'. http://feriadellibropoliticodemadrid.org/ediciones-anteriores/.
Fernàndez, Anna, and Miró, Ivan. 2016. *L'economia social i solidària a Barcelona*. Barcelona: La Ciutat Invisible and Ajuntament de Barcelona (Comissionat d'Economia Cooperativa, Social i Solidària). https://www.laciutatinvisible.coop/wp-content/uploads/2016/02/essb_def3.pdf.
Fernández, Fruela. 2017. '"Voy a empeñar la Edad de Oro": Historia, música y política en la crisis española (2011–2016)'. *Romance Quarterly* 64 (3): 135–146.
Fernández, Fruela. 2018. 'Podemos: politics as a "task of translation"'. *Translation Studies* 11 (1): 1–16.
Fernández, Fruela. 2020a. 'Toolbox, tradition, and capital: the many roles of translation in contemporary Spanish politics'. *Translation Studies* 13.
Fernández, Fruela. 2020b. 'Commons'. In *The Routledge encyclopedia of citizen media*. Abingdon: Routledge.
Fernández, Joseba, Sevilla, Carlos, and Urbán, Miguel, coords. 2012. *¡Ocupemos el mundo! Occupy the World!* Barcelona: Icaria.
Fernández, Joseba, Sevilla, Carlos, and Urbán, Miguel, coords. 2013. *De la nueva miseria. La universidad en crisis y la nueva rebelión estudiantil*. Madrid: Akal.
Fernández-Savater, Amador. 2012a. '¿Cómo se organiza un clima?'. *Fuera de Lugar*, 9 January. http://blogs.publico.es/fueradelugar/1438/%C2%BFcomo-se-organiza-un-clima.
Fernández-Savater, Amador. 2012b. 'Olas y espuma. Otros modos de pensar estratégicamente'. *Eldiario.es*, 10 September. https://www.eldiario.es/zonacritica/Olas-espuma-modos-pensar-estrategicamente-15m-25s_6_46255376.html.
Fernández-Savater, Amador. 2013a. *Fuera de lugar. Conversaciones entre crisis y transformación*. Madrid: Acuarela.
Fernández-Savater, Amador. 2013b. 'Fuerza y poder. Reimaginar la revolución'. *Eldiario.es*, 19 July. https://www.eldiario.es/interferencias/Fuerza-poder-Reimaginar-revolucion_6_155444464.html.
Fernández-Savater, Amador. 2019. 'Una disputa antropológica: crisis y movimientos en España, 2008-2017'. In Jorge Cagiao and Isabelle Touton (eds.), *España después del 15M*. Madrid: La Catarata, 21–38.
Fernández-Savater, Amador, and García-Ormaechea, Álvaro. 2011. 'Alain Badiou y el 15-M: "una modificación brutal de la relación entre lo posible y lo imposible"'. *Público*, 24 June. https://blogs.publico.es/fueradelugar/636/alain-badiou-y-el-15-m-una-modificacion-brutal-de-la-relacion-entre-lo-posible-y-lo-imposible.
Fisher, Mark. 2009. *Capitalist realism: Is there no alternative?* Winchester: Zero Books.
Fisher, Mark. 2012. 'What is hauntology?'. *Film Quarterly* 66 (1): 16–24.
Fisher, Mark. 2013. 'The metaphysics of Crackle: Afrofuturism and hauntology'. *Dancecult: Journal of Electronic Dance Music Culture* 5 (2): 42–55.
Fisher, Mark. 2014. *Ghosts of my life*. Winchester: Zero Books.

Bibliography

Flanagan, Mary. 2009. *Critical play: Radical game design*. Cambridge MA: MIT Press.

Flesher Fominaya, Cristina. 2015a. 'Debunking spontaneity: Spain's 15-M/Indignados as autonomous movement'. *Social Movement Studies* 14 (2): 142–163.

Flesher Fominaya, Cristina. 2015b. 'Redefining the crisis/redefining democracy: Mobilizing for the right to housing in Spain's PAH movement'. *South European Society & Politics* 20 (4): 465–485.

Flesher Fominaya, Cristina. 2017. 'European anti-austerity and pro-democracy protests in the wake of the global financial crisis'. *Social Movement Studies* 16 (1): 1–20.

Folbre, Nancy. 1991. 'The unproductive housewife: Her evolution in nineteenth-century economic thought'. *Signs* 16 (3): 463–484.

Fontana, Josep. 2012. 'Prólogo'. In Juan Andrade Blanco, *EL PCE y el PSOE en (la) transición*. Madrid: Siglo XXI, 7–12.

Forgacs, David. 1989. 'Gramsci and Marxism in Britain'. *New Left Review* 176: 70–88.

Forti, Steven, and Russo Spena, Giacomo. 2019. *Ada Colau, la ciudad en común*. Translated by Lucía Martínez Pardo. Barcelona: Icaria.

Fortún, Gloria. 2017. 'Mansplaining'. In Lucas Platero, María Rosón and Esther Ortega (eds.), *Barbarismos queer y otras esdrújulas*. Barcelona: Bellaterra, 288–294.

Foucault, Michel. 1971. 'Nietzsche, la généalogie, l'histoire'. In Michel Foucault. 2001. *Dits et écrits 1, 1954–1975*. Edited by Daniel Defert and François Ewald. Paris: Gallimard, 1004–1024.

Foucault, Michel. 1974. 'Prisons et asiles dans le mécanisme du pouvoir'. In Michel Foucault. 2001. *Dits et Écrits* 1. Edited by Daniel Defert and François Ewald. Paris: Gallimard, 1389–1392.

Foucault, Michel. 2004. *Naissance de la biopolitique. Cours au Collège de France (1978–1979)*. Paris: Seuil/Gallimard.

França, João. 2015. 'El Observatorio DESC, un referente para el nuevo gobierno de Barcelona'. *Eldiario.es*, 5 July. https://www.eldiario.es/catalunya/Observatorio-DESC-referente-gobierno-Barcelona_0_405959777.html.

Fraser, Nancy. 2017. 'Crisis of care? On the social-reproductive contradictions of contemporary capitalism'. In Tithi Bhattacharya (ed.), *Social reproduction theory*. London: Pluto Press, 21–36.

Fritsch, Kelly, O'Connor, Clare, and Thompson, AK. 2016. 'Introduction'. In Kelly Fritsch, ClareO'Connor and AK Thompson (eds.), *Keywords for radicals. The contested vocabulary of late-capitalist struggle*. Oakland: AK Press, 1–21.

Fuentes Vega, Alicia. 2017. *Bienvenido, Mr. Turismo. Cultura visual del boom en España*. Madrid: Cátedra.

Fundación de los Comunes. 2015. 'La Fundación'. https://fundaciondeloscomunes.net/la-fundacion/.

Fundación de los Comunes. 2018. *La crisis sigue. Elementos para un nuevo ciclo político*. Madrid: Traficantes de Sueños.

Fundéu BBVA. 2013. 'gentrificación, neologismo válido en español'. *Fundéu*, 24 April. https://www.fundeu.es/recomendacion/gentrificacion/.

Fundéu BBVA. 2016. 'populismo, palabra del año 2016 para la Fundéu BBVA'. https://www.fundeu.es/recomendacion/populismo-palabra-del-ano-2016-para-la-fundeu-bbva/.

Fundéu BBVA. 2017a. 'turismofobia, neologismo válido'. https://www.fundeu.es/recomendacion/turismofobia-neologismo-valido/.

Fundéu BBVA. 2017b. 'machoexplicación, alternativa a mansplaining'. https://www.fundeu.es/recomendacion/condescendencia-machista-alternativa-a-mansplaining/.

Fundéu BBVA. 2018. '«Nacionalpopulismo», escrita en una sola palabra, es una alternativa válida al anglicismo «alt-right»'. *Twitter*, 11 October. https://mobile.twitter.com/Fundeu/status/1050313571446521856.

Fuster, Mayo, Subirats, Joan, Berlinguer, Marco, Martínez, Rubén, and Salcedo, Jorge. 2015. *Procomún digital y cultural libre*. Barcelona: Icaria.

Gabarre, Manuel. 2019. *Tocar fondo. La mano invisible detrás de la subida del alquiler*. Madrid: Traficantes de Sueños.

Gaber, Sherief. 2016. 'What word is this place? Translating urban social justice and governance'. In Mona Baker (ed.), *Translating dissent: Voices from and with the Egyptian revolution*. London: Routledge, 97–106.

Gago, Verónica, and Cavallero, Luci. 2017. 'Argentina's life-or-death women's movement'. *Jacobin*, 7 March. https://www.jacobinmag.com/2017/03/argentina-ni-una-menos-femicides-women-strike/.

Galcerán, Montserrat. 2012. 'Presencia de los feminismos en la Puerta del Sol madrileña'. *Youkali*, 12: 31–36.

Galegas 8M. 2018. 'Folga de coidados'. *Galegas 8M*. http://galegas8m.gal/folga-de-coidados/.

Garcés, Joan. 2008. *Soberanos e intervenidos: Estrategias globales, americanos y españoles*. Madrid: Siglo XXI.

García Alcalá, Julio Antonio. 2001. *Historia del "Felipe" (FLP, FOC y ESBA): de Julio Cerón a la Liga Comunista Revolucionaria*. Madrid: Centro de Estudios Políticos y Constitucionales.

Gaxie, Daniel. 1977. 'Économie des partis et rétributions du militantisme'. *Revue française de science politique* 27 (1): 123–154.

Genette, Gérard. 1987. *Seuils*. Paris: Éditions du Seuil.

Gerbaudo, Paolo. 2012. *Tweets and the streets. Social media and contemporary activism*. London: Pluto Press.

Gerbaudo, Paolo. 2017. *The mask and the flag. Populism, citizenism and global protest*. London: Hurst.

Gerbaudo, Paolo. 2019. *The digital party. Political organisation and online democracy*. London: Pluto Press.

Gibert, Lluís. 2018. 'Tradueixo. Anem fent autonomisme per garantir una bona pagueta amb l'excusa de trobar consensos per plantejar coses impossibles'. *Twitter*, 16 December. https://mobile.twitter.com/lluisgibert/status/1074230522220560384?p=v.

Gil, Andrés. 2015. 'Qué significa el "Omnia sunt communia!" con el que han prometido el cargo concejales de Carmena'. *Eldiario.es*, 13 June. http://www.eldiario.es/politica/Omnia-communia-investidura-Manuela-Carmena_0_398260311.html.

Gil, Iván. 2015. '"Understanding Podemos", el documento de Pablo Iglesias que devora la City londinense'. *El Confidencial*, 2 June. http://www.elconfidencial.com/espana/2015-06-02/understanding-podemos-el-documento-de-pablo-iglesias-que-devora-la-city-londinense_866070/.

Gil, Javier, and Sequera, Jorge. 2018. 'Expansión de la ciudad turística y nuevas resistencias. El caso de Airbnb en Madrid'. *Empiria. Revista de Metodología de Ciencias Sociales* 41: 15–32.

Gil, Silvia. 2011. *Nuevos feminismos. Sentidos comunes en la dispersión*. Madrid: Traficantes de Sueños.

Gilman-Opalsky, Richard. 2016. *Specters of revolt*. London: Repeater Books.

Gimeno, Beatriz. 2018. 'Le discours contre le néolibéralisme est aujourd'hui très fort dans le mouvement féministe espagnol'. *Mouvements* 94: 118–125.

Bibliography

GOB. 2019. 'Sobre nosaltres. Què és el GOB?'. *GOB Mallorca*. https://www.gobmallorca.com/gob/sobre-nosaltres.

Gómez Ramos, Antonio. 2016. 'Koselleck y la Begriffsgeschichte. Cuando el lenguaje se corta con la historia'. In Reinhart Koselleck. *historia/Historia*. Madrid: Trotta, 9–23.

Goteo. 2016. 'Think Global, Print Local: Pensar desde los comunes'. https://www.goteo.org/project/think-global-print-local.

Goteo. 2017. 'Tot inclòs. Danys i conseqüències del turisme a casa nostra. EL DOCUMENTAL'. https://ca.goteo.org/project/tot-inclos.

Goutsos, Dionysis, and Polymeneas, George. 2017. 'Self-constructed and ascribed identity of the Greek protesters in Syntagma Square'. In Ourania Hatzidaki and Dionysis Goutsos (eds.), *Greece in crisis: Combining critical discourse and corpus linguistics perspectives*. Amsterdam and Philadelphia: John Benjamins, 191–222.

Gramsci, Antonio. 1988. *The Gramsci Reader. Selected Writings 1916–1935*. Edited and translated by David Forgacs. New York: Schocken Books.

Grueso, Stéphane. 2012. 'El 15-M, una rebelión copyleft'. *Público*, 5 May. https://www.publico.es/espana/15-m-rebelion-copyleft.html.

Guedán, Manuel. 2016. *Podemos. Una historia colectiva*. Madrid: Akal.

Guerrilla Translation. 2017. 'Acerca de'. http://www.guerrillatranslation.es/acerca-de/.

Guerrilla Translation. 2019a. 'Our governance model'. https://www.guerrillatranslation.org/our-governance-model/.

Guerrilla Translation. 2019b. 'Our Story and Founding Principles'. https://www.guerrillatranslation.org/the-guerrilla-translation-manifesto.

Guerrilla Translation. 2019c. 'Guerrilla Translation!'. *YouTube*. https://www.youtube.com/channel/UCFz-pDMJjiwo8zX9OSqTO9A.

Guerrilla Translation. 2019d. 'Distributed Cooperative Organization (DisCO) Governance Model V 3.0'. *Guerrilla Media Collective Wiki*. http://wiki.guerrillamediacollective.org/index.php/Distributed_Cooperative_Organization_(DisCO)_Governance_Model_V_3.0#Credit_Estimation.2C_Translation_Value_and_the_Sliding_Scale.

Gunter, Joel. 2011. '"Wherever there was news, we went": Libya's "A-Team" fixers on getting the story out'. *Journalism.co.uk*, 17 November. https://www.journalism.co.uk/news-features/-wherever-there-was-news-we-went–libya-s-a-team-fixers-on-getting-the-story-out/s5/a546770/.

Guo, Ting. 2008. 'Translation and activism: Translators in the Chinese Communist movement in the 1920s–30s'. In Pieter Boulogne (ed.), *Translation and Its Others. Selected Papers of the CETRA Research Seminar in Translation Studies 2007*. Available online: https://www.arts.kuleuven.be/cetra/papers/files/guo.pdf.

Gutiérrez, Bernardo. 2017. *Pasado mañana. Viaje a la España del cambio*. Barcelona: Arpa.

Gutiérrez, Icíar, and Borraz, Marta. 2018. 'Angela Davis visita Madrid: "El racismo siempre ha estado en el centro del fascismo"'. *Eldiario.es*, 24 October. https://www.eldiario.es/desalambre/Angela-Davis-racismo-siempre-fascismo_0_828367470.html.

Gutiérrez, Miren. 2018. *Data Activism and Social Change*. London: Palgrave Macmillan.

Gutiérrez, Raquel, and Salazar Lohman, Huáscar. 2015. 'Reproducción comunitaria de la vida'. *El Apantle* 1: 15–50.

Gutiérrez Aguilar, Raquel. 2019. 'The radical subversion of the world'. In Camille Barbagallo, Nicholas Beuret and David Harvie (eds.), *Commoning*. London: Pluto Press, 39–43.

Hacia la huelga feminista. 2019. 'Puntos de cuidados en la Comunidad de Madrid'. http://hacialahuelgafeminista.org/wp-content/uploads/2019/03/8m_actualizado_el_5m.pdf.

Hands, Joss. 2010. *@ is for activism*. London: Pluto Press.
Harvey, David. 2003. 'The right to the city'. *International Journal of Urban and Regional Research* 27 (4): 939–941.
Harvey, David. 2004. 'The 'new' imperialism: accumulation by dispossession'. *Socialist Register* 40: 63–87.
Harvey, David. 2005. *A brief history of neoliberalism*. Oxford: Oxford University Press.
Harvey, David. 2008. 'El derecho a la ciudad'. *Sinpermiso*, 5 October. http://www.sinpermiso.info/textos/el-derecho-a-la-ciudad.
Harvey, David. 2012. *Rebel cities. From the right to the city to the urban revolution*. London: Verso.
Heilbron, Johan. 1999. 'Toward a sociology of translation: Book translations as a cultural world-system'. *European Journal of Social Theory* 2 (4): 429–444.
Hernández, Esteban. 2018. 'Y luego dicen que por qué fracasa la izquierda'. *El Confidencial*, 28 January. https://blogs.elconfidencial.com/espana/postpolitica/2018-01-28/y-luego-dicen-que-por-que-fracasa-la-izquierda_1512110/.
Herrero, Yayo. 2018. 'Prólogo'. In Janet Biehl, *Las políticas de la ecología social*. Translated by Colectividad Los Arenalejos. Barcelona: Virus, 7–17.
Hessel, Stéphane, and Uría, Lluís. 2013. *¡No os rindáis! Con España, en la trinchera por la libertad y el progreso*. Barcelona: Destino.
Hessel, Stéphane. 2011a. *¡Indignaos!* [orig. *Indignez-vous!*]. Translated by Telmo Moreno. Barcelona: Destino.
Hessel, Stéphane. 2011b. *¡Comprometeos!* [orig. *Engagez-vous!*]. Translated by Rosa Alapont. Barcelona: Destino.
Heyes, Cressida. 2018. 'Identity politics', *The Stanford Encyclopedia of Philosophy*, available online: https://plato.stanford.edu/archives/fall2018/entries/identity-politics/.
Hobsbawm, Eric, and Rudé, George. 1969. *Captain Swing*. London: Lawrence and Wishart.
Hochschild, Arlie. 2000. 'Global care chains and emotional surplus value'. In Anthony Giddens and Will Hutton (eds.), *On the edge: Globalization and the new millennium*. London: Sage Publishers, 130–146.
Hochschild, Arlie, and Machung, Anne. 2012. *The second shift: Working parents and the revolution at home*. Revised and updated edition. London: Penguin.
Horrillo, Patricia. 2019. 'Sobre mí'. *Procesos de cambio*. http://patriciahorrillo.com/sobre-mi/.
Iglesias, Pablo. 2007. 'Las clases peligrosas. La interfaz boliviana en la resistencia global al capitalismo'. In Jesús Espasandín and Pablo Iglesias (eds.), *Bolivia en movimiento. Acción colectiva y poder político*. Barcelona: El Viejo Topo, 259–284.
Iglesias, Pablo. 2008. 'Multitud y acción colectiva postnacional: un estudio comparado de los Desobedientes de Italia a Madrid (2000–2005)'. PhD diss., Universidad Complutense de Madrid.
Iglesias, Pablo. 2011. *Desobedientes. De Chiapas a Madrid*. Madrid: Editorial Popular.
Iglesias, Pablo. 2014. *Disputar la democracia: política para tiempos de crisis*. Madrid: Akal.
Iglesias, Pablo. 2015a. 'Understanding Podemos'. *New Left Review* 93: 7–22. Translated by Fruela Fernández.
Iglesias, Pablo. 2015b. *Politics in a Time of Crisis: Podemos and the Future of European Democracy*. Translated by Lorna Scott Fox. London: Verso.
Iglesias, Pablo. 2016. 'La Política contra la Historia. El maestro Tronti juega en otra liga; la que cura los adanismos (y la tontería)'. *Twitter*, 15 October. https://twitter.com/pablo_iglesias_/status/787325672633032704?lang=es.

152 Bibliography

Iglesias, Pablo. 2017. 'Hobsbawm sobre la necesidad de los historiadores como 'recordadores' profesionales de lo que algunos quieren olvidar (economía y política)'. *Twitter*, 3 January. https://twitter.com/Pa'lo_Iglesias_/status/816244122071822336/photo/1.

Iglesias, Pablo, and Monedero, Juan Carlos. 2011. *¡Que no nos representan! El debate sobre el sistema electoral español*. Madrid: Editorial Popular.

Iglesias, Pablo, and Nega. 2013. *¡Abajo el régimen!* Barcelona: Icaria.

Iglesias-Onofrio, Marcela, Rodrigo-Cano, Daniel, and Benítez-Eyzaguirre, Lucía. 2018. 'Marea Verde y Marea Blanca: nuevas formas de comunicación y acción colectiva'. *Revista Científica de Información y Comunicación*, 15: 193–221.

ILO. 2006. *Freedom of Association: Digest of decisions and principles of the Freedom of Association Committee of the Governing Body of the ILO*. Fifth (revised) edition. Geneva: International Labour Office.

Jakobson, Roman. 1959. 'On linguistic aspects of translation'. In Reuben A. Brower (ed.), *On translation*. Cambridge, MA: Harvard University Press, 232–239.

JM. 2018. 'Tradueixo la part del final: ambdós governs es compromenten a convèncer als seus respectius ciutadans de que cal una reforma de l'Estatut'. *Twitter*, 20 December. https://mobile.twitter.com/JM9barris/status/1075864307345358852?p=v.

Jones, Henry. 2019. 'Searching for statesmanship: a corpus-based analysis of a translated political discourse'. *Polis. The Journal for Ancient Greek and Roman Political Thought*, 36: 216–241.

Jones, Owen. 2012. *Chavs: la demonización de la clase obrera* [orig. *Chavs: the Demonization of the Working Class*]. Translated by Íñigo Jáuregui. Barcelona: Capitán Swing.

Jones, Owen. 2015. *El Establishment. La casta al desnudo*. Translated by Javier Calvo. Barcelona: Seix Barral.

Jorge(r). 2018. 'Os traduzco: EXPLOTACIÓN LABORAL'. *Twitter*, September 4. https://twitter.com/Revanchaa/status/1036972656694845440.

Juliana, Enric. 2015. 'Entre la ira y la reforma; entre Peter Pan y el Estado'. In Pablo Iglesias, *Una nueva Transición. Materiales del año del cambio*. Madrid: Akal, 11–20.

Juliana, Enric, and Palà, Roger. 2017. *Esperant els robots. Mapes i transicions polítiques: algunes idees sobre l'endemà*. Barcelona: Icaria.

Juste de Ancos, Rubén. 2016. 'El último Botín: España, en manos de Blackrock, el gigante silencioso'. *Ctxt*, 9 March. https://ctxt.es/es/20160309/Politica/4697/Botin-Santander-Blackrock-Fink-Ana-Patricia.htm.

Juventud sin Futuro. 2011. *Juventud sin Futuro*. Barcelona: Icaria.

Kadet, Anne. 2011. 'The Occupy Economy'. *Wall Street Journal*, 15 October. http://online.wsj.com/article/SB10001424052970204002304576631084250433462.html.

Karagiannopoulos, Vasileios. 2018. *Living with hacktivism: From conflict to symbiosis*. London: Palgrave Macmillan.

Katakrak. 2019. 'Catálogo'. https://katakrak.net/cas/editorial/catalogo.

Keady, Joseph. 2018. '*Between theory and action: White nationalist narratives of invasion and resistance*'. Paper presented at the international conference La traduzione come atto politico, Università degli Studi di Perugia, 10 May.

Kelly, Christine. 2016. 'Care'. In Kelly Fritsch, Clare O'Connor, and AK Thompson (eds.), *Keywords for radicals. The contested vocabulary of late-capitalist struggle*. Oakland: AK Press, 71–77.

Kioupkiolis, Alexandros, and Giorgos Katsambekis. 2014. 'Introduction'. In Alexandros Kioupkiolis and Giorgos Katsambekis (eds.), *Radical democracy and collective movements today: The biopolitics of the multitude versus the hegemony of the people*. Oxford and New York: Routledge, 8–21.

Kluge, Alexander, and Negt, Oskar. 2015. *En tiempo de amenaza, el camino del medio lleva a la muerte*. No place: Libros del Marrón.

Knibiehler, Yvonne. 2017. *Histoire des mères et de la maternité en Occident*. Paris: Presses Universitaires de France.

Kornetis, Kostis. 2014. '"Is there a Future in this Past?" Analyzing 15M's Intricate Relation to the Transición'. *Journal of Spanish Cultural Studies* 15 (1–2): 83–98.

Koselleck, Reinhart. 2006. 'Crisis'. *Journal of the History of Ideas*, 67 (2): 357–400. Translated by Michaela Richter.

La Haine. 2015. 'Surge el colectivo Libros del Marrón'. *La Haine*, 28 July. https://www.lahaine.org/mm_ss_est_esp.php/surge-el-colectivo-editorial-quot.

La Hidra Cooperativa. 2017. 'La revolución jurídica de los bienes comunes'. http://lahidra.net/la-revolucion-juridica-de-los-bienes-comunes/.

La Ingobernable. 2018a. 'Máster en comunes urbanos'. https://ingobernable.net/2018/05/18/master/.

La Ingobernable. 2018b. 'Imaginando la transición más allá del capital: una conversación con Paul Mason (autor de Postcapitalismo, 2016)'. *La Ingobernable*, https://ingobernable.net/2018/11/16/postcapitalismo/.

La Ingobernable. 2019a. 'Nosotras'. *La Ingobernable*, https://ingobernable.net/nosotras/.

La Ingobernable. 2019b. 'UNEDI'. *La Ingobernable*, https://ingobernable.net/category/unedi/.

La Ingobernable. 2019c. 'Encuentro: Manifiesto de un feminismo para el 99%'. *La Ingobernable*, https://ingobernable.net/2019/03/13/encuentro-manifiesto-de-un-feminismo-para-el-99/.

La Ingobernable. 2019d. '#Hilo Del Ayuntamiento antidesahucios que desalojó #Argumosa11'. *Twitter*, 22 May. https://twitter.com/csingobernable/status/1131233498067607553.

La Ingobernable. 2019e 'Mañana miércoles debatimos con la analista alemana Lisa Vollmer dentro de la gira de presentación del libro "Estrategias contra la gentrificación", de @katakrak54'. *Twitter*, 4 June. https://twitter.com/csingobernable/status/1135799091676368897.

La Lleialtat Santsenca. 2019. 'Inici'. https://www.lleialtat.cat/.

La Oveja Roja2019. 'Catálogo'. http://www.laovejaroja.es/catalogo.htm.

La Tuerka. 2012. 'Violentos y antisistema: ¿quién agita la calle?'. Tele-K, 8 March.

La Tuerka. 2013. '#100Tuerkas'. Canal 33, 26 June.

La Tuerka. 2014. 'Antología de Antonio Gramsci'. PúblicoTV, 27 February.

La Tuerka. 2017a. 'Otra Vuelta de Tuerka – Pablo Iglesias con Anna Gabriel'. PúblicoTV, 9 January.

La Tuerka. 2017b. 'Otra Vuelta de Tuerka – Conversación con Perry Anderson'. *Youtube*. https://www.youtube.com/watch?v=E-VJGyzaSFs.

La Vanguardia. 2011. 'Hessel vende más de 40.000 ejemplares de "¡Indignaos!" en España'. *La Vanguardia*, 27 May. https://www.lavanguardia.com/libros/20110527/54161963607/hessel-vende-mas-de-40-000-ejemplares-de-indignaos-en-espana.html.

La Vanguardia. 2007. 'No tendrás casa en tu puta vida'. *La Vanguardia*, 27 August. https://www.lavanguardia.com/vida/20070829/53389384382/no-tendras-casa-en-tu-puta-vida.html.

La Vanguardia. 2018. 'CCOO lanza un "diccionario" para traducir términos que endulzan precariedad'. *La Vanguardia*, 23 April. https://www.lavanguardia.com/local/sevilla/20180423/442889625547/ccoo-lanza-un-diccionario-para-traducir-terminos-que-endulzan-precariedad.html.

La Vorágine. 2019. 'Qué somos'. https://lavoragine.net/que-somos/.
Labrador, Germán. 2014. '¿Lo llamaban democracia? La crítica estética de la política en la Transición española y el imaginario de la historia en el 15M'. *Kamchatka* 4: 11–61.
Labrador, Germán. 2017. *Culpables por la literatura. Imaginación política y contracultura en la transición española (1968–1986)*. Madrid: Akal.
Laclau, Ernesto. 2005. *On Populist Reason*. London: Verso Books.
Laclau, Ernesto, and Mouffe, Chantal. 1985. *Hegemony and socialist strategy*. London: Verso Books.
Lacol and La Ciutat Invisible. 2018. *Habitar en comunidad. La vivienda cooperativa en cesión de uso*. Madrid: La Catarata.
Lacorte, Rocco. 2010. 'Translatability, language and freedom in Gramsci's Prison Notebooks'. In Peter Ives and Rocco Lacorte (eds.), *Gramsci, language, and translation*. Lanham, MD: Lexington Books, 213–224.
Lebron, Christopher. 2017. *The making of Black Lives Matter: A brief history of an idea*. Oxford: Oxford University Press.
Lengua de Trapo. 2019. 'Colecciones'. https://lenguadetrapo.com/colecciones/.
Lenore, Víctor. 2014. *Indies, hipsters y gafapastas*. Barcelona: Capitán Swing.
León, Carolina. 2019. 'aparte de una sobreabundancia de "libro feminista" que dentro de seis meses no va a recordar nadie y no pasaría el más mínimo filtro de rigor'. *Twitter*, 4 May. https://mobile.twitter.com/carolinkfingers/status/1124745244870938625.
León de Aranoa, Fernando. 2016. *Política. Manual de instrucciones*. Madrid: Reposado Producciones.
Lerner, Gerda. 2017. *La creación del patriarcado*. Translated by Mònica Tussell. Pamplona: Katakrak.
Lerner, Gerda. 2019. *La creación de la conciencia feminista*. Translated by Ivana Palibrk. Pamplona: Katakrak.
Linebaugh, Peter. 2008. *The Magna Carta manifesto*. Berkeley: University of California Press.
Linebaugh, Peter. 2013. *El manifiesto de la Carta Magna. Comunes y libertades para el pueblo*. Translated by Yaiza Hernández and Astor Díaz. Madrid: Traficantes de Sueños.
Linksvayer, Mike. 2012. 'Creative Commons: governing the intellectual commons from below'. In David Bollier and Silke Helfrich (eds.), *The wealth of the commons. A world beyond market & state*. Amherst: Levellers Press. http://wealthofthecommons.org/essay/creative-commons-governing-intellectual-commons-below.
Llaneras, Kiko. 2016. 'El CIS evidencia la brecha entre votantes de nuevos y viejos partidos'. *El Español*, 8 May. http://www.elespanol.com/espana/20160507/122987812_0.html.
López, Isidro. 2016. 'Tras el 26J, ¿hacia dónde va Podemos?' *Contraparte*, 28 June. http://blogs.publico.es/contraparte/2016/06/28/tras-el-26j-hacia-donde-va-podemos/.
López, Isidro. 2019. 'Nadia al volante: hacia un nuevo suicidio de la izquierda'. *El Salto*, 17 December. https://www.elsaltodiario.com/opinion/nadia-al-volante-hacia-un-nuevo-suicidio-de-la-izquierda.
López, Isidro, and Rodríguez, Emmanuel. 2011. 'The Spanish model'. *New Left Review* 69: 5–29.
López Alós, Javier. 2017. 'El debate sobre el populismo en España (2014–2017). Un estado de la cuestión'. *Pensamiento al margen* 7: 146–177.
Lopez de Etxezaharreta, Garazi, and Gonzalez Ruiz de Larramendi, Iñigo. 2011. 'Auzolan y Batzarre, ¿bases para la democracia del siglo XXI en Euskal Herria?'.

Nabarralde, 22 March. https://nabarralde.eus/auzolan-y-batzarre-ibases-para-la-democracia-del-siglo-xxi-en-euskal-herria/.
López-Terra, Federico. 2017. 'Spain's freedom of speech repression is no joke'. *The Conversation*, 13 April. https://theconversation.com/spains-freedom-of-speech-repression-is-no-joke-75889.
Madison, Michael, Frischmann, Brett, and Strandburg, Katherine. 2019. 'Knowledge commons'. In Blake Hudson, Jonathan Rosenbloom and Dan Cole (eds.), *Routledge handbook of the study of the commons*. Abingdon: Routledge, 76–90.
Madrilonia. 2011. *La Carta de los Comunes*. Madrid: Traficantes de Sueños.
Maeckelbergh, Marianne. 2011. 'Doing is believing: Prefiguration as strategic practice in the alterglobalization movement'. *Social Movement Studies* 10 (1): 1–20.
Malets, Olga, and Zajak, Sabrina. 2014. 'Moving culture: Transnational social movement organizations as translators in a diffusion cycle'. In Britta Baumgarten, Priska Daphi, and Peter Ullrich (eds.), *Conceptualizing culture in social movement research*. London: Palgrave, 251–274.
Manetto, Francesco. 2015. 'Pablo Iglesias: "Temo que Don Winslow me distraiga en campaña"'.10*El País*, December. http://cultura.elpais.com/cultura/2015/12/04/babelia/1449254582_923051.html.
Manifestolibri. 2018. *#quellavoltache. Storie di molestie*. Rome: La Talpa.
Manifiesto ILP. 2011. 'Contra la condena hipotecaria, por el derecho a la vivienda'. Deleted site, archived under https://web.archive.org/web/20120310045229/http://www.quenotehipotequenlavida.org/?page_id=34.
Marcos, Laura. 2018. 'Comment'. *Facebook*, 20 December. https://www.facebook.com/groups/225313300642/permalink/10162203855485643/.
Marías, Javier. 2018. 'Palabras que me impiden seguir leyendo'. *El País Semanal*, 16 October. https://elpais.com/elpais/2018/12/10/eps/1544456326_569657.html.
Mariátegui, José Carlos. 1928. 'Aniversario y balance'. *Amauta* 17: 1–2.
Martin, Brian. 2007. 'Activism, Social and Political'. In Gary L. Anderson and Kathryn G. Herr (eds.), *Encyclopedia of activism and social justice*, vol. 1. Thousand Oaks/London: SAGE, 19–27.
Martínez, Guillem. 2012. 'El concepto CT'. In Guillem Martínez (ed.), *CT o la Cultura de la Transición. Crítica a 35 años de cultura española*. Barcelona: Mondadori, 13–23.
Martínez, Guillem. 2016. *La gran ilusión. Mito y realidad del proceso indepe*. Barcelona: Debate.
Martínez, Guillem. 2017a. 'Procesando el Proceso (I)'. *Ctxt*, 23 February. https://ctxt.es/es/20170222/Politica/11299/Catalu%C3%B1a-proces-mas-puigdemont-referendum-soberanismo.htm.
Martínez, Guillem. 2017b. 'Black friday de reforma constitucional'. *Ctxt*, 28 November. https://ctxt.es/es/20171122/Politica/16380/proces-gobierno-catalunya-elecciones-155.htm.
Martínez, Ion. 2017. 'Más allá de la ciudad. El derecho a la vida urbana'. In Henri Lefebvre, *El derecho a la ciudad*. Madrid: Capitán Swing, 7–13.
Martínez, Laura. 2018. 'Te vendes en el mercado laboral, te vendes en el matrimonial, o te vendes en la calle con tu cuerpo, ¿acaso la vagina es sagrada?' *Eldiario.es*, 1 December. https://www.eldiario.es/cv/femilenial/Entrevista-Silvia-Federici_6_841025916.html.
Martínez López, Gladys, and Elorduy, Pablo. 2017. 'Pablo Iglesias: "Cometeríamos un error si pensáramos que nos tenemos que parecer al PSOE"'. *El Salto*, 21 May. https://www.elsaltodiario.com/podemos/cometeriamos-un-error-si-pensaramos-que-para-atraer-a-descontentos-con-el-psoe-nos-tenemos-que-parecer-al-psoe.

Marx, Karl. 1867. *Capital. A Critique of Political Economy.* Volume I. Translated by Samuel Moore and Edvard Aveling [1867]. Marxists Internet Archive. https://www.marxists.org/archive/marx/works/1867-c1/.

Mattei, Ugo. 2013. *Bienes comunes. Un manifiesto.* Translated by Gerardo Pisarello. Barcelona: Trotta.

Medina, Miguel Ángel. 2018. 'Los fondos buitre nos están agrediendo de forma salvaje'. *El País*, 17 September. https://elpais.com/ccaa/2018/09/16/madrid/1537117776_968961.html.

Mehrez, Samia (ed.). 2012. *Translating Egypt's revolution: the language of Tahrir.* Cairo: American University Press.

Meiksins Wood, Ellen. 1986. *The retreat from class. A new 'true' socialism.* London: Verso Books.

Meiksins Wood, Ellen. 2017. *The origin of capitalism.* London: Verso.

Miguel, Luna. 2019. 'El reto viral definitivo: únete al #AliadoChallenge'. *Eldiario.es*, 20 January. https://www.eldiario.es/zonacritica/reto-viral-definitivo-unete-AliadoChallenge_6_858874113.html.

Milano, Claudio, and Mansilla, José. 2019. 'La cuestión turística: el activismo turístico y la turistificación de los movimientos sociales'. In Ernest Cañada and Ivan Murray (eds.), *Turistificación global. Perspectivas críticas en turismo.* Barcelona: Icaria, 367–380.

Milano, Claudio, Novelli, Marina, and Cheer, Joseph. 2019. 'Overtourism and degrowth: a social movements perspective'. *Journal of Sustainable Tourism* 27 (12): 1857–1875.

Mills, Jane. 1989. *Womanwords: A vocabulary of culture and patriarchal society.* London: Longman.

Milton, John. 2006. 'The resistant political translations of Monteiro Lobato'. *The Massachusetts Review*, 47 (3): 486–509.

Mir García, Jordi. 2013. 'Hessel, la indignación y el 15M'. *Público*, 27 February. http://www.publico.es/actualidad/hessel-indignacion-y-15m.html.

Mogo Castro, Cristian. 2018. 'Alquiler: ¿problema o burbuja?' *El Salto*, 8 May. https://www.elsaltodiario.com/tribuna/alquiler-problema-o-burbuja-pah.

Monedero, Juan Carlos. 2011. *La Transición contada a nuestros padres.* Madrid: Los Libros de la Catarata.

Montero, Justa. 2009. 'Granada, treinta años después, aquí y ahora'. In *Treinta años después: aquí y ahora. Jornadas Feministas Estatales.* Granada: Asamblea de Mujeres de Granada/Federación de Organizaciones Feministas del Estado Español, 877–879.

Monterroso, Iliana, Cronkleton, Peter, and Larson, Anne. 2019. 'Commons, indigenous rights, and governance'. In Blake Hudson, Jonathan Rosenbloom and Dan Cole (eds.), *Routledge Handbook of the Study of the Commons.* Abingdon: Routledge, 376–391.

Mora, Miguel, Gallego Díaz, Soledad, and Rivero, Jacobo. 2015. 'Íñigo Errejón: La campaña de infamias y de acoso va a ir a más'. *Ctxt*, 15 January. http://ctxt.es/es/20150115/politica/92/Entrevista-%C3%8D%C3%B1igo-Errej%C3%B3n-Mujica-Constituci%C3%B3n-Maduro.htm.

Moreno, Lara. 2019. 'Hola, a 2 de junio, en Carabanchel bajo, barriobajero, estando presentes @rubiodemarzo, @gabrielawiener, @JairoExtre, @PeioHR, decidimos que vamos a dejar de hablar de mansplaining y empezar a hablar de #macholección'. Twitter, 2 June. https://twitter.com/lara_morenom/status/1135238875876679680.

Moreno-Caballud, Luis. 2015. *Cultures of anyone: Studies on cultural democratization in the Spanish neoliberal crisis.* Translated by Linda Grabner. Liverpool: Liverpool University Press.

Moreno Pestaña, José Luis. 2019. *Retorno a Atenas. La democracia como principio antioligárquico*. Madrid: Siglo XXI.
Morozov, Evgeny. 2013. *To Save Everything, Click Here: The Folly of Technological Solutionism*. New York: Public Affairs.
Mouffe, Chantal. 2018. *For a left populism*. London: Verso Books.
Mowbray, Mike. 2010. 'Blogging the Greek riots: between aftermath and ongoing engagement'. *The Resistance Studies Magazine* 1: 4–15.
Mudde, Cas, and Rovira Kaltwasser, Cristóbal. 2019. *Populismo: una breve introducción*. Translated by María Enguix. Madrid: Alianza.
Muller, Sandra. 2017. 'La journaliste Sandra Muller revient sur le phénomène #balancetonporc qu'elle a lancé'. *Le Monde*, 30 December. https://www.lemonde.fr/idees/article/2017/12/30/sandra-muller-la-blague-lourdingue-cet-argument-qui-excuse-tout_5235930_3232.html.
Munar, Pere. 2017. *Salvem Sa Dragonera. Història dels ecologismes a Mallorca*. Palma: Illa Edicions.
Munárriz, Ángel. 2019. 'Miguel Urbán: "Decir que haciendo políticas sociales junto al PSOE se frena a la extrema derecha es propaganda"'. *InfoLibre*, 2 December. https://www.infolibre.es/noticias/politica/2019/11/29/miguel_urban_decir_que_con_politicas_sociales_con_psoe_frena_extrema_derecha_propaganda_101459_1012.html
Murray, Ivan. 2015. *Capitalismo y turismo en España. Del "milagro económico" a la "gran crisis"*. Translated by Macià Blàzquez. Barcelona: Alba Sud.
N'Asturies Podemos. 2016. 'Los nuevos desafíos de la Europa del cambio'. https://asturias.podemos.info/portfolio/los-nuevos-desafios-la-europa-del-cambio-brexit-la-troika/.
Negri, Antonio, and Michael Hardt. 2009. *Commonwealth*. Cambridge, MA: Harvard University Press.
Negri, Antonio, and Michael Hardt. 2017. *Assembly*. Cambridge, MA: Harvard University Press.
Neilson, Brett. 2009. 'Opening translation'. *Transeuropéennes*, November 5. http://www.transeuropeennes.org/en/articles/107/Opening_translation.html.
Nergaard, Siri, and Arduini, Stefano. 2011. 'Translation: A new paradigm'. *Translation* 0: 8–17.
Nez, Heloïse. 2016. '"We must register a victory to continue fighting". Locating the action of the Indignados in Madrid'. In Marcos Ancelovici, Pascale Dufour, and Heloïse Nez (eds.), *Street politics in the age of austerity. From the Indignados to Occupy*. Amsterdam: Amsterdam University Press, 121–145.
NH3 and Grumer. 2017. 'Benvingut turisme insostenible'. *Tot Inclòs* 4: 12–13.
Nociones Comunes. 2013. 'Los comunes urbanos'. *Traficantes de Sueños*, March. https://www.traficantes.net/nociones-comunes/los-comunes-urbanos.
Nociones Comunes. 2018. 'Movimiento #HaciaLaHuelgaFeminista-S3-¿Dónde están los movimientos?' *Soundcloud*. https://soundcloud.com/fundaciondeloscomunes/donde-estan-los-movimientos-s3-movimiento-hacialahuelgafeminista.
Noël, Sophie. 2012. *L'édition indépendante critique. Engagements politiques et intellectuels*. Paris: Presses de l'ENSSIB.
Observatori DESC. 2008. '10 d'octubre. Jornades: El dret a l'habitatge i a la ciutat en el marc de la crisi. Un debat pendent'. *Observatori DESC*, October. https://observatoridesc.org/ca/10-doctubre-jornades-dret-lhabitatge-i-ciutat-marc-crisi-debat-pendent.
Observatorio da Mariña pola Igualdade. 2013. 'Trivial Feminista do Observatorio da Mariña pola Igualdade'. http://observatorioigualdade.org/2013/04/16/trivial-feminista-do-observatorio-da-marina-pola-igualdade-3/.

158 Bibliography

Observatorio Metropolitano de Madrid. 2015. 'Introducción'. In Observatorio Metropolitano de Madrid (ed.), *El mercado contra la ciudad. Sobre globalización, gentrificación y políticas urbanas*. Collective translation. Madrid: Traficantes de Sueños.

Oliveres, Arcadi. 2011. *Les veus de les places*. Barcelona: Icaria.

Oneto, José. 2015. 'Pablo Iglesias se quiere comer a Pedro Sánchez'. *República de las Ideas*, 3 June. http://www.republica.com/viva-la-pepa/2015/06/03/pablo-iglesias-se-quiere-comer-a-pedro-sanchez/.

Ortiz, Ana María. 2016. 'Del "no fui al 15M" de Pablo Iglesias al "fue una pocilga" de Esperanza Aguirre'. *El Mundo*, 8 May. https://www.elmundo.es/papel/historias/2016/05/08/572c8937ca4741dd208b4624.html.

Ostrom, Elinor. 1990. *Governing the commons: The evolution of institutions for collective action*. Cambridge, UK: Cambridge University Press.

P2P Foundation. 2019. 'About'. https://p2pfoundation.net/the-p2p-foundation/about-the-p2p-foundation.

PAH. 2011a. 'PSOE y PP declaran la guerra a l@s ciudadan@s afectad@s por las hipotecas!'. *PAH*, 23 February. https://afectadosporlahipoteca.com/2011/02/23/psoe-y-pp-declaran-la-guerra-a-los-ciudadanos-afectados-por-las-hipotecas/.

PAH. 2011b. 'Menos comisión y más democracia real'. *PAH*, July. https://afectadosporlahipoteca.files.wordpress.com/2011/07/texto-pah-comisic3b3n-congreso.pdf.

PAH. 2011c. 'Elecciones #20N: PSOE y PP en contra de l@s hipotecad@s y desahuciad@s #NoLesVotes'. *PAH*, 18 November. https://afectadosporlahipoteca.com/2011/11/18/elecciones-20n-psoe-y-pp-en-contra-de-ls-hipotecads-y-desahuciads-nolesvotes/.

PAH. 2012. 'Lo llaman Crisis, pero es una estafa. Lo llaman Suicidio, pero es #GenocidioFinanciero La PAH convoca'. *PAH*, 25 October. https://afectadosporlahipoteca.com/2012/10/25/lo-llaman-crisispero-es-una-estafa-lo-llaman-suicidio-pero-es-genocidiofinanciero-la-pah-convoca/.

PAH Barcelona. 2016. '@profdavidharvey Hoy viene a conocer @LA_PAH para intercambiar experiencias sobre el derecho a la ciudad y movimientos sociales. ¡Gracias!'. *Twitter*, 14 November. https://twitter.com/PAH_BCN/status/798166594589511680.

PAH Barcelona. 2018. 'Presentación del informe «Radiografías de la situación del derecho a la vivienda, la pobreza energética y su impacto en la salud en Barcelona»'. *PAH BCN*, 10 April. https://pahbarcelona.org/presentacion-del-informe-radiografias-de-la-situacion-del-derecho-a-la-vivienda-la-pobreza-energetica-y-su-impacto-en-la-salud-en-barcelona/.

PAHC Sabadell. 2014. 'Les imprescindibles (article d'Oriol Sorolla, membre de la PAHC de Sabadell)'. *PAHC*, 13 November. http://www.afectatscrisisabadell.cat/2014/11/les-imprescindibles-article-doriol-sorolla-membre-de-la-pahc-de-sabadell/.

Pallicer, Antoni, and Blàzquez, Macià. 2017. 'Turismo y caciquismo hotelero en las Baleares. La publicación Tot Inclòs y la quiebra del consenso social'. *Ecología Política* 52: 88–92.

Palomera, Jaime. 2018. 'Prólogo'. In David Madden and Peter Marcuse, *En defensa de la vivienda*. Translated by Violeta Arranz. Madrid: Capitán Swing, 11–20.

Partido Comunista de los Pueblos de España. 2011. 'Declaración del CE del PCPE sobre las movilizaciones iniciadas el 15 M'. *PCPE*, 19 May. https://www.pcpe.es/index.php/comite-central/item/268-sobre-las-movilizaciones-iniciadas-el-15-m.

Pellizzetti, Pierfranco. 2019. *El fracaso de la indignación. Del malestar al conflicto*. Translated by Alejandro Pradera. Madrid: Alianza Editorial.

Pepitas de Calabaza. 2019. 'Ensayo'. http://www.pepitas.net/catalogo/ensayo.

Pérez-González, Luis. 2010. '"Ad-hocracies" of translation activism in the blogosphere: A genealogical case study'. In Mona Baker, Maeve Olohan and María Calzada Pérez (eds.), *Text and context: Essays on translation and interpreting in honour of Ian Mason*. Manchester: St. Jerome, 259–287.

Pérez-González, Luis. 2016. 'The politics of affect in activist amateur subtitling: a biopolitical perspective'. In Mona Baker and Bolette Blaagaard (eds.), *Citizen media and public spaces: Diverse expressions of citizenship and dissent*. London: Routledge, 118–135.

Pérez Orozco, Amaia. 2009. 'Feminismo anticapitalista, esa Escandalosa Cosa y otros palabros'. In *Treinta años después: aquí y ahora. Jornadas Feministas Estatales*. Granada: Asamblea de Mujeres de Granada/Federación de Organizaciones Feministas del Estado Español, 713–720.

Pieterse, Jan. 2009. *Globalization and culture: Global melange*. Lanham MD: Rowman & Littlefield Publishing Group.

Piketty, Thomas. 2018. 'Brahmin left vs merchant right: Rising inequality & the changing structure of political conflict'. World Inequality Database, Working Paper Series, March.

Pillow, Wanda. 2003. '"Bodies are dangerous": using feminist genealogy as policy studies methodology'. *Journal of Education Policy* 18 (2): 145–159.

Piróth, Attila, and Baker, Mona. 2019. 'The ethics of volunteerism in translation. Translators without borders and the platform economy'. *Attila Piróth's website*, October. http://www.pirothattila.com/Piroth-Baker_The_Ethics_of_Volunteerism_in_Translation.pdf.

Platero, Lucas, María Rosón, and Esther Ortega. 2017. 'Introducción'. In Lucas Platero, María Rosón and Esther Ortega (eds.), *Barbarismos queer y otras esdrújulas*. Barcelona: Bellaterra, 9–18.

Postico, Daniel. 2016. 'Owen Jones, gurú británico de Podemos: 'Venezuela está en un estado horrible''. *El Español*, 1 June. http://www.elespanol.com/mundo/20160531/128987433_0.html.

Pouly, Marie-Pierre. 2017. 'Formations of Class and Gender/Des femmes respectables. Remarques sur la traduction en sciences sociales'. *Biens symboliques/Symbolic Goods*, 1. https://revue.biens-symboliques.net/119.

Prádanos, Luís. 2018. *Postgrowth imaginaries. New ecologies and counterhegemonic culture in post-2008 Spain*. Liverpool: Liverpool University Press.

Prentoulis, Marina, and Thomassen, Lasse. 2013. 'Autonomy and hegemony in the squares: the 2011 protests in Greece and Spain'. In Alexandros Kioupkiolis and Giorgos Katsambekis (eds.), *Radical democracy and collective movements today: The biopolitics of the multitude versus the hegemony of the people*. Abingdon: Routledge, 193–212.

Público. 2017. 'La conferencia del filósofo Zizek que colapsó el Círculo de Bellas Artes'. *Público*, 29 June. https://www.publico.es/culturas/conferencia-filosofo-zizek-colapso-circulo-bellas-artes.html.

Puche, Paco. 2015. *El gobierno y uso de los bienes comunes según Elinor Ostrom*. Málaga: Ediciones del Genal/El Acebuche Libertario.

Quaglieri, Alan, and Sánchez, Sheila. 2019. 'Alojamiento turístico y "economía colaborativa": una revisión crítica'. In Ernest Cañada and Ivan Murray (eds.), *Turistificación global. Perspectivas críticas en turismo*. Barcelona: Icaria, 343–365.

Ramis, Margalida. 2017. 'NO Limits. El miratge del creixement illimitat'. *Tot Inclòs*, 4: 18.

Rancière, Jacques. 1996. *El desacuerdo* [orig. *La mésentente*]. Translated by Horacio Pons. Buenos Aires: Nueva Visión.

Rancière, Jacques. 2009. *The emancipated spectator*. Translated by Gregory Elliott. London: Verso Books.
Ranea, Beatriz. 2019. *Feminismos. Antología de textos feministas para uso de las generaciones más jóvenes, y de las que no lo son tanto*. Madrid: La Catarata.
Razquin, Adriana. 2017. *Didáctica ciudadana: la vida política en las plazas. Etnografía del movimiento 15M*. Granada: Universidad de Granada.
Reitan, Ruth. 2007. *Global activism*. Abingdon: Routledge.
Rendueles, César. 2013. *Sociofobia. El cambio político en la era de la utopía digital*. Barcelona: Capitán Swing.
Rendueles, César. 2016. 'Las ideas del nuevo milenio'. *El País*, 18 June. http://cultura.elpais.com/cultura/2016/06/16/babelia/1466077843_289600.html.
Rendueles, César, and Sola, Jorge. 2015. 'Podemos and the paradigm shift'. *Jacobin*, 13 April. https://www.jacobinmag.com/2015/04/podemos-spain-pablo-iglesias-european-left/.
Ritzen, Yarno. 2018. 'Rising internet shutdowns aimed at silencing dissent'. *Al Jazeera*, 29 January. https://www.aljazeera.com/news/2018/01/rising-internet-shutdowns-aimed-silencing-dissent-180128202743672.html.
Rivero, Ángel, Zarzalejos, Javier, and del Palacio, Jorge. 2018. *Geografía del populismo*. Madrid: Tecnos.
Rivero, Jacobo. 2014. *Conversación con Pablo Iglesias*. Madrid: Turpial.
Rivero, Jacobo. 2015. *Podemos. Objetivo: asaltar los cielos*. Barcelona: Planeta.
Rizzo, Sergio, and Stella, Gian. 2015. *La casta. De cómo los políticos se volvieron intocables*. Translated by Martín López Vega. Barcelona: Capitán Swing.
Rodríguez, Emmanuel. 2015. *Por qué fracasó la democracia en España. La Transición y el régimen de '78*. Madrid: Traficantes de Sueños.
Rodríguez, Emmanuel. 2016. *La política en el ocaso de la clase media. El ciclo 15M-Podemos*. Madrid: Traficantes de Sueños.
Rodríguez, Emmanuel, and López, Isidro. 2016. 'El utopismo liberal no ha sido vencido. Leer a Polanyi hoy'. In Karl Polanyi, *La gran transformación. Crítica del liberalismo económico*. Barcelona: Virus, 9–19.
Roggeband, Conny. 2007. 'Translators and transformers: International inspiration and exchange in social movements'. *Social Movement Studies* 6 (3): 245–259.
Romanos, Eduardo. 2016. 'De Tahrir a Wall Street por la Puerta del Sol: la difusión transnacional de los movimientos sociales en perspectiva comparada'. *Revista Española de Investigaciones Sociológicas* 154: 103–118.
Romanos, Eduardo. 2018. 'Immigrants as brokers: dialogical diffusion from Spanish indignados to Occupy Wall Street'. *Social Movements Studies* 15 (3): 247–262.
Romero, Ricardo, and Tirado, Arantxa. 2016. *La clase obrera no va al paraíso*. Madrid: Akal.
Roy, Arundhati. 2011. *Walking with the comrades*. London and New York: Penguin.
Rubio-Pueyo, Vicente. 2017. *Municipalism in Spain. From Barcelona to Madrid, and beyond*. New York: Rosa Luxemburg Foundation.
Ruiz Marull, David. 2016. 'Cómo explicar a un intelectual inglés la grave crisis interna del PSOE'. *La Vanguardia*, 29 September. http://www.lavanguardia.com/politica/20160929/41661561035/owen-jones-crisis-psoe-pedro-sanchez.html.
Sainz Borgo, Karina. 2015. 'Pablo Iglesias no para de hablar, ni siquiera en inglés: Verso Books lo lleva fuera de España'. *Vozpópuli*, 13 July. http://www.vozpopuli.com/cultura/Ensayos-Podemos-Pablo_Iglesias-Verso_Books-Politics_in_a_time_of_crisis-_Podemos_and_the_Future_of_Democracy_in_Europe_0_824617551.html.

Sánchez, Juan Luis. n.d. 'Los primeros 40 de Sol'. *Periodismo humano*. https://periodismohumano.com/temas-destacados/los-primeros-40-de-sol.html.

Sánchez, Juan Luis. 2018. 'De la pancarta arrancada del 15M a la victoria política del 8M'. *Eldiario.es*, 10 March. https://www.eldiario.es/juanlusanchez/pancarta-arrancada-victoria-politica_6_748635145.html.

Sánchez Cedillo, Raúl. 2011. 'El 15m como insurrección del cuerpo máquina'. In *Democracia distribuida. Miradas de la Universidad Nómada al 15M*, 49–65. Trasversales, October 7. http://www.trasversales.net/ddun15m.pdf.

Sangre Fucsia. 2017. 'Un año después de Feminismos Reunidos: reimpresión y reflexión'. *Sangre Fucsia*, 12 December. https://sangrefucsia.wordpress.com/2017/12/12/reimpresion-feminismos-reunidos/.

Sangre Fucsia. 2019a. 'Nosotras'. *Sangre Fucsia*. https://sangrefucsia.wordpress.com/about/.

Sangre Fucsia. 2019b. 'Sangre Fucsia'. *Ivoox*. https://www.ivoox.com/podcast-podcast-sangre-fucsia_sq_f162460_1.html.

Santos, Boaventura de Sousa. 2006. *The rise of the global left: The World Social Forum and beyond*. London: Zed Books.

Sapiro, Gisèle. 2009a. 'Mondialisation et diversité culturelle: les enjeux de la circulation transnationale des livres'. In Gisèle Sapiro (ed.), *Les contradictions de la globalisation éditoriale*. Paris: Nouveau Monde, 275–301.

Sapiro, Gisèle. 2009b. 'Modèles d'intervention politique des intellectuels. Le cas français'. *Actes de la recherche en sciences sociales* 176–177: 8–31.

Schavelzon, Salvador. 2015. 'La formación de Podemos: Sudamérica, populismo postcolonial y hegemonía flexible'. *Rebelión*, 24 December. http://www.rebelion.org/docs/207136.pdf.

Selim, Samah. 2016. 'Text and context: translating in a state of emergency'. In Mona Baker (ed.), *Translating Dissent: Voices from and with the Egyptian revolution*. London and New York: Routledge, 77–87.

Senda de cuidados. 2018. 'Newsletter de abril'. https://tinyurl.com/yffvsly6.

Serry, Hervé. 2002. 'Constituer un catalogue littéraire. La place des traductions dans l'histoire des Éditions du Seuil'. *Actes de la recherche en sciences sociales* 144: 70–79.

Sharma, Sarah. 2014. 'Because the night belongs to lovers: Occupying the time of precarity', *Communication and Critical/Cultural Studies* 11 (1): 5–14.

Shirley, Sheryl. 2001). 'Zapatista organizing in cyberspace: Winning hearts and minds?'. *Latin American Studies Association*, http://lasa.international.pitt.edu/Lasa2001/ShirleySheryl.pdf.

Shubert, Adrian. 1987. *The road to revolution in Spain: The coal miners of Asturias, 1860–1934*. Champaign: University of Illinois Press.

Siglo XXI. 2019. 'Historia'. https://www.sigloxxieditores.com/coleccion/historia/.

Simó Comas, Marta. 2015. 'Conciencia democrática e industria editorial en los primeros años de la Transición española: la *Biblioteca de divulgación política*'. *Amnis* 14. http://amnis.revues.org/2634.

Simón, Pablo. 2012. 'La Constitución de 1978 y la crisis del régimen'. *Politikon*, 9 December. http://politikon.es/2012/12/09/la-constitucion-de-1978-y-la-crisis-del-regimen/.

Sitrin, Marina, and Azzellini, Dario. 2014. *They can't represent us! Reinventing democracy from Greece to Occupy*. London: Verso Books.

Smith, Neil. 1996. *The new urban frontier. Gentrification and the revanchist city*. London: Routledge.

162 Bibliography

Solnit, Rebecca. 2016a. *Los hombres me explican cosas*. Translated by Paula Martín. Madrid: Capitán Swing.

Solnit, Rebecca. 2016b. *Els homes m'expliquen coses*. Translated by Marina Espasa. Barcelona: Angle.

Soriano, Domingo, and Muro, Miriam. 2015. 'Pablo Iglesias admite que su "objetivo fundamental" para este año no es ganar al PP sino liquidar al PSOE'. *Libertad Digital*, 2 June. http://www.libertaddigital.com/espana/2015-06-02/pablo-iglesias-admite-que-su-objetivo-fundamental-para-este-ano-no-es-ganar-al-pp-sino-sustituir-al-psoe-1276549519/.

Sorinas Giménez, Bernat. 2015. 'Recuperar derechos entre cadáveres de la especulación'. *Eldiario.es*, 5 July. https://www.eldiario.es/catalunya/opinions/Recuperar-derechos-cadaveres-especulacion_6_406019409.html.

Soto-Trillo, Eduardo. 2015. 'El laboratorio boliviano de Íñigo Errejón'. *Estudios de Política Exterior*, 16 June. http://www.politicaexterior.com/actualidad/el-laboratorio-boliviano-de-inigo-errejon/.

Srnicek, Nick. 2017. *Platform capitalism*. Cambridge: Polity.

Steger, Manfred. 2013. *Globalization: a very short introduction*. Third edition. Cambridge: Cambridge University Press.

Stiglitz, Joseph. 2002. *Globalization and its discontents*. New York/London: WW Norton.

Streeck, Wolfgang. 2015. 'The rise of the European consolidation state'. Max-Planck-Institut für Gesellschaftsforschung Discussion Paper 15/1.

Subcomandante Marcos and Le Bot, Yvon. 1997. *El sueño zapatista*. Barcelona: Anagrama.

Subirats, Joan, and Rendueles, César. 2016. *Los (bienes) comunes. ¿Oportunidad o espejismo?* Barcelona: Icaria.

Sylone. 2019. 'Inicio'. http://www.sylone.org/.

Sztulwark, Diego. 2019. *La ofensiva sensible*. Buenos Aires: Caja Negra.

Taibo, Carlos. 2011. *Nada será como antes. Sobre el movimiento 15-M*. Madrid: Los Libros de la Catarata.

Taibo, Carlos, and Domènech, Antoni, eds. 2011. *La rebelión de los indignados*. Madrid: Editorial Popular.

Tarrow, Sidney. 2006. *The new transnational activism*. Cambridge: Cambridge University Press.

Tarrow, Sydney. 2013. *The language of contention. Revolutions in words, 1688–2012*. Cambridge: Cambridge University Press.

Terraferida. 2015. 'Què som?'. *Terraferida*. https://terraferida.cat/que-som/.

The Commons Transition Primer. 2019. 'Welcome'. https://primer.commonstransition.org/.

Thompson, Edward Palmer. 1971. 'The moral economy of the English crowd in the eighteenth century', *Past & Present*, 50: 76–136.

Thompson, Edward Palmer. 2015. *La formación de la clase dominante y otros textos*. No place: Libros del Marrón.

Torres, Juan. 2010. '¿Es inevitable sufrir la dictadura de los mercados?' *ATTAC España*, 25 July. https://www.attac.es/2010/07/25/es-inevitable-sufrir-la-dictadura-de-los-mercados/.

Toscano, Alberto. 2015. 'Portrait of the Leader as a Young Theorist'. *Jacobin*, 19 December. https://www.jacobinmag.com/2015/12/podemos-iglesias-europe-austerity-elections-spain-theory-laclau/.

Tot Inclòs. 2017. 'Lluites'. *Tot Inclòs*, 4: 22–23.

Tot Inclòs. 2019a. 'Balanç de la legislatura 2015–2019'. *Tot Inclòs*. https://totinclos.noblogs.org.
Tot Inclòs. 2019b. 'Traduccions'. *Tot Inclòs*. https://totinclos.noblogs.org/traduccions/.
Tot Inclòs. 2019c. 'Descarregar el documental'. *Tot Inclòs.cat*. http://totinclos.cat/descarregar/.
Toupin, Louise. 2018. *Wages for housework. A history of an international feminist movement*. Translated by Käthe Roth. London: Pluto Press.
Touton, Isabelle. 2016. 'Memoria y legado de las militancias feministas de la transición en la España post-15M: algunas pistas de reflexión'. In Claudia González and Aránzazu Sarría Buil (eds.), *Militancias radicales. Narrar los sesenta y los setenta desde el siglo XXI*. Madrid: Postmetrópolis, 179–208.
Touton, Isabelle. 2019. 'Cultura colaborativa, autogestionada y feminista post-15M: el ejemplo de Sevilla'. In Jorge Cagiao and Isabelle Touton (eds.), *España después del 15M*. Madrid: La Catarata, 218–250.
Traficantes de Sueños. 2019a. 'Proyecto editorial'. https://www.traficantes.net/proyecto-de-la-editorial.
Traficantes de Sueños. 2019b. 'Historia'. https://www.traficantes.net/colecciones/historia-0.
Traficantes de Sueños. 2019c. 'Mapas'. https://www.traficantes.net/colecciones/mapas.
Traficantes de Sueños. 2019d. 'Prácticas constituyentes'. https://www.traficantes.net/colecciones/practicas-constituyentes-0.
Traverso, Enzo. 2016. *Left-wing melancholia. Marxism, history, and memory*. New York: Columbia University Press.
Tymoczko, Maria. 2000. 'Translation and political engagement: Activism, social change and the role of translation in geopolitical shifts'. *The Translator* 6 (1): 23–47.
Tzul Tzul, Gladys. 2015. 'Sistemas de gobierno comunal indígena: la organización de la reproducción de la vida'. *El Apantle* 1: 125–140.
United Nations. 2017. 'Spain's eviction violated family's human rights, say UN experts'. *UN News*, 5 July. https://news.un.org/en/story/2017/07/560982-spains-eviction-violated-familys-human-rights-say-un-experts.
Urquizu, Ignacio. 2016. *La crisis de representación en España*. Madrid: Libros de la Catarata.
Vaga de totes. 2014. 'Què és la vaga de totes?'. *Vaga de totes*. https://vagadetotes.wordpress.com/manifest-2/inici/.
Vaga Feminista. 2018. 'Punts de cura'. https://www.vagafeminista.cat/punts-de-cura/.
Valdivielso, Joaquín, and Moranta, Joan. 2019. 'The social construction of the tourism degrowth discourse in the Balearic Islands'. *Journal of Sustainable Tourism* 27 (12,): 1876–1892.
Vallejo Pousada, Rafael. 2015. '¿Bendición del cielo o plaga? El turismo en la España franquista, 1939–1975'. *Cuadernos de Historia Contemporánea* 37: 89–113.
Vega García, Rubén. 2002a. *Hay una luz en Asturias: Las huelgas de 1962 en Asturias*. Gijón: Ediciones Trea.
Vega García, Rubén. 2002b. *Las huelgas de 1962 en España y su repercusión internacional: el camino que marcaba Asturias*. Gijón: Trea.
Venuti, Lawrence. 1995. *The translator's invisibility*. London and New York: Routledge.
Venuti, Lawrence. 1998. *The scandals of translation: Towards an ethics of difference*. London: Routledge.
Verkami. 2018a. 'Hestóricas pioneras'. *Verkami*. https://www.verkami.com/projects/20755-herstoricas-pioneras.

Verkami. 2018b. 'Ménades editorial: publiquemos a mujeres'. *Verkami*. https://www.verkami.com/projects/22422-menades-editorial-publiquemos-a-mujeres.
Viejo, Raimundo, ed. 2011. *Les raons del indignats*. Barcelona: Pòrtic.
Viejo, Raimundo. 2019. '¿Qué vota tu biblioteca? La mía vota Colau!'. *Facebook*, 18 May. https://www.facebook.com/raimundo.viejo.v/photos/a.402578433259206/1167225520127823/?type=3 [The account was deleted in November 2019].
Vila, Salvador. 2007. 'El mito de la burbuja inmobiliaria'. *Levante*, 19 July. https://www.levante-emv.com/opinion/3598/mito-burbuja-inmobiliaria/322154.html.
Vilarós, Teresa. 1998. *El mono del desencanto. Una crítica cultural de la transición española (1973–1993)*. Madrid: Siglo XXI.
Villacañas de Castro, Luis. 2013. 'Chavs, chonis, y el nuevo socialismo (si lo hubiera)'. *Res Publica: Revista de Filosofía Política* 29: 89–98.
Villacañas, José Luis. 2015. *Populismo*. Madrid: La Puerta Grande.
Villacañas, José Luis. 2018. '¿Falta de teoría?'. *Levante*, 20 February. https://www.levante-emv.com/opinion/2018/02/20/falta-teoria/1681577.html.
Villacañas, José Luis, and Ruiz Sanjuán, César, coord. 2018. *Populismo versus republicanismo*. Madrid: Biblioteca Nueva.
Virus Editorial. 2019a. 'Ensayo'. http://www.viruseditorial.net/editorial/coleccion/ensayo.
Virus Editorial. 2019b. 'Sobre la editorial'. http://www.viruseditorial.net/editorial/sobre-editorial.
Vivas, Esther, and Antentas, Josep Maria. 2011. *Las voces del 15-M*. Madrid: Los Libros del Lince.
Vivas, Esther;, and Antentas, Josep Maria. 2012. *Planeta indignado*. Madrid: Ediciones Sequitur.
Von Flotow, Louise. 1991. 'Feminist translation: Contexts, practices and theories'. *TTR* 4 (2): 69–84.
Wall, Derek. 2014. *The commons in history. Culture, conflict, and ecology*. Cambridge MA: MIT Press.
Wark, Mckenzie. 2019. *Capital is dead*. London: Verso Books.
Wennerhag, Magnus. 2010. 'Another modernity is possible? The global justice movement and the transformations of politics'. *Distinktion: Scandinavian Journal of Social Theory* 11 (2): 25–49.
Williams, Raymond. 1975. *Keywords. A vocabulary of culture and society*. Second edition [1983]. London: Longman.
Wolf, Michaela. 2012. 'The sociology of translation and its "activist turn"'. *Translation and Interpreting Studies* 7 (2): 129–143.
Wolfson, Todd, and Funke, Peter. 2016. 'The contemporary epoch of struggle. Anti-austerity protests, the Arab uprisings and Occupy Wall Street'. In Mona Baker (ed.), *Translating Dissent: Voices from and with the Egyptian revolution*. London: Routledge, 60–73.
WWF. 2019. 'Deforestation in the Amazon'. *WWF*, https://wwf.panda.org/our_work/forests/deforestation_fronts/deforestation_in_the_amazon/.
Xiao, Qiang. 2011. 'The Battle for the Chinese Internet'. *Journal of Democracy* 22 (2): 47–61.
Yrigoy, Ismael. 2018. 'Transforming non-performing loans into re-performing loans: Hotel assets as a post-crisis rentier frontier in Spain'. *Geoforum* 97: 169–176.

Zaldua, Beñat. 2012. 'PP y CiU preparan la enésima reforma del Código Penal'. *Naiz*, 27 July. http://www.naiz.eus/es/actualidad/noticia/20120727/la-enesima-reforma-del-codigo-penal#.

Zazo, Óscar, and Torres, Steven, eds. 2019. *Spain after the Indignados/15M Movement*. London: Palgrave Macmillan.

Zubero, Imanol. 2012. 'De los "comunales" a los "commons": la peripecia teórica de una práctica ancestral cargada de futuro'. *Documentación social*, 165: 15–48.

Index

15M movement 2, 7, 9, 11, 22, 24, 26, 49–50, 54; and feminism 70–74, 81–85; and housing activism 92, 94; and its political limits 47, 70, 108–109, 129–131; and its relationship with the past 28, 36–37, 39; origins and composition 26–28, 32–33; and Podemos 107–109, 111, 115–117, 120, 123–124, 126; and the book industry 33, 37–38, 40–45, 76; and the commons 50, 52, 54, 56, 57, 62, 67; and the intellectual field 31, 124–125, 126–127; and the *Transición* 30–31, 38; and translation 3, 6, 33–35, 40–45, 48, 120, 126–127, 131–135

activism 9, 29, 41, 48; against the commodification of housing 93–96; against the excesses of tourism 97–101; and concepts 49–50, 78–79, 94–97; and feminism 70, 75, 79–80; and globalisation 11–24; and translation 17–24, 61, 102, 106; in Translation Studies 17–18, 24–25; and the environment 102–103
Agamben, Giorgio 120
aganaktismenoi (protest movement) 34, 48
Ahora Madrid (political platform) 7, 41, 56, 63, 87
Akal (publisher) 37, 41, 42
Anderson, Perry 122
Antentas, Josep Maria 3, 31–32, 131
Anti-globalization movement *see* Global justice movement
Arab uprisings 2–3, 23, 28, 92, 130; *see also* Tahrir
Assemblea de Barris pel Decreixement Turístic (activist group) 97–100, 105
Asturian (language) 8, 40, 102, 120

Babels (activist network) 19, 20
Badiou, Alain 33–34, 48
Baker, Mona 3, 7, 11–12, 17–19, 23, 61, 90, 99
Barcelona en Comú (political platform) 7–8, 32, 50, 63–65, 67, 95, 107, 124
Basque (language) 8, 48, 66, 99
Bauman, Zygmunt 1, 117
boardgames 74
Bollier, David 50, 55–56, 59–60
Bourdieu, Pierre 43, 45, 49, 107, 115, 120–123, 127, 132
Butler, Judith 6, 15, 33, 75, 118, 120–121, 124–125, 134

Caffentzis, George 50, 52, 54–55, 63
Cano, Germán 48, 116–118, 127
capitalist realism (concept) 14, 36, 80, 93
Capitán Swing (publisher) 37, 41, 42, 44, 126
care (political concept) 10, 69, 86–88, 132–133; history of the concept 78–80; and the care strike 80–85; translational difficulties 81, 88.
Carrasco, Cristina 79–82, 89
casta (political concept) 112, 123
Casus Belli (publisher) 37, 41, 42
Catalan (language) 8, 34, 54–55, 81–82, 84, 88, 96, 98, 99, 102–103, 106
Catalan pro-independence movement 113, 119, 129, 131
cipotudo (political concept) 120; *see also cuñadismo*
Colau, Ada 64, 93–96, 110, 124
Comisiones Obreras (trade union) 119
commons 4, 95, 101, 105, 132; and feminism 74, 84–85, 87; and Spanish activism 56–63; and political controversies 63–65, 67–68; history of the concept

50–53; translational complexities 53–56, 66
comunes see commons
Contra el diluvio (activist group) 48, 102–103, 105
cuidados see care
Cul de Sac see El Salmón
Cultura de la Transición (political concept) 31, 38, 40, 43–44, 119, 120, 123, 133; *see also* Spanish Transition to Democracy
cuñadismo (political concept) 88; *see also cipotudo*

Davis, Angela 33, 75
democracy: and contemporary activism 21; and the 15M 26–28, 32, 36, 38, 108–109, 111, 135; and the movement of the squares 15, 130; as concept 49, 52
Derrida, Jacques 36
Doerr, Nicole 2, 6, 20, 65, 117, 135
Domènech, Xavier 32, 108

Egypt 2–3, 15, 23, 28, 97, 108, 129; *see also* Arab uprisings; Tahrir
El Salmón (publisher) 37–38, 41–42, 102–105, 133
El Salto (magazine) 116, 119
Errejón, Íñigo 27, 30–33, 123, 127; clashes within Podemos 107–108; reflections on populism 109–114; reflections on translation 115–116; and the national question 112–113; *see also* Gramsci, Antonio; Iglesias, Pablo; Laclau, Ernesto; Mouffe, Chantal; Podemos
Even-Zohar, Itamar 33, 42, 123, 126, 132
EZLN *see* Zapatistas

Federici, Silvia 4, 33; and care 79–83, 87–88; and the commons 52, 54–55, 63, 74, 95; *see also* care; commons; Feminism
feminism: and care 78–80, 80–87; and contemporary activism 15–16, 61; and genealogy 73–76; and the book industry 76–78; and the feminist strike 69–70, 80–87; in Spain 4–5, 7, 10, 45, 70–73, 105, 109, 119–120, 132–133; *see also* care
Feria del Libro Político de Madrid (book fair) 38–39
Fernández-Savater, Amador 3, 27, 29, 33–34, 108, 123

Fisher, Mark 14, 36, 80
Foucault, Michel 14, 37, 73
Francoism 29–30, 38, 40, 91
Fraser, Nancy 63, 79–80
Fundación de los Comunes (activist network) 7, 56, 59, 64, 130

Galician (language) 8, 81, 85, 88, 99, 102
gentrification 63, 94, 96, 99, 101; *see also* Plataforma de Afectados por la Hipoteca; right to the city
Global justice movement 14–19
Globalisation 9, 11–22, 24, 40, 101, 110, 130–131
GOB (environmentalist group) 98–99
Gramsci, Antonio 4, 6, 110–113, 115, 117, 123, 132; *see also* Errejón, Íñigo; Laclau, Ernesto; Mouffe, Chantal
Greece 2, 15, 28, 39–40, 108, 129
Grup Balear d'Ornitologia i Defensa de la Naturalesa *see* GOB
Guerrilla Translation (cooperative) 50, 55, 60–62

Harvey, David 4, 12–13, 52, 94–95, 122; *see also* Plataforma de Afectados por la Hipoteca; right to the city
hauntology (concept) 36–40, 46, 58
Hessel, Stéphane 34–35
Hobsbawm, Eric 38, 122
Hochschild, Arlie 80
Hoja de Lata (publisher) 37, 133

Iglesias, Pablo 32, 107, 127–128, 132–133; and *casta* 112; and communication as translation 115–118; and intellectual networks 120–121; and the national question 113; and translation as capital 121–122; criticisms 123–126; relationship with the 15M 32, 109–110; *see also* Errejón, Íñigo; Podemos
indignados see 15M movement

Jones, Owen 112, 124, 126–127, 132
Juventud sin Futuro (protest movement) 29, 31, 36

Katakrak (publisher) 37, 41–42, 48, 56, 78
Koselleck, Reinhart 1–2

La Hidra (cooperative) 56, 59
La Ingobernable (social centre) 7, 50, 57, 62–63, 67, 69, 84

168 Index

La Tuerka (TV show) 109, 113, 115, 118, 121–123
Laclau, Ernesto 15, 33–34, 48, 110–114, 123, 125, 130; *see also* Errejón, Íñigo; Gramsci, Antonio; Mouffe, Chantal
Lefebvre, Henri 94
Lengua de Trapo (publisher) 32, 37, 41–42, 44
Lerner, Gerda 78
Linebaugh, Peter 51, 56, 58
López, Isidro 5, 45; and the Spanish economic model 26, 30, 90–92; criticisms to Podemos 112–113, 126, 129; *see also* Rodríguez, Emmanuel
Luis Buñuel (social centre) 62, 88

Madrilonia (activist collective) 56–58
mansplaining 87–88
Mareas (protest movement) 7
Mariátegui, José Carlos 111–112
Marx, Karl 44, 51, 95
Marxism 4, 21, 38, 94, 117, 122
Meiksins Wood, Ellen 51, 125
Ménades (publisher) 77
Morales, Evo 110
Moreno Pestaña, José Luis 47, 135
Moreno-Caballud, Luis 3, 5, 30–31, 91, 93, 125
Mouffe, Chantal 15, 27, 32, 110–114, 121, 124, 130; *see also* Errejón, Íñigo; Gramsci, Antonio; Laclau, Ernesto
movement of the squares (activist wave) 5, 7; and activist translation 22–24, 33–35, 44; and the 15M 3, 27–28; and the commons 52; and housing activism 93; and regional politics 63; in historical context; 15–17; origins 2; and political limits 108, 129–130
Municipalismo see Municipalist movement in Spain
Municipalist movement in Spain 7, 12, 45, 65, 129

Negri, Antonio: and the 15M 33–34, 48; and the commons 52; and translation 6, 33–34, 48, 134; support to new parties 121, 124
neoliberalism: and feminism 71, 80, 84; and globalisation 11–15; and hauntology 36, 40; and populism 111; and the right to the city 95–96; and the Spanish crisis 29–30; impact on activism 18–19, 24; transformation of concepts 49–50

New Left Review (journal) 102, 121–122, 128, 132; *see also* Anderson, Perry

Observatori DESC (think-tank) 95
Occupy Wall Street 6, 24, 44, 88, 128
Ostrom, Elinor 51–52, 60

PAH *see Plataforma de Afectados por la Hipoteca*
Partido Popular (political party) 47, 62, 72, 94, 114; *see also* Partido Socialista Obrero Español
Partido Socialista Obrero Español (political party) 30–31, 66, 70, 81, 94, 128–129; *see also* Partido Popular
Pasolini, Pier Paolo 104
Patio Maravillas (social centre) 29, 62
Pepitas de Calabaza (publisher) 41–42
Pérez Orozco, Amaia 80–81
Pimentel, Rafaela 81, 84
Pisarello, Gerardo 64, 95
Plataforma de Afectados por la Hipoteca (housing movement) 64, 93–96, 104–105, 108; *see also* gentrification; right to the city
Podemos (political party) 9, 10, 12, 41–44, 63; and Latin America 109–113; and populism 111–114; and translated intellectuals 110–113, 121–122, 126–127; and translation 115–118, 110–122; criticisms 123–126; relationship with the 15M 32–33, 48, 108–109
Polanyi, Karl 44–45
politically committed book publishers 36–46, 76–78; *see also* Akal; Capitán Swing; Casus Belli; El Salmón; Feria del Libro Político de Madrid; Hoja de Lata; Katakrak; Lengua de Trapo; Ménades; Pepitas de Calabaza; Sylone; Traficantes de Sueños; Virus
Populism 4; and Podemos 107, 109–113, 123, 132; attacks on 113–114
PP *see* Partido Popular
prefiguration (political concept) 27, 60
Procomún *see* Commons
PSOE *see* Partido Socialista Obrero Español

radical publishers *see* politically committed book publishers
Rancière, Jacques 33–34, 121, 135
Rendueles, César 16, 50, 53, 108, 115, 126

representation (political concept) 32, 34–35, 48, 108, 117
right to the city (concept) 94–95, 105; *see also* Harvey, David; *Plataforma de Afectados por la Hipoteca*
Rodríguez, Emmanuel 45; and the 15M 3, 7, 27–28, 31, 70, 108–109; and the Spanish economic model 5, 26, 31, 90–92; and the Transition to Democracy 30

Sangre Fucsia (radio show) 74–75
Santos, Boaventura de Sousa 6, 16, 21, 118, 124, 134
Sin Permiso (journal) 23, 95, 102
Sol (square in Madrid) 26, 47, 69, 71–72
Spanish Transition to Democracy: and feminism 72; and the publishing sector 36–38, 44–45; and the Spanish economy 91; and translation 40, 44–45, 131; debates and criticisms 29–31, 42, 58; *see also Cultura de la Transición*
squares *see* movement of the squares
Subcomandante Marcos *see* Zapatistas
Subirats, Joan 50, 53–54, 64
Sylone (publisher) 41–42

Tahrir (square in Cairo) 28, 34, 49; *see also* Arab uprisings; Sol
Tarrow, Sydney 6, 16, 49, 51, 82
Terraferida (activist group) 98
Territorio Doméstico (association) 81, 84
Thompson, E.P. 28, 45–46
Tot Inclòs (journal and collective) 97–99, 105

tourism 90–92, 97–101; *see also* activism; *Assemblea de Barris pel Decreixement Turístic*; *Tot Inclòs*
Traficantes de Sueños (publisher) 37, 41–42, 45, 76, 88, 96; and the commons 50, 54, 56–60
Transición see Spanish Transition to Democracy
translation: and activism 2–10, 17–25; and care 78–85; and climate change 101–103, 106; and expanded translation 4, 9, 25, 47, 67, 85, 87–88, 132–133; and feminism 73–78, 87–89; and housing activism 94–97; and Podemos 109–128; and political critique 118–120; and Social Movements studies 5–6, 135–136; and the 15M 3–4, 33–46; and the commons 53–66; and tourist activism 97–101; and volunteering 19–20, 22–23, 61–62, 127

V de Vivienda see Plataforma de Afectados por la Hipoteca
Venuti, Lawrence 3, 132
Verso Books (publisher) 121, 126, 132
Villacañas, José Luis 113, 124
Virus (publisher) 37, 41–42, 44–45, 54

Wages for Housework (feminist network) 79–80, 83; *see also* Federici, Silvia
Wikipedia 52, 74
World Social Forum 16, 19–21, 118

Zapatistas 21–22, 110
Žižek, Slavoj 33, 120–121